Growling Tiger, Roaring Dragon

INDIA, CHINA
AND THE
NEW WORLD
ORDER

DAVID SMITH

GROWLING TIGER ROARING DRAGON

Douglas & McIntyre
VANCOUVER/TORONTO/BERKELEY

Douglas & McIntyre Ltd.
2323 Quebec Street, Suite 201
Vancouver, British Columbia
Canada V5T 4S7
www.douglas-mcintyre.com

Library and Archives Canada Cataloguing in Publication
Smith, David, 1954 Apr. 3–
Growling tiger, roaring dragon : India, China and the new world order / David Smith.

Includes index.
First published London : Profile Books, 2007 under title: The dragon and the elephant.

ISBN 978-1-55365-334-9

1. China—Economic conditions—21st century. 2. India—Economic conditions—
21st century. 3. International economic relations. 4. Geopolitics. 5. Economic
forecasting—China. 6. Economic forecasting—India. I. Title.

HC412.S59413 2007   330.951′06   C2007-903038-6

First published in Great Britain in 2007
by Profile Books Ltd. as *The Dragon and the Elephant*

Cover design by Peter Cocking
Typeset by MacGuru Ltd
Printed and bound in Canada by Friesens
Printed on acid-free paper that is forest friendly
(100% post-consumer recycled paper) and has been processed chlorine free
Distributed in the U.S. by Publishers Group West

We gratefully acknowledge the financial support of the Canada Council for the
Arts, the British Columbia Arts Council, the Province of British Columbia through
the Book Publishing Tax Credit, and the Government of Canada through the Book
Publishing Industry Development Program (BPIDP) for our publishing activities.

Contents

For Jane

Introduction: India, China and the New World Order

The genesis of this book came, not in Beijing or Shanghai, or Delhi or Mumbai, or even from gazing into an economic crystal ball. Instead, it came at the end of a talk I was giving to a group of businessmen, mainly industrialists, one evening in London a few years ago. I had run through the usual diet of topics for a business audience: what might happen to inflation and interest rates; whether the UK was likely to join the European single currency (this was a while ago), the dollar, oil prices, and so on. They listened politely, asked some questions, and then the discussion turned to an issue that had not been part of my talk. 'What,' somebody asked, 'about China and India?' There was a nodding of heads around the room, and from the conversation that followed a definite view emerged, one that was pessimistic, even fatalistic. Manufacturing jobs were being lost to China at an alarming pace, and the service sector was following a similar passage to India. A seismic shift was taking place in the global economy, in which China was claiming the lion's share of the world's manufacturing and India was rapidly sewing up services. Things would never be the same again. The men and women around the table would not be as much affected as their children and grandchildren. Where would the jobs of the future be when there was nothing that countries like Britain could do more competitively than China and India, with their enormous pools of cheap labour, increasingly educated workforces and ability to embrace the latest technology? What would we do when China and India could do everything? Britain and the other rich economies were sleepwalking their way to long-run economic decline. We were in London, but it could have been Toronto, Toulouse or Tokyo, Chicago or Cologne.

As I thought about this, I realised that these business people were not alone. One of the biggest mailbags I received at the *Sunday Times* was in response to a piece I wrote about China. Whenever we wrote about the outsourcing of jobs to India, the reaction was similar. Not only were manufacturing jobs going, but so too were the service sector posts that had come along to replace them. China and India had become the hot story. The Chinese authorities were locked in a battle with the United States over the value of China's currency, the renminbi, because of its growing trade surplus with America. China was simultaneously keeping prices down in the West, by producing manufacturing goods at ever lower prices, and pushing its costs up with its gargantuan appetite for raw materials and oil. Was the China effect benign or damaging? What about India? The headlines told of back office and call centre jobs being outsourced to the subcontinent, but the stories also foresaw the day when everything – from stockbrokers' research to medical testing and diagnosis – could be done in Bangalore and Mumbai. Had anybody moved up the value chain as quickly as China and India were doing? What about the millions of graduates they were producing? What hope for the young people of Canada, the US, Britain or Europe? Should everybody start praying, and learning Mandarin?

The story of India (the tiger) and China (the dragon) did not suddenly emerge. Indians quite like the idea of their country as a lumbering elephant, which will slowly but steadily win the race, like the tortoise of Aesop's fable. But for more than a decade, India has performed more like another of her national symbols, the tiger. China's modern-day miracle stretches back further, more than a quarter of a century. What seems to have happened, however, is that both reached the point where they were impacting significantly on the rest of the world quite recently. In the 1990s, when the dot.com boom competed for the headlines with the 1997–8 Asian financial crisis, neither China nor India received as much attention as they should have done. Perhaps we did not quite believe the China–India story.

On a visit to Shenzhen from Hong Kong in the summer of 1998, I recall the train from Kowloon carrying me towards what at first looked like a mirage – ghostly images of shimmering skyscrapers rising out of nothing. I knew there were skyscrapers behind me – Hong Kong's world-famous landmarks – but I had not expected to see buildings on a similar scale in communist China. But they were real, the embodiment of Deng Xiaoping's ambition to have a twenty-first-century city on the edge of communist China, looking out on and every bit as impressive and successful as capitalist Hong Kong. To me, however, these gleaming new buildings did not seem quite like the real thing. My reaction, I suppose, was a bit like that of the writer J. B. Priestley who, on seeing the smart new art deco industrial assembly plants on London's Great West Road, like the iconic Hoover building, in the 1930s declared that they were merely playing at being factories; the real things were much grittier and grimier. That, it seemed, also applied to Shenzhen's new skyscrapers. They were playing at being office blocks, an impression reinforced when I was told that most of them lacked tenants. The impression, less than a decade ago, was of a city pretending to be a metropolis. It was chaotic and a little dangerous, a combination of giant building site and frontier town, with plenty of dodgy characters to go with it. A façade was being constructed, but was it any more substantial than those they put up on the set of a cowboy movie? It was certainly solid enough, as subsequent events have proved. Today Shenzhen is at the heart of a special economic zone numbering 10 million people. Thanks to Deng, China's economic visionary, it became the country's first modern city, a magnet to workers from rural areas and other towns. Even by China's standards this is a crowded place, with the highest population density of any city in the country, which has the local authority worrying about how to manage its success. It is also China's busiest sea port. Shenzhen's factories turn out products in vast quantities, many of them destined for the US market. Wal-Mart, the world's biggest company, whose success is inextricably intertwined with that of China, has its global procurement centre there, ensuring that production stays high and prices low.

China is developing, and it is doing so at a breakneck pace. The first thing experienced by visitors to Shanghai, its financial capital, is the futuristic Mag-Lev train from the airport, which, disappointingly, only takes you so far into the city centre. The second impression is one of tremendous growth. Shanghai's city plan for 2020, put together with the help of international architects and planners, includes nine satellite cities, each with a projected population of 800,000 people. Close by will be Dongtan, intended to be the world's first eco city. Shanghai will have huge industrial parks, to cater for every possible industry, including mass-market motor manufacture and petrochemicals. A network of modern subway and metro trains will, when they have been constructed, make the Mag-Lev look dated. By the time of the 2010 World Expo, its riverfront site and the surrounding area will have been redeveloped. It is an ambitious plan for a city that, even more than Shenzhen, has more than a flavour of Lower

Manhattan about it. And it is deliberately symbolic, intended to demonstrate that China is planning for a dazzling, high-technology future. For those whose image of China is of a sweatshop economy it is an awakening. And who would doubt the country's determination or its record of powerful economic growth, averaging more than 9 per cent a year, now stretching back over more than a quarter of a century?

In India, the symbolism is less obvious. India sells itself as 'the world's fastest-growing democracy', and the figures support it: an average growth rate of 6 per cent a year over two decades (and more than 9 per cent recently). India's impressive rise has only recently begun to impact significantly on the West, the drop in international telecommunications charges highlighting its low labour costs and high-quality labour force. While China has become the manufacturing location of choice for multinationals, India has become the favoured location for the outsourcing of a range of service sector activities, from software development and call centres through to sophisticated research reports. Highly paid analysts on Wall Street and in London top and tail company research reports put together by Indian staff working at a fraction of the cost. The tower blocks and office complexes being developed in Mumbai, India's financial capital, will, according to Dr Manmohan Singh, the country's prime minister, make people 'forget about Shanghai' within five years as Mumbai becomes 'a talking point' for the world. But Mumbai also exposes the other India, one of grinding and highly visible poverty. Four hundred thousand slum dwellers were cleared from their homes to make space for the gleaming towers, without being rehoused. No visitor to India can fail to be struck by the extremes of poverty that exist, side by side, with the country's modern-day economic miracle. Nearly one in ten children dies before reaching the age of five. India is indeed the world's largest democracy but she is also a country of clear and striking contrasts. Perhaps it is the ultimate experiment in trickle-down economics. Like China she has large, mainly poorly educated masses, only gradually being touched by the prosperity that characterises her expanding middle class.

The rise of China and India, which I shall avoid calling 'Chindia', will be the outstanding development of the early decades of the century, raising fundamental questions about the structure of the world economy and the balance of global geopolitical power. Imagine the world by the middle of the century. If the forecasters are right, the world's three biggest economies will be, in order, China, the United States and India. Beijing, Washington and New Delhi will be where global power lies. Their climb will have been astonishing. Even now, China and India together are only half the size of Japan and barely a fifth of the United States in terms of gross domestic product (GDP). China and India's journey over the next forty to fifty years will be a fascinating one, full of huge opportunities and pitfalls, both for the countries themselves and for the rest of us. Is their growth sustainable or will it peter out, just as we are coming to rely on it as the motor of the global economy? Will it be a gold rush for international businesses that ends up with disappointed hopes? Or is this the time, after many false hopes, that firms will start to make money in China and India? If we no longer rub our eyes at China's extraordinary progress, we do still wonder at India – the world's fastest-growing democracy or not – which only a couple of decades ago seemed destined to remain an economic basket case, most of its people condemned to permanent poverty.

This time, however, it really does look different. China began to turn the corner in the late 1970s, India – though there is some debate about this – in the early 1990s. Walt Rostow, the great American economic historian, defined the conditions for what he called 'the take-off into self-sustained growth', notably high levels of investment and the transfer of workers from the land on a large scale. Both countries have achieved those conditions. There can be no going back to backward, agrarian-based economies. For both China and India the future that looms – and before very long – is Rostow's final stage of economic development, the era of mass consumption. That is not to say the emergence of China and India will be free of tensions. In China the fundamental tensions between an increasingly free market economy and a repressive and undemocratic regime have yet to be resolved. But what about India, whose growing population and gilt-edged economic prospects appear to guarantee prosperity? Never in modern times has a developing country been so powerful. Yet that is what India still is – with *per capita* GDP levels a fraction of those in the rich Western economies and only half those of China. The rise of India, like that of China, will shift the balance of global power. It will also challenge our attitudes to rich and poor countries. After the devastating Indian Ocean tsunami of 26 December 2004, in which 200,000 people died, including at least 12,000 in India, the Indian government declared it did not want assistance from other countries, an important rite of passage. The supplicant has become the competitor. The poor country is becoming a powerful nation; a new economic powerhouse. Currently, 200 million people in China and 300 million in India live on less than a dollar a day. But, as the World Bank has pointed out, the economic rise of these countries has been the single most important factor in reducing global poverty over the past two decades.

The purpose of this book is to try to answer some key questions which go beyond the concerns of economists and politicians. 'What will we do when China and India do everything?' is indeed an important question. Businessmen, seeing their markets claimed by Chinese-manufactured goods, and their back-office functions 'offshored' to India, wonder about the future. But there are others. What about the impact of these new economic superpowers on the global stage? Will China be a benign presence, as Japan was in the 1980s? How worried should we be that China already has the economic lock over America with vast dollar holdings? How aggressive will a superpower China be? What about India? Are its tensions with Pakistan a foretaste of a new instability? Will India turn the economic tables on its old imperial master, Britain, in the way America did?

This book starts by trying to solve a mystery. We know that China and India were powerful economic forces at the beginning of the nineteenth century. How did they come to be so important then, only to sink into economic obscurity a few decades later? Chapter One: The Return of History is an attempt to trace the economic rise and fall of the two countries from ancient times to relatively recent days, in order to set their modern rise in context. Chapter Two: Enter the Dragon is about China's modern rise. Mao Tse-tung is still revered in China, but it was only after his death that his country first began to see the glimmerings of economic hope. I happened to be in Beijing in September 2006 on the thirtieth anniversary of his death and queued, with tens of thousands of others, to file into the mausoleum on Tiananmen Square and walk past his embalmed body. People bought chrysanthemums to place at the feet of his statue at the entrance to the building. The older visitors bowed down, while some gasped as they filed past the perspex coffin and saw the embalmed body, smaller than you would expect but unmistakably Mao. Images of him are everywhere, on the banknotes and in public places. To an extent, perhaps, it is the authorities' way of maintaining the link with the past. But Deng Xiaoping, the architect of a renaissance that was by both accident and design, is far less visible. In China it took a death – that of Mao – to create the conditions for the country's rise. And as described in Chapter Three: India Rising, it also took a death – the brutal assassination of former prime minister and Congress Party leader Rajiv Gandhi in 1991 and a simultaneous economic crisis, to persuade India's people, businesses and politicians that things could not continue as they were. Chapter Four: China Roars, the World Listens, and Chapter Five: India's Networked Economy, look at the impact of the two countries now and their likely impact in the future. How big will their markets be, and how accessible? How much of the current strength is real, and how much will pass, perhaps as a result of the problems of success? Chapter Six: China versus India does something that politicians of the two countries always claim not to do, it compares their strengths and weaknesses. Some say the combination of favourable demographics and democratic government means that India will be the best bet in the long run, even though it is starting from a long way back. But what about the environment, or the social and political tensions created by those who have been left behind? Is China best placed to manage these potential hurdles, or is India? Finally, I offer some broad conclusions, in Chapter Seven: Ten Ways China and India will (and won't) Change the World. I'll leave those until you get there.

A final word might be useful to set the book in context. It takes a lifetime, they say, to understand China and perhaps longer, if that were possible, to get to grips with India. There are plenty of great books written by old China hands and by those whose experience of India dates from the time of the Raj. Local writers, who are perhaps best placed of all to tell the story of their country's changes, have also been responsible for some excellent accounts. I cannot attempt to compete with this kind of local knowledge. So, while Mahatma Gandhi said India 'lives in her villages', I cannot offer village-level anecdotes of the country's rise. Similarly, my perspective on China has to be that of a visitor. But from that perspective, I hope, it is possible to avoid the problem of not seeing the woods for the trees. The aims of this book are to explain China and India's rise, to assess whether we should be alarmed or cheered by it, and to try to assess where these two huge countries are heading, and what it means for the rest of us. You will judge whether it has succeeded in these aims.

1

The Return of History

'India is the cradle of the human race, the birthplace of human speech, the mother of history, the grandmother of legend, and the great grandmother of tradition. Our most valuable and most instructive materials in the history of man are treasured up in India only.'

Mark Twain (attributed), visiting India in 1896

'Histories of the world omitted China; if a Chinaman invent the compass or movable type or gunpowder we promptly "forgot it" and named their European inventors. In short, we regarded China as a sort of different and quite inconsequential planet.'

William Edward Burghardt Du Bois

The ancient pillars

Where do you start looking at China and India's past? The obvious answer is a long time ago. The story of their place in the world is, at one level, simply told. These two huge countries, with their large and resourceful populations, were dominant once and, it appears, will be dominant again, taking their traditional place at the heart of the global economy. The rise of Europe, North America and Japan has been, on this view, just a brief interlude in the grand historical sweep. The surprise, perhaps, is that China and India ever went away. Certainly that is the way it looks from the numbers. The extent of their dominance in the past is striking. For most of the ancient and modern eras they were the twin pillars of the world economy, bastions of wealth and progress. The numbers, in this context, are mainly those of Angus Maddison, the British-born economic historian who has done more than anybody else to give us a statistical narrative to complement descriptive accounts of the world's past. Maddison's calculations, carefully set out in his masterwork *The World Economy: A Millennial Perspective*,[1] show that 2,000 years ago China and India between them held a 59 per cent share of the world economy (of which India had 33 per cent, China 26 per cent). The precise numbers can be debated, but the broad picture he suggests goes unchallenged. At the birth of Christ, India made up a third of the global economy, China more than a quarter. History, it seems, is on China and India's side. Their current rise is mainly just the return of the *status quo*.

It is, though, a bit more complicated than that, otherwise we would be looking forward to the return to prominence of all the ancient empires. Civilisations rise and fall. There is nothing preordained about the fact that once-great powers will reassert themselves; indeed the opposite is more often true. As is the case for ancient Egypt, Greece or Rome, it was common until relatively recently to regard history as more of a burden for India and China than as a harbinger of future greatness. So it is worth reminding ourselves of the historical backdrop.

Indus roots

Two thousand years ago, India and China had a lot of economic history behind them. At the dawn of Christianity, India was already prosperous. The Harappan or Indus valley civilisation, among the world's oldest and certainly one of the most sophisticated, peaked between 3000 and 1700 BCE, though there is evidence of settlement 3,000 or more years before that. Excavations, the first of which began at the end of the nineteenth century, have uncovered not only what may have been the world's first cities, but well-engineered systems of drainage, irrigation and household water supply that were probably superior to those in many parts of present-day India and Pakistan. Civic life and organised politics thrived in the Indus valley. There were religious rites, based around sacred animals and male and female fertility symbols. Agricultural efficiency provided for urban prosperity, the valley's farmers producing surpluses beyond their subsistence needs. Archaeological excavations suggest they grew wheat, barley, sesame, mustard and dates. Cotton was cultivated, the first anywhere in the world. Animals, including dogs, cats, pigs and cattle, were domesticated. They may have domesticated the elephant; Indus carvings and seals suggest elephants were used for hauling timber and transporting produce. The Indus valley civilisation also had a tax system. Agricultural production was taxed by the authorities, farmers being required to transfer a portion of their production into public granaries and other storage facilities.

This civilisation reached out commercially to the other developed societies of the time. There was 'evidence for trade contact with the surrounding cultures in the Arabian Gulf, West and Central Asia and peninsular India', according to Jonathan Mark Kenoyer, professor of anthropology at the University of Wisconsin and a noted expert.[2] After 1700 BCE the Indus valley civilisation gradually declined or fragmented for reasons that are not entirely clear. Environmental change appears to have played a part, with the Indus river changing its course, parts of it suffering from drought and others destructive floods. But that did not stop other civilisations developing and thriving, notably the Aryans.[3] These successor civilisations were also sophisticated – trading, breeding cattle and horses, using iron and copper, and making pottery.

The Aryans, even more than the Indus valley civilisation, give us the thread that takes us through to modern India. The 'Aryan-speaking peoples' consisted of many tribes but shared a common Aryan – Indo-European – language. The Aryans initially settled the vast Indo-Gangetic plain, stretching from the Indus river to the Punjab plain and the Ganges delta. There, as the political economist Deepak Lal writes, they gradually evolved 'from semi-nomadic cattle-breeding pastoralists into settled agriculturalists'. There, too, they evolved the caste system, 'which has provided the basic social framework for the daily lives of the people of the subcontinent, now called Hindu. It has survived innumerable foreign invasions – from the barbarians in the north and most recently by sea in the south – internal turmoil, colonisation, and economic vicissitudes, so much so that after over two thousand years it still remains of vital importance in understanding the society and politics of India.'[4] This era is also the subject of contemporary controversy. Did the Aryans invade from Central Asia, thus making them 'non-Indian' in origin? Or is there an unbroken line of Indian peoples stretching back to 6000 BCE, from the Vedic era, through the Indus valley civilisation and the Aryans to modern times? India, on this view, was the true cradle of civilisation and owes little to other cultures, the Aryan invasion being a colonialist myth. The Bharatiya Janata Party (BJP), when it came into government in 1998, pushed this strongly, ordering school textbooks to be rewritten to reflect this version of India's history as a Hindu continuum. Crucial to the new theory was that the horse was not brought to India by Aryan invaders, but was used extensively by the Harappans. The jury is still out on that.

China's dynastic development

If you wander round the Forbidden City – officially the Palace Museum – in the centre of Beijing, you are struck by two things. One is the sheer size of the place – 720,000 square metres – which means you soon become overwhelmed by the number of exhibits on display. The other is the long sweep of Chinese history. The Forbidden City, so called because it was for centuries off limits to ordinary people, has artefacts that are 5,000 or more years old, including sophisticated ceramics. It provides a glimpse into China's past, right through to the opulence of the Ming (1368–1644) and Qing (1644–1911) dynasties.

China's economic development significantly pre-dates that of India. The earliest Chinese pottery has been dated to 9000 BCE: bowls and jars from southern China, made from thick clay and primitively decorated using stone knives. Chinese agriculture has been traced back to around 7000 BCE. In farming settlements such as Banpo in northern China, millet was grown and kept in grain-storage pits, and dogs and pigs were domesticated. The cultivation of rice, modern China's staple crop, began in the lowlands of the Yangtze river delta around 6000 BCE. Agriculture-based prosperity led to invention and innovation. By about 3000 BCE farmers of the Longshan culture in eastern China had invented the potter's wheel and were making delicate, eggshell-thin pottery. Walled settlements began to appear, too, as did the stratification of society; archaeologists have been able to distinguish between rich and poor burials. Shortly afterwards farmers first began raising silkworms and weaving silk, another crucial building block in China's development.

The first of China's ancient dynasties, the Xia, emerged out of this Longshan culture. Lasting from about 2200 to 1750 BCE, the Xia dynasty built palaces and elaborate tombs, and manufactured bronze vessels. The

Shang dynasty, dating from 1766 to 1122 BCE, overlapped for a few years with the Xia dynasty. In the Shang period millet (then the staple crop) was farmed and beans cultivated on the giant north China plain. Peasants and labourers, required to work on walls, palaces and monuments, were effectively slaves, and had to make themselves available for military service. The Shang dynasty left behind a treasure trove for archaeologists, most notably the so-called oracle bones: inscriptions made on the shoulder blades of oxen or on turtle shells. These bones, either in the form of questions to the oracle or predictions about harvests, the weather and future events, offer important insights into the way Shang society was organised under the ruler. Bronze vessels, many of which have survived, were manufactured during this period.

China's economy continued to develop under the third of the ancient dynasties, the Zhou, which ran from 1122 to 256 BCE (usually divided between the earlier Western Zhou and later Eastern Zhou periods). Metal agricultural tools came into use, initially bronze implements in the Yangtze valley, later iron and steel. Primitive tokens of exchange gave way to minted metal coinage around the sixth and fifth centuries BCE, the time of Kong Fuzi (or, to Westerners, Confucius), who lived from around 551 to 479 BCE. A formal system of taxation was in existence in Lu, the north-eastern state where Confucius was born, during his lifetime. There was a communal system of agriculture, each plot of land divided into nine – eight farmed by individual farmers and the ninth collectively, its produce delivered to the ruler. Farming provided the basis for the ancient Chinese economy but so did trade. This was when the division of Chinese society into the 'four occupations' began, 'placing the warrior nobility (later replaced by imperial officials) at the top, followed by farmers, artisans and, lastly, merchants. While farmers, whose labour fed all others, were held in high esteem, the ruling class scorned merchants as parasites who contributed little of real value to the wealth of the realm. However, this hierarchy of occupations represented a political ideal rather than social reality. Successful merchants often amassed great fortunes, while the vast majority of peasants lived in the shadow of poverty.'[5] There is a parallel here with the development of India's rather more rigid caste system, which also has ancient roots. While innovation and modernisation characterised the Zhou dynasty, so did military conflict, making it a time of 'rapid but unstable expansion'.[6] By about the sixth century BCE new weapons had been developed, including the crossbow, iron sword and body armour, and armies of up to 600,000 men were raised. *The Art of War* by Sun Tzu, a modern-day bestseller, dates from this period, the so-called Warring States period.

Population and wealth

Wars aside, both India and China had made significant economic progress 2,000 years ago. Then, as now, they also had the weight of large populations on their side. By the standards of the time both countries were heavily populated. Maddison estimates China's population to have been just below 60 million and that of India 75 million. For comparison, western Europe had a population of less than 25 million. The world's centre of gravity was in Asia. Including Japan, with its population of just 3 million, three-quarters of the globe's total population of about 230 million was in Asia. Perhaps China and India had too much too soon, and became complacent. That is the view of Deepak Lal, certainly of India's great wealth in the pre-Christian era. 'If reports like those of the Greek traveller Megasthenes, who spoke of India's fabulous wealth, and of subsequent visitors like the Chinese pilgrim Huan Tsiang (AD 606–47) are accurate, India must have attained a standard of living higher than other civilisations of the time well before the beginning of the Christian era,' he has written.[7] Indeed, it is his contention that because India achieved prosperity early she effectively rested on her laurels, settling at what he describes as a 'high level equilibrium trap', with *per capita* income remaining roughly stagnant from around 300 BCE until the modern era. At the start of that long period India was a rich country; at the end it had been left behind by just about everybody else.

This is not the place for a detailed account of Chinese and Indian history up to the present day, though it is instructive to highlight some of the most important economic developments. In terms of the broad economic numbers, relatively little changed during the first Christian millennium, the only significant development being the relative rise of Africa. In the year 1000, China and India's combined share of the global economy, according to Maddison, was almost 52 per cent. India was still ahead on 29 per cent, with China at 23 per cent (you begin to see why China's current lead rankles so much). The next 500 years (1000–1500 CE) saw the beginnings of the rise of western Europe, from a 9 to an 18 per cent share. It also saw the Chinese economy catch up with, and overtake, India. By the time of the Renaissance, China and India accounted for nearly half of global economic activity between them. China's population remained stable at just under 60 million from 0 to 1000 CE, rising to more than 100 million by 1500. This was in spite of the loss of some 30 million people as a result of the Mongol invasions of the thirteenth and fourteenth centuries. Mongol horsemen invaded north China in 1234, south China in 1279, and brought bubonic plague to China in the middle of the fourteenth century.

The numbers tell some of the story, but what was happening to the Indian and Chinese economies in terms of their development? Before answering that question, it is worth reminding ourselves of a fundamental difference between India and China, a point made by the economist Meghnad Desai. While China has sought unity as a single national entity, a country, in the more than 2,000 years since the era of the Warring States, this has not been true of India, as he reminds us.

While both India and China have a long history, their histories are very different.

> China has been by and large a stable, centrally-run state through its
> history with limited periods of instability and lack of a single authority.
> India's history has been exactly the reverse. The periods when a single
> King or political authority ruled over even the major part of India's
> territory can be counted on fingers of one hand ... In India's case there
> never was any authority which has ruled over all of India ... India has
> been an idea in world culture for millennia but its borders were fixed only
> in the late 19th century sometime after the British gave up on Afghanistan
> and drew the Durand line.[8]

Chinese invention

What most people know about early and medieval China, of course, is its extraordinary inventiveness. China's record on inventions is not only impressively long but, thanks to the slow diffusion of technology between countries and continents in the past, anticipated Western (European) discoveries by hundreds, and in some cases thousands, of years. Ancient China invented and used implements such as the iron plough and weapons including the crossbow. To this can be added lacquer, the kite (including for manned flight), the compass, paper, steel, the use of petroleum and natural gas as fuel, the trace-efficient horse harness, the wheelbarrow and the first canals for transportation. Chinese invention and innovation were driven by a combination of the need, particularly in the case of agriculture, to provide more efficient and plentiful sources of food supply; and curiosity, as with the desire to know more about the planets. 'The Chinese drew no sharply defined line between scientific and technological pursuits,' writes the historian Peter Golas,

> Indeed, the very concepts of 'science' and 'technology' as they are understood in the West did not exist in traditional Chinese thought. It is therefore not difficult to think of instances in which at least partly 'scientific' concerns stimulated technological responses. The desire to discover order in the universe by means of astronomical and astrological observations, for example, prompted the invention of many instruments over the first millennium [CE], eventually culminating in the eleventh-century clock tower invented by Su Song, which represented the crowning mechanical achievement of traditional China. The clock tower's escapement system – which consisted of pouring water into successive cups on the periphery of the driving waterwheel – allowed the slow and regular rotation of the wheel and of the armillary sphere, celestial globe, and timekeeping jackwork that were linked to it.[9]

By the same token, the Chinese fascination with magnetism led directly to the invention of the compass, while experiments in alchemy led to the discovery of the ingredients for the manufacture of gunpowder, another noted Chinese invention.

In the case of food supply, the Chinese were highly inventive when it came to agricultural tools and innovative in respect of farming methods. The big shift, which came after the collapse of the Han dynasty (206 BCE–220 CE), was from the staple crop of millet to rice. 'Large-scale migration of Chinese settlers into the Yangtze River valley began during the Fifth and Sixth centuries,' writes Lal. 'At first the land was cleared by fire, flooded, and then abandoned. But gradually, settled farming developed with wet-rice cultivation. This was accompanied by the development of new tools, crop rotations, and new kinds of seeds. Wet rice required a radically different technology from the dry farming of the north.'[10] The rise in agricultural productivity appears to have been extraordinary, particularly in the period when China's population began to soar. Chinese agriculture followed the pattern set out by agricultural economist Ester Boserup in her classic work *The Conditions of Agricultural Growth* (1965).[11] Boserup herself cited the capacity of Chinese peasants for hard work, notably in comparison with their Indian counterparts. 'Boserupian' growth in agricultural output, as distinct from the Malthusian idea that limits on food production would be reached, was achieved, as Lal explains, 'with rising labour intensity of cultivation, and hence rising output per acre as the population per acre rose'.[12]

China was also well ahead of the West when it came to maritime technology, and thus sea power, notably from the eleventh to the fifteenth centuries CE. The first Chinese professional navy was created in 1232 to protect coastal areas against Mongol attacks and grew over the following hundred years to twenty squadrons and more than 50,000 men. China, having invented the compass, also invented stern-post rudders, which could be raised or lowered according to water depth, and human-powered paddle-wheel ships. Chinese sails, constructed out of bamboo matting, were strong. Chinese ships, usually featuring a series of separated watertight compartments, could sail on after suffering partial damage. At the peak of Chinese maritime power, in the early fifteenth century, its fleet ventured far and wide, sailing across the India Ocean as far as the Red Sea and the coast of Africa. Giant 'treasure' ships, five times the size of European vessels, were the embodiment of Chinese power. Under the fifteenth-century emperor Yung-lo, the long voyages undertaken by these ships appear to have been for good will purposes rather than trade, although one mission returned to China with African livestock, including giraffes and zebras.

Needham's 'Grand Question'

Any account of Chinese inventiveness cannot ignore the contribution of Joseph Needham (1900–1995), the Cambridge biochemist who made his life's work the study of China's scientific and technological past. His interest, sparked by working with Chinese scientists in Cambridge in the 1930s, blossomed when he was posted to China for four years in 1942, and resulted in the seven-volume (so far) work *Science and Civilisation in China*, the first volume of which was published in 1954, and which has been continued by his students and collaborators after his death. Needham, whose other legacy is the Needham Research Institute in Cambridge, was the foremost Western sinologist of his time and was once described as 'the Erasmus of the twentieth century'. He blotted his copybook only in the early 1950s, when he supported Chinese and Korean communist claims that the Americans had used biological weapons during the Korean War. For all his discoveries, however, and his contribution to the understanding of how much China contributed to scientific and technological progress, he is perhaps best remembered for his 'grand question'. Put simply, this is: why did modern science, as opposed to ancient and medieval science, only develop in the West, and not China? And, even more pertinently, why did the first industrial revolution occur in western Europe, when China had such a head start? After all, as the economic historian David Landes points out, China was almost there, and much earlier, turning out 125,000 tonnes of pig iron annually as long ago as the eleventh century, seven hundred years before Britain achieved that level of production.[13]

One explanation is the nature of Chinese technical progress itself. The Chinese got there early but they did not follow-through. Chinese water clocks were well ahead of their time, and should have been the precursors of the mechanical clock. The mechanical clock, however – much more precise and durable than the water clock – was developed in Europe and became a Western monopoly for three centuries. Unlike in modern times, where China has been quick to copy Western technology, in medieval times it held back. As Landes again points out, this was 'not for want of interest: the Chinese imperial court and wealthy élites were wild about these machines; but because they were reluctant to acknowledge European technological superiority, they sought to trivialise them as toys. Big mistake.'[14] There are other examples. China's discovery of gunpowder should have put her in a powerful position when it came to weaponry. It was Europe, however, which developed the technology. Gunpowder, in primitive form, was not particularly effective. Only when it was developed in Europe in the form of kernels or pebbles did it achieve real firepower. Chinese gunpowder was mainly useful for fireworks.

A second explanation is that, just at the point when China should have been able to exploit her technology internationally, and develop it, she turned her back on the world. The grand voyages of the treasure ships, which were only tangentially for the purposes of trade, were China's somewhat half-hearted attempt to engage with the rest of the world. They were also to represent the high watermark of such engagement for years.

The cost of the expeditions was high and prompted a fiscal crisis. Indeed, they came to be held in such low regard that the records of the expeditions were destroyed. In the fifteenth century an outward-looking China became inward-looking. Merchants, always held in low regard by the authorities, were formally banned from engaging in foreign trade. Trade promotes economic development and technical progress; China's withdrawal from trade ensured such development was halted. China's technological lead persisted but without the appetite to exploit it. Europe, on the other hand, was never too proud to adopt Chinese technology. 'Until the fifteenth century, European progress in many fields was dependent on transfers of technology from Asia or the Arab world,' writes Maddison. 'In 1405–33, Chinese superiority in shipping technology was evident in seven major expeditions to the "Western Oceans". Chinese ships were much bigger than those of the Portuguese, more seaworthy and more comfortable, with watertight compartments, many more cabins, and a capacity to navigate over large distances to Africa. Thereafter, China turned its back on the world economy, and its maritime technology decayed.'[15]

The most plausible rationale for the lack of follow-through in China is, however, cultural. Between 500 and 600 years ago, China stopped trying. Some scholars, like Mark Elvin, have emphasised the emergence of neo-Confucian philosophy, which was profoundly anti-scientific in attitude, instead valuing introspection, intuition and subjectivity. For Elvin, 'the consequences of this philosophy for Chinese science were disastrous. As the result of a highly sophisticated metaphysics there was always an explanation – which of course was no explanation at all – for anything puzzling ... Here then was the reason why China failed to create a modern science of her own accord, and the deepest source of her resistance to the assimilation of the spirit of Western science both in the 17th century and later.'[16]

Partly related to this, and of even more relevance to present-day China, was the nature of its society and the way it was governed. China, as Desai notes, has long been ruled from the centre. The more powerful the control by the state, the less room for individual initiative. The Chinese, famous for their entrepreneurial abilities, have, it appears, been obliged for centuries to give vent to them only outside China, so sapping has been this control. Even in pre-communist times its citizens were subject to what amounted to totalitarian control. Landes certainly finds this highly plausible, citing Etienne Balazs, author of *Chinese Civilization and Bureaucracy*:

The ingenuity and inventiveness of the Chinese, which have given so much to mankind – silk, tea, porcelain, paper, printing and more – would no doubt have enriched China further and brought it to the threshold of modern industry, had it not been for this stifling state control ... It is the State that kills technological progress in China. Not only in the sense that it nips in the bud anything that goes against it or seems to go against its interests, but also by the customs implanted inexorably by the *raison d'Etat*. The atmosphere of routing, of traditionalism, and of immobility, which make any innovation suspect, and initiative that is not commanded and sanctioned in advance, is unfavourable to the spirit of free inquiry.[17]

The Hindu Equilibrium

There is no equivalent of the Needham question when it comes to India. Though Indians had more than their share of mathematical and scientific breakthroughs (including a string of claims to being the inventors of the negative number and much of modern mathematics), unlike the Chinese they were in no position to challenge the industrial emergence of Britain and other economies in western Europe. India started well. Even 2,000 years ago its agricultural sector was well developed. The range of crops grown in ancient India, and for that matter the agricultural methods used, would have been familiar to any nineteenth-century observer. It included most obviously rice, but also wheat, millet, many pulses, gourds, sugar cane, oil seeds, betel, garlic, peppers, ginger, a variety of spices, cotton, silk, hemp and jute. Indian agriculture was highly labour-intensive, and did not benefit, or perhaps did not require, the kind of technological breakthroughs characteristic of early China. As the historian Dietmar Rothermund has argued, India adopted 'appropriate technology', the traditional Indian economy being

> geared to small-scale production in family units of peasants and artisans. Land and labour as factors of production were abundant, and therefore the third factor – capital – which is substituted for the other factors whenever they are scarce, was not required. There was, of course, some capital formation in trade and also in terms of the construction of wells and tanks for local irrigation, but there was no capital accumulation that would lead to a concentration of the ownership of the means of production. The tools and implements were simple and could be made

locally and cheaply. The manufacturers sponsored by some rulers for the making of arms or of luxury goods were very rare indeed. Wealth was sometimes amassed by successful merchants or victorious warlords, but such wealth was usually lost as quickly as it had been gained.[18]

Small-scale farmers were the backbone of the economy, providing taxes or tribute to local rulers. The vagaries of the climate, and in particular the monsoon, made harvest failures a common occurrence. Peasant farmers, however, bore the risk.

While wealth did not percolate down to the peasants, it existed, as did a relatively sophisticated economic structure. Peter Robb quotes early evidence of 'some very large-scale individual enterprises engaged in manufacture and distribution – pottery, cotton and silk textiles in particular'. There was also trade.

> Within India and beyond, there was a good deal of land, river and sea-borne trade. It is impossible to measure the quantities but the range is plain, implying networks that stretched from Gandhara in the north-west to Bengal in east, and from north Bihar to the southern coasts of India – horses from the north-west; elephants from Assam; coral, pearls and sandalwood from the south; gold and iron from south Bihar; and so on ... A spice trade with the Roman empire was long important along the west coast; Indian as well as Arab traders plied the western Indian ocean as far as Africa.[19]

The idea of India's economic development being frozen for centuries has been touched on earlier, in Lal's Hindu equilibrium, or 'high-level equilibrium trap'. While India did not move forward very much, however, it would be wrong to imply that the economy was unchanging. From about 1000 CE onwards, India was subject to frequent invasions by cavalry troops from Turkey and Afghanistan. Power struggles between the Muslim invaders and the Hindu kingdoms, during the Delhi sultanate from 1192 to 1526, succeeded in further fragmenting the Indian economy. Transport was difficult; most areas were not even linked by roads suitable for bullock carts. The fragmentation of the country meant, according to Rothermund, that 'there was a well-developed trade and a great deal of sophistication in dealing with money and credit, but all this was never institutionalised or guaranteed by any authority. Credit was based on personal relations and not on an impersonal legal system. Therefore all established channels of trade were well financed, but new ventures and investments would rarely find the necessary credit. Among the most well-established branches of trade was the export trade.'[20]

How do we square India's patchy economic development with the great wealth of the Mughal dynasty (1526–1858), which provided such a magnet for Europeans? This line of Muslim emperors left behind grand architectural monuments, most notably the Taj Mahal, built in Agra in the 1630s by the distraught Mughal emperor Shah Jahan after the death of his favourite wife, Mumtaz Mahal. Was this not a reflection of great economic progress? The answer – which is not to deny that wealth – is that India was an extraordinarily unequal society. A Russian merchant, Afanasiy Niktin, who spent four years in central India (the Bahmani sultanate) in the fifteenth century, wrote of the huge contrast between the nobility's wealth and the poverty of the great mass of the population. Later visitors from Europe, accustomed to grinding poverty at home, were struck by similar contrasts. Under the Mughal emperors, the nobility and the courts, as well as a growing number of bureaucrats and moneylenders, enjoyed high living standards and access to the finest products the world could offer. But the largely rural majority population, stuck in the fields, lived a subsistence existence, with one basic meal of rice, millet or pulses a day, their efforts largely providing for the prosperity of the Mughal court.

At the Birth of the Industrial Revolution

For economists and commentators of the modern era analysing the phenomenon of India and China, it is sobering to discover that in this, as in many other things, Adam Smith got there first. In his *Wealth of Nations (An Inquiry into the Nature and Causes of the Wealth of Nations)*, published in 1776, Smith noted that 'China has been long one of the richest, that is, one of the most fertile, best cultivated, most industrious, and most populous countries in world'.[21] But Smith, even then, was able to record that China's economic development 'seems, however, to have been long stationary' and that 'Marco Polo, who visited it more than five hundred years ago, describes its cultivation, industry and populousness almost in the same terms in which they are described by travellers in the present times. It had perhaps, even long before his time, acquired that full complement of riches which the nature of its laws and institutions permits it to acquire.'

Smith, even from his distant vantage point in Scotland, was aware of the grim condition of China's poor, worse than anything in eighteenth-century Britain, although he perhaps chose to emphasise his point through exaggeration. 'The poverty of the lower ranks of people in China far surpasses that of the most beggarly nations in Europe,' he wrote.

In the neighbourhood of Canton many hundred, it is commonly said, many thousand families have no habitation on the land, but live constantly in little fishing boats upon the rivers and canals. The subsistence which they find there is so scanty that they are eager to fish up the nastiest garbage thrown overboard from any European ship. Any carrion, the carcase of a dead dog or cat, for example, though half putrid and stinking, is as welcome to them as the most wholesome food to the people of other countries. Marriage is encouraged in China, not by the profitableness of children, but by the liberty of destroying them. In all great towns several are every night exposed in the street, or drowned like puppies in the water. The performance of this horrid office is even said to be the avowed business by which some people earn their subsistence.[22]

Smith was struck by India's great wealth alongside the low wages of its working people. It was left, however, to James Mill, another product of the Scottish Enlightenment and a near-contemporary of Smith's, to produce the definitive account of India of the time. His six-volume *History of India*, published in the winter of 1817/18, the fruit of twelve years' labour, was described by the historian Thomas Macaulay as 'on the whole the greatest historical work which has appeared in our language since that of Gibbon', and earned him a post with the East India Company, rising to the position of chief examiner. Mill's *History* was comprehensive, telling the story of 'The Hindus' and 'The Mahomadens' and intertwining the country's history with that of the East India Company. If Smith debunked some of the contemporary myths of China, Mill did so for India, although without visiting the country. Mill's version of India was not one where great wealth and natural resources were waiting to be plundered by a determined colonial power. India was inhospitable and making money there was challenging. Looked at from a modern perspective, however, Mill's debunking went too far.

According to the economist Amartya Sen, Mill's *History* 'tells us probably as much about imperial Britain as about India':

James Mill disputed and rejected practically every claim ever made on behalf of Indian culture and intellectual traditions, but paid particular attention to dismissing Indian scientific works. Mill rebuked early British administrators (particularly, Sir William Jones) for having taken the natives 'to be a people of high civilization, while they have in reality made but a few of the earliest steps in the progress to civilization'. Indeed, since colonialism need not be especially biased against any particular colony compared with any other subjugated community, Mill had no great difficulty in coming to the conclusion that the Indian civilization was at par with other inferior ones known to Mill: 'Very nearly the same with that of the Chinese, the Persians, and the Arabians', and also the other 'subordinate nations, the Japanese, Cochin-Chinese, Siamese, Burmans, and even Malays and Tibetans'. Mill was particularly dismissive of the alleged scientific and mathematical works in India. He denied the generally accepted belief that the decimal system (with place values and the placed use of zero) had emerged in India, and refused to accept that Aryabhata and his followers could have had anything interesting to say on the diurnal motion of the earth and the principles of gravitation.[23]

Smith and Mill were writing for their time, but what they correctly deduced was that by the eighteenth and early nineteenth centuries economic power was shifting away from China and India. Smith saw the price of labour, a proxy for what today we would call *per capita* income, as highest in the Netherlands, followed by England, France, Britain's North American colonies, Spain, Spain's American colonies, China and Bengal. Maddison calculates that *per capita* incomes in Europe overtook those in China during the fourteenth century. But population counts for a lot, then as now. Thanks in large part to their huge populations, as recently as 1820 China and India together accounted for 49 per cent of the world economy (China 33 per cent, India 16 per cent), compared with 24 per cent for western Europe, 9 per cent for eastern Europe and less than 2 per cent for America. The writing, however, was on the wall.

Economic Backwaters

Over the centuries China failed to exploit her technological lead and India suffered from a lack of genuine economic progress. Even so, the fall from grace of both countries was spectacular. One moment, it seemed, everybody wanted to plunder their wealth. The next, they seemed to have little to offer. 'Somewhere between the mid-eighteenth and early nineteenth centuries, both these countries became, in the European eyes, bywords for stagnant, archaic, weak nations,' writes Desai. 'For China, this happened between the adulation of Voltaire and the cooler judgment of Montesquieu; in India's case, it was the contrast between Sir William Jones's desire to learn things Indian and James Mill's dismissal of Indian history as nothing but darkness. The 20th century brought nothing but a deepening of the perception of the two countries as bywords for misery and the perceptions were not too far behind actual conditions of the two countries.'[24]

Why was this? At some point, China's population ceased to be a source of economic advantage and became a burden. Chinese technology could not always meet the food demands of sharply growing numbers. Between 1400 and 1800, China's population grew from 65 million to roughly 400 million. Food shortages meant hunger and, sometimes, severe famine. They also meant repeated outbreaks of civil unrest, particularly in the eighteenth and nineteenth centuries. China's rejection of Western technology was by now instinctive and came from the very top. In an oft-told, near-legendary story, in 1793 Lord Macartney, George III's ambassador, took what today would be described as a trade mission to Beijing, complete with an impressive cargo of European technologies to lay before the Chinese emperor, Qian Long, including telescopes, globes, barometers, lenses, clocks, airguns, swords, Wedgwood pottery and three carriages. The emperor was unimpressed, telling the deflated Macartney that his offerings were mere 'amusements for children' and that: 'There is nothing we lack – we have never set much store on strange or ingenious objects, nor do we want any more of your country's manufactures.'[25] The conventional view is that the emperor committed a huge blunder, depriving his country of access to this new technology. Some historians have argued, however, that there was method in Qian Long's madness. He knew that China could not compete in these products, and merely feigned a lack of interest in them. These things come full circle. Today Jane Macartney, a descendant of Lord Macartney, reports for *The Times* from Beijing on China's economic ascent.

Whatever the motivation, without technology, and without ambition, China continued to go backwards. *Per capita* GDP in 1950 was only three-quarters of its 1820 level, over a period in which living standards in Europe and America were racing ahead. The cultural explanation for Chinese economic failure came to the fore. Individualism and entrepreneurial activity were discouraged, or simply failed to bloom, even before the republican and communist eras of the twentieth century. The penny dropped in the second half of the nineteenth century, from around the 1860s, towards the end of the Qing dynasty, prompting a deliberate policy of what was described as 'self-strengthening', partly prompted by China's military vulnerability. Now China was open to outside influences, and outside technologies. Foreign-language schools were opened in Beijing, Shanghai and other cities, foreign books were translated into Chinese, and a delegation was sent to America to seek purchases of capital goods or, as they were described, 'machines to make machines'. A shipyard was constructed in Shanghai to build steamships based on Western technology. Remington rifles were made under licence in the 1870s. In that decade too, there was a new emphasis on the establishment of heavy industry and the exploitation of the country's vast coal reserves. Half a century after George Stephenson China built and tested its first steam locomotive, the *Rocket of China*. A textiles industry also developed. The Shanghai Cotton Cloth Mill produced nearly 4 million metres of cloth in 1892 but was destroyed by fire the following year, and the financial loss – it was uninsured – meant it was never rebuilt.

Self-strengthening did not work, although it brought some industry to China. In some cases costs in China were simply too high, in contrast to present-day circumstances. The Shanghai shipyard produced only fifteen ships, all expensive and, by the time they were completed, obsolete. The workers manufacturing Remington rifles could never achieve the standards of accuracy required; the resulting guns were not only costly to produce but could not shoot straight. The historian J. A. G. Roberts offers a range of explanations for this failure but finds none of them entirely convincing. One is the incompatibility of Confucianism with the needs of a modern state. Another is what he describes as Chinese obscurantism but, as he points out, the case study usually offered in support of this is flawed, 'the often-quoted example being the case of a short stretch of railway which was built to connect Shanghai and Wusong. This railway, which was constructed by a British consortium in 1876, was later bought by Chinese officials and destroyed. Their action was derided as irrational and superstitious, but it has been shown that they destroyed the railway because it had been built on Chinese soil by Westerners who had not obtained permission, and because a fatality on the line had aroused local peasants and threatened disorder.'[26]

There are other explanations. Was the Chinese élite's traditional hostility towards commerce and the merchant class responsible for the failure of the self-strengthening policy? Alternatively, did the élite come to rely too heavily on merchants to finance some of these long-term, economy-building projects, designed to give China an industrial infrastructure, when all those merchants were really interested in was making a fast buck? Certainly, the kind of long-term capital needed to finance China's belated development was not in plentiful supply. Or was it simply the case, as has been argued for India, that China was held down by Western imperialism? Not only was China trying to make up lost ground but, because she was weak militarily in comparison with the Western powers, she had to divert resources that could have been used for modernising the industrial base into armaments.

Gunboat Diplomacy

Having lost her economic power, and lacking military might, in the nineteenth century China was prey to the imperialist ambitions of the great trading nations of Europe, and subject to foreign invasion and influence. The First Opium War of 1839–42 culminated in the capture of Hong Kong by British gunboats. The opium–for–tea trade instigated by the British East India Company was too important to be blocked. Hong Kong's capture was necessary to ensure the free passage of Indian opium in exchange for Chinese tea. The so-called 'Arrow' war of 1856–60, sparked by the seizure by the Chinese of the British-registered ship *Arrow*, saw the opening-up of China's inland waterways to the Anglo-French allies. Weakened by internal uprisings and major rebellions, China was in no position to resist. In 1860 it handed over a large area of territory to Russia, including what became the port of Vladivostok. International treaties, beginning with the 1842 Treaty of Nanjing, forced China to maintain low tariffs and legalised the opium trade. They also saw the establishment of so-called treaty ports, which eventually numbered more than ninety, open to foreign trade and foreign residents. A weakened China was also prey to the attentions of Japan, and suffered defeat in the 1894–5 Sino-Japanese War. China was forced to recognise Korea and cede territory to Japan, including Taiwan. In the aftermath, according to Roberts, there was 'a scramble for China', a huge amount of overseas interest in areas previously regarded as closed to outsiders. 'The scramble for concessions was accompanied by a rapid increase in foreign investment in China,' he writes. 'For example, France took a large share in the Russo-Chinese Bank, which financed the Chinese Eastern Railway, the line constructed across Manchuria. Belgium played an important part in the financing of the Beijing–Hankou Railway, which was completed in 1905. After the Treaty of Shimonoseki had permitted the establishment of industries in the treaty ports, foreign investment in industry increased quickly.'[27]

Railway projects precipitated a boom in inward investment that lasted decades, through the Boxer Rebellion of 1900, the 1911 revolution that saw China become a republic, the First World War and the turbulence and labour unrest of the 1920s. There were periods when this invest-ment appeared to be paying dividends; Chinese industrial production rose by 300 per cent between 1916 and 1928. But, as the economic writer Joe Studwell has recounted in detail, the hopes of foreign investors were not to be fulfilled. Nobody made much money in China. By the time of a second major act of aggression by the Japanese, the invasion of Manchuria in 1931, the writing was on the wall. By the start of the Sino-Japanese War in 1937, it was all over. China's 400 million consumers proved as difficult to charm as the emperor Qian Long had been in 1793. Money and reputa-tions were lost and the railways, 'victims of both economic fantasy and Chinese economic reality', according to Studwell, provided an enduring symbol of that failure: 'If there were returns, they were meagre. In many cases the bonds issued to finance railway construction went unpaid and are today historical curiosities bought and sold by collectors.'[28] For China they were a symbol of its story of relative economic decline.

Tales from the Raj
What of India? Just as there is a version of the Chinese story that attri-butes its downward drift to the malign effects of Western imperialism,

so there are many accounts that relate India's decline to Western, and in particular British, exploitation. China was opened up for trade, and so was India. The British East India Company, which eventually came to rule India from offices in Leadenhall Street in the City, was originally intended to be purely a trading company. Established in 1600 and given exclusive rights to bring products into Britain from India, it was charged with the task of challenging Dutch–Portuguese control of the spice trade. In the first 150 years of its existence it mainly did just that, operating as a significant trading presence at various points along the Indian coast. But the strains were there. After all, India was the focus of domestic and international rivalries. Former journalist Daniel Litvin, in his 2003 book *Empires of Profit*, records the two stages of 'the Company's' development:

> The first stage, which covers the period from the Company's establishment in 1600 until the 1750s shows the employees in India struggling to keep to the stated corporate policy that they should engage only in peaceful trade. Instead they became heavily embroiled in local politics, often contrary to the instructions of their bosses in London. Such was the failure of headquarters to understand and control the situation on the ground that the Company took its first steps towards the invasion of an entire subcontinent in an unplanned, almost accidental way.[29]

After Sir Robert Clive's victory at Plassey in 1757, which saw the French quickly reduced to a marginal role in India, the British East India Company fought to gain control of the country. Warren Hastings was the first East India Company governor-general of India from 1773 to 1785. Charles Canning, Viscount Canning, was the last, from 1856 to 1858, ruling the country during the Indian Mutiny. After it, when India became a more conventional imperial possession, Canning was the first viceroy.

The East India Company changed the nature of the Indian economy. When it took over India was an exporter of process products, including manufactures, and an importer of bullion. By the time of the mutiny India had assumed a more normal colonial position, exporting raw materials and importing manufactures from the colonial power. The Company also forced India into the peculiar three-way trade in which opium, cotton and silver were exported to China in return for tea and silk. These were then mainly returned to Britain along with produce from India.

How exploited was India? 'It is well known to all, that in this age the people of Hindoostan, both Hindoos and Mohammedans, are being ruined under the tyranny and oppression of the infidel and treacherous English,' read the declaration of the Indian mutineers in 1857.[30] All imperial powers exploit; the question is whether British rule effectively condemned India to a subservient economic role, preventing her emergence. 'Did the British impoverish India?' asks Procter & Gamble's former CEO in India Gurcharan Das in his 2002 book *India Unbound*.[31] This is one of the most hotly debated topics in modern Indian history. A powerful body of nationalist and Marxist opinion, taking its lead from Karl Marx himself, argues that this indeed was the case. Marx, writing in the *New York Herald Tribune* in June 1853, put it graphically:

> There cannot, however, remain any doubt but that the misery inflicted by the British on Hindostan is of an essentially different and infinitely more intensive kind than all Hindostan had to suffer before. All the civil wars, invasions, revolutions, conquests, famines, strangely complex, rapid, and destructive as the successive action in Hindostan may appear, did not go deeper than its surface. England has broken down the entire framework of Indian society, without any symptoms of reconstitution yet appearing. This loss of his old world, with no gain of a new one, imparts a particular kind of melancholy to the present misery of the Hindoo, and separates Hindostan, ruled by Britain, from all its ancient traditions, and from the whole of its past history.[32]

Such views are not uncommon a century and a half on. The British, it is often said, plundered, exploited and impoverished India, destroying its economic potential to benefit its own manufacturers. Did not India's share of world industrial output drop from 25 per cent in 1750 to just 2 per cent by 1900? Most modern writers, however, see the role of Britain as somewhat more balanced.

'There is no question that in the 18th century the British plundered and looted India's wealth, as all conquerors have done in history,' writes Das.[33]

> The more important historical question is if Britain systematically exploited its colony by creating ongoing institutions that were to India's detriment. This has to do with the nature and theory of colonialism. I

have already said that the British did not de-industrialise India. It was
the industrial revolution that threw millions of weavers out of work.
It would have happened anyway when the new technologies reached
India. British government policy could have cushioned the impact by
erecting trade barriers, but protecting handlooms would have been a
temporary palliative at best. Odd as it may seem, Britain did not 'exploit'
India enough. Had it made the massive investments in India as it did in
the Americas, India would have become prosperous and a much bigger
market for British goods. An impoverished India was certainly not in
Britain's economic interest.

India's economy was not going anywhere when the British came along.
The centuries-long period of stagnation was continuing and the Mughal
dynasty was crumbling. But India did have the world's biggest cotton
industry in the seventeenth and eighteenth centuries. Could not this,
rather than the Lancashire cotton industry, have been mechanised and
developed? Landes suggests not. The Indian cotton industry was heavily
labour-intensive and locked into that mode of production. If output
needed to be increased, it was simply a question of hiring more people,
though in practice it was more of a cottage industry of self-employed
craftsmen. The spinners and weavers had no interest in technological
innovation, and neither did the Indian middlemen merchants. It was not
the responsibility of the East India Company to force machinery and new
methods on reluctant Indian workers when to have done so would have
been seen as acting against the interests of workers and mill-owners back
in Britain. Innovation in India, as Landes puts it, 'took place within the
conventional manual context, and a big conceptual and social difference
separates machines and hand tools'.[34]

While Europe was moving towards industrial revolution, India was in
a technological blind alley, having made no serious scientific progress for
centuries. Perhaps in the right circumstances the first industrial revolution could have happened in China. In India it was a non-starter. As it was,
according to Lal: 'I could find no evidence, despite nationalist hagiogra-
phy, that there were any prospects for indigenous Promethean growth
emerging in medieval India, growth allegedly blocked by British colonialism. In fact, it was under British aegis that India became one of the pio-
neers of industrialization in the Third World.'[35] A 2004 National Bureau of

Economic Research paper, 'Industry's De-industrialization under British Rule' by David Clinginsmith and Jeffrey Williamson,[36] concludes that the decline of Indian industry arose mainly as a result of the chaotic demise of the Mughals, not the malign influence of the British.

What we do know, however, is that the Indian economy did make some progress, particularly after 1857. Cotton mills, modern for their time, were started by Indian businessmen in the 1850s, mainly in Bombay (Mumbai), selling about half their output of coarse yarns to China and Japan. The jute industry, based around Calcutta (Kolkata), and mainly owned and run by Scots, also developed rapidly in the second half of the nineteenth century. Coal output from Bengal mines rose to 15.7 million tonnes a year by the outbreak of the First World War, and met the demands of India's fast-expanding railway industry. The first Indian steel mill was opened by the Tata Company in 1911 (which nearly a century later successfully bid for Corus, and thus most of what remained of Britain's steel industry). Indian industry grew during the First World War, when imports from Britain were restricted, textiles and steel being particular beneficiaries of being given a free run at the domestic market. It continued to expand in the period after the war. The *swadeshi* movement, which promoted economic nationalism, had from early in the twentieth century urged a boycott of British goods and services, from industrial products to banking and insurance. In the 1920s, official policy endorsed this by implementing a series of tariff increases to protect Indian industry. In the early 1930s, when all governments resorted to protectionism following the introduction of America's Smoot–Hawley Tariff of 1930, the barriers against imports were further increased. By 1934, imports of cotton cloth were subject to a 50 per cent tariff. The results were dramatic. From a turn-of-the-century position where Indian mills supplied only 8 per cent of the cotton bought domestically, the proportion was 62 per cent by 1936 and 76 per cent by 1945. Indian industry was expanding, growing by nearly 6 per cent a year on average between 1913 and 1938, nearly double the rate of increase of industrial production in the rest of the world. Indian industrial output by the time of independence was 6.5 times its level in 1900. Was this economic exploitation? It certainly does not look like it.

The Balance Sheet of Empire

Against this has to be set the fact that colonial rule carried significant costs. Most of the managerial, supervisory and technical jobs in India were occupied by the British. Most of the population remained in rural poverty; Maddison notes that by the time of independence in 1947 just 3 million people were employed in large-scale industry, and a further 12 million in small-scale industry and handicrafts, out of a labour force of 160 million. Britain, as the colonial power, also extracted its 'rent' from India. 'Home charges' – transfers back to Britain – reached £50 million a year by the 1930s. Maintaining a highly paid British administration was another burden for the Indian economy. The drain on the Indian economy as a result of government pensions, interest on official debt and commercial profits averaged 1.5 per cent of gross domestic product in the 1920s and 1930s, and was higher before that. The balance sheet of British rule in India has entries on both sides.

Time has healed. Manmohan Singh, the reforming finance minister who went on to become prime minister, received an honorary degree from Oxford University in July 2005 and praised the legacy Britain had bestowed on India. 'Today, with the balance and perspective offered by the passage of time and the benefit of hindsight, it is possible for an Indian prime minister to assert that India's experience with Britain had its beneficial consequences too,' he said. 'Our notions of the rule of law, of a constitutional government, of a free press, of a professional civil service, of modern universities and research laboratories have all been fashioned in the crucible where an age old civilisation met the dominant empire of the day.'[37] Other benefits, according to Desai, include the English language 'which facilitates even today India's access to global markets', the legal system of property rights and the Western orientation of the country's élite. Britain also, he says, attempted to develop the Indian economy ahead of its old rival: 'India began to acquire railroads and modern industry a quarter of century earlier than China – in the 1850s rather than the 1870s. More foreign capital *per capita* was poured into India than in China.' British rule may also have given India the considerable modern advantage of being a single country. The alternative, Desai speculates, could have been that the spoils of India were divided between Portuguese, British, French, Dutch and Danish trading companies, different regions speaking different languages and subject to different colonial masters. 'The India we talk of today is a 19th century product in more than one sense,' he concludes.[38]

Eclipse

For the nineteenth century and most of the twentieth century, however, Chinese and Indian economic power ebbed away. The period from 1820 to the outbreak of the First World War in 1914 was Europe's golden age; the full flowering of the industrial revolution that began in Britain and spread through the Continent. China and India, of course, had had much earlier industrial revolutions. The twentieth century was America's. The twin pillars of the world economy became backwaters and economically backward. Global economic power rested with the old world of Europe, the new world of North America and the industrial might of Japan. The choices made by India after independence in 1947 and China in the communist era after 1949 are highly relevant and will feature as the backdrop to the modern revival of the two economies. But if we scroll forward a century and a half from 1820 to 1973 – a watershed year for the world economy – the eclipsing of China and India appears almost complete. By the early 1970s western Europe had a 26 per cent share of the global economy, the United States and Canada 25 per cent, while China and India's share was less than 8 per cent (with China rather bigger than India) – equivalent to that of Japan. But Japan's population was a fourteenth of the size of the two Asian giants combined. When, in response to the first oil crisis of the modern era, a grouping of the major economic powers was put together – what eventually became the Group of Seven – there were places for the United States, Japan, Germany, Britain, France, Italy and Canada. Ideological and other differences aside, nobody thought of inviting China and India. They simply were not important enough. Their success stories, it seemed then, were all behind them.

2

Enter the Dragon

'Poverty is not socialism. To be rich is glorious.'

Deng Xiaoping

'The "rise" of China has suddenly become the all-absorbing topic for those professionally concerned with the future of the planet.'

Robert Skidelsky

Pariah State

When did China make the transition from economic backwater to driving force of the global economy? When did worries about human rights and the absence of democracy start to be outweighed by China's economic importance? While it is hard to be precise, and no doubt some will claim to have spotted China's emergence almost from the moment Deng Xiaoping embarked on his liberalising reforms in 1978, perceptions about China have changed dramatically in the space of just a few years. The shadow of the Tiananmen Square massacre of 1989 in Beijing, when hundreds of civilian protestors were killed and thousands injured, loomed large over Western attitudes to China for most of the 1990s. It is fair to say that China did not really come of age as an economic force to be reckoned with until the twenty-first century was under way. Tiananmen, while confirming the brutally repressive nature of the Chinese regime, also appeared to underline its schizophrenic attitude to reform.

The story of the Tiananmen Square massacre is well known, the events that led up to it less so. Tiananmen, to set the location in context, is Beijing's historic gathering place, latterly the symbol of Communist Party power. It was there in 1949 that Mao proclaimed the People's Republic. The student protests that led to the massacre began with the death in April 1989 of Hu Yaobang, the liberal reformer sacked two years earlier by Deng as General Secretary of the Communist Party. Hu was popular, his ousting in response to earlier student protests being widely seen as unfair. The 1989 protests began as marches to mourn his death, students gathering in Tiananmen Square on the day of Hu's funeral and demanding a meeting with Li Peng, the prime minister. When the students were accused of plotting turmoil by an officially ordered editorial in the *China People's Daily*, 50,000 took to the streets in protest. The protests escalated over the following weeks, with up to a thousand students taking part in a hunger strike. On 30 May, ten days after the declaration of martial law, the protestors erected a statue carved by art students, the Goddess of Democracy, in the square. This was too much for the authorities, though Zhao Ziyang, Party general secretary, urged a negotiated settlement and, like his predecessor Hu, lost his job as a result. The troops were ordered in on 4 June and, despite heavy resistance from students and Beijing residents, succeeded in quelling the protests by use of extreme force. The enduring image of the protests, which was broadcast around the world, was that of a lone protestor standing in front of a government tank and refusing to move. While he has not been identified with certainty, it is thought that his fate, like that of many of the other protestors, was to be executed a few days later by firing squad. The Chinese Red Cross estimates that 2,600 protestors died and several thousand were injured.

Beyond the human tragedy of the Tiananmen Square massacre, the effect was to cast doubt, both inside and outside China, on the liberalising reforms being pursued under Deng. Many in the Party hierarchy saw the protests as evidence that the reforms had gone too far, too fast, while others saw them as a signal that the process of economic liberalisation had to reach out to sections of the population that were missing out on the benefits. As it was, the collapse of communism in the Soviet Union and eastern Europe did more than any internal debate in China to settle the argument for further reform.

Appalling Old Waxworks

Tiananmen's legacy, including an embargo on arms sales by the United States and the European Union, and delays in Chinese membership of the World Trade Organisation, persisted well into the 1990s. It also coloured attitudes to the return by Britain of Hong Kong to China in 1997. An air of gloom surrounded the event, the fear being that a vibrant, Western-orientated remnant of empire was about to be swallowed up by a grey and repressive Chinese regime. At the handover ceremony on 30 June 1997, Chris Patten, the last British governor of Hong Kong, who had frequently clashed with Beijing during his five-year posting, spoke of Britain's contribution having been 'the rule of law, clean and light-handed government, the values of a free society', and 'the beginnings of representative government and democratic accountability'. The fear, which turned out to be wrong, was that none of this was necessarily secure under Chinese rule. The Prince of Wales, who also attended the ceremony, was rather less diplomatic. Excerpts from his private diaries, which came to light several years later, refer to goose-stepping Chinese soldiers, and 'the appalling old waxworks' which comprised China's political leadership. Prince Charles's diary entry, headed 'The Great Chinese Takeaway', frets about the future of democracy and about 'creeping corruption and the gradual undermining of Hong Kong's greatest asset – the rule of law'.[1]

The West's engagement with China, therefore, was characterised by extreme suspicion, even until relatively recently. In 1998, when Bill Clinton made a presidential visit to China, the most significant icebreaking episode after Tiananmen, the big issue was still the country's human rights record rather than its economic potential. 'How Bad is China?' asked *Time* magazine, in its curtain-raising piece on the visit.[2] Most Americans still regarded China as 'morally and politically beyond the pale', and the presidential visit was highly controversial. Most of the focus of the trip, indeed, was on a human rights record that was improving only 'glacially' and a Chinese system 'that does not permit any freedoms that might challenge the control of the ruling Communist Party in word or deed and arbitrarily punishes anyone who tries to do so. These issues are most directly antithetical to American values but do not lend themselves to quick, dramatic solutions. China's government does not allow freedom of expression or association, peaceful demonstration or independent labour unions; it does employ detention, torture, the denial of due process.' Not only that, but China's policy of exporting weapons to regimes unfriendly to America was a highly destabilising factor in the post-cold war world, which ran counter to Washington's interests. There was an economic purpose to Clinton's visit, but even that was open to debate. China was good at exporting low-cost manufactured goods to America (it still is) but was unwilling to open her market to imports: 'The Chinese market remains largely untapped because Beijing works at keeping it closed.'[3] China also showed scant respect for intellectual property rights, piracy being apparently an accepted business practice – a topic that was to become a central issue in negotiations over Chinese membership of the World Trade Organisation.

Attitudes to China were by no means uniform during the 1990s but such wariness was widespread. China's economic power was always hidden behind other factors: human rights, the political nature of the regime, and the suspicion of Beijing's motives on the international stage. After the Soviet Union's collapse, perhaps, the West was too quick to see China immediately stepping into its shoes as an aggressive communist super-power. Perhaps, too, China did not do enough to help her own cause. Even now, Tiananmen casts it shadow. In January 2006, when the inter-net search engine Google controversially agreed to comply with China's domestic censorship rules, one of the issues was the ability of Chinese citizens to search for online information about the massacre. The result of the censorship was that Chinese users entering 'Tiananmen' into Google would be greeted only with peaceful pictures of the square.

Mr Biggs Goes to Beijing

One episode illustrates the West's uncertain, even idiosyncratic, attitude to China as a budding economic power in the 1990s. In September 1993 Barton Biggs, then Morgan Stanley's chief market strategist, and a man with a huge reputation in the financial markets, left New York for a short trip to China. He returned, apparently a changed man, quick to share his discoveries with his clients. 'After eight days in China, I'm tuned in, overfed and maximum bullish,' he wrote.[4] His investment note, headed simply 'China!', reflected his new-found enthusiasm. China, he said, would be 'the mother of all bull markets' for investors, and buying shares in Hong Kong – then four years ahead of the British handover – was the way to take advantage of it. 'The wild bull markets in Hong Kong (1970s),

Singapore (late 1970s) and Taiwan (late 1980s) will seem like child's play,' he wrote. 'Not only will prices rise several thousand per cent, I believe, but the supply of stock outstanding will double year after year.' He was very taken with the economy, and the people in control of it. 'We were all stunned by the enormous size of China,' he wrote. 'We were also very impressed with the calibre of the people running China. The vice-governor of the People's Bank said in perfect English: "We are out of the woods".' When Biggs spoke, Wall Street listened. He, after all, had predicted the worldwide stock market crash of October 1987. He was untroubled by the seamier side of China's reputation, describing Western media attitudes as 'sanctimonious'. 'I did not sense pervasive corruption or decadence in China as I have in other developing countries,' he wrote. Chinese leaders were 'smart, tough, friendly people with a definite vision' and good at working the crowds. Morgan Stanley increased its holdings of Hong Kong shares and so did many other investors. The market soared.

Others, however, had their doubts. At the time Zhu Rongji, the Chinese vice-premier with responsibility for the economy (he was christened the 'economic tsar'), was implementing a programme designed to curb a rapidly emerging inflation problem, runaway credit growth and widespread fraud and corruption. His sixteen-point austerity plan had been launched in July, two months ahead of the Morgan Stanley visit. By the autumn there were doubts about whether the authorities would follow-through with the plan, designed to put the economy on a surer footing, and older China hands were worried. 'Barton Biggs went to China and bought the gospel,' said Ranjan Pal, chief regional economist at Jardine Fleming Securities. 'I am less optimistic about the future and really worried about the easing of China's austerity programme. I think they will have to hit the brakes much harder next year. It's going to be bad for all concerned.' Biggs also found himself up against the formidable Milton Friedman, Nobel laureate and one of the greatest economists of the twentieth century. He too had been following the Chinese economy and did not like what he saw. 'There is no evidence the government wants to give up control of the market,' he said. 'They have been following a stop–go policy, using blunt instruments to try to cool the economy and control inflation. It is hard to tell what will happen. The momentum is going to be held back, and perhaps later stymied.' As a monetarist, he was also concerned about the prospect of runaway inflation.

Investors, however, preferred the Biggs version, until a couple of months later in November 1993, when another note from the Morgan Stanley strategist pulled the rug away from beneath their feet. This time the tone was different. 'It is not clear who the winners and losers will be in the struggle for economic policy in China,' he wrote. He was also concerned about the boom in Hong Kong share prices that his earlier optimism had sparked, saying that 'the craziness content about the magic of China is beginning to look like a bubble'. His then colleague David Roche (not to be confused with Stephen Roach, Morgan Stanley's chief economist at the time of writing), who had accompanied Biggs on the trip, said: 'There are important risks in China. Income differentials are growing like wildfire. Keeping a lid on political reform can be dangerous. The People's Liberation Army could become the problem. So could protectionism.' Because of this, Morgan Stanley was reducing its Hong Kong holdings, 'taking a third of our chips off the table', in Biggs's words.[5] The gambling analogy was appropriate. Many investors lost out heavily and complained to Hong Kong's market regulators, but to no avail. It was a lesson that there was money to be lost as well as made in China.

Too Big to Ignore

What has changed to make China noticed more as an economic threat – and opportunity – than as a pariah state? The short answer is that she has achieved critical mass; her economy has become too large and influential to ignore. The country's economic growth rate, averaging 9.5 per cent a year in real terms since 1978, has long been spectacular. But to exert significant influence economies need to combine growth and size. In the early years of China's long expansion, in the 1980s, even her growth rate of over 9 per cent was equivalent to perhaps a tenth of global economic growth, sometimes less; a relatively minor contribution. In the 1990s, when post-Tiananmen doubts were at their height, attention focused in any case on the booming US economy. The dot.com boom and America's longest-ever economic expansion diverted attention away from the fast-emerging Chinese economy. That was always going to change, and it took the bursting of the dot.com bubble, together with the effects on the US economy of the 9/11 terrorist attacks, to bring it home. Over the period from 2001 to 2005, China accounted for as much as a third of global economic growth. By the end of 2004, the Council on Foreign Relations in Washington could look forward to the prospects for 2005 as 'a US–China story', these being the twin locomotives of the world economy. 'China's sheer size, coupled with its rapid growth, makes it a major player in the global economy,' said Anne Krueger, deputy managing director of the International Monetary Fund, in a speech in 2005.[6] She noted that while 'this is an economy with a lot of catching up to do', with low *per capita* incomes and widespread poverty, China had become the major economic force in Asia. 'As an engine of regional growth, it is clear that China has overtaken Japan. With Japan barely growing in recent years, the buoyancy of the Chinese economy has been crucial for other Asian economies.' China had also fitted into the gap vacated on the other side of the world by a slow-growing Europe, pulling in imports – notably commodities – that Latin American countries would normally have exported to the European Union. The focus on China was deliberate. It has become common to refer to the BRICs (Brazil, Russia, India and China) economies, christened as such by Goldman Sachs to capture the four fastest-growing, large emerging economies. 'Of course, China is not the only fast-growing emerging economy that is making waves around the world,' wrote Pam Woodall in the *Economist*.

> But China really does loom much larger: its contribution to global GDP growth since 2000 has been almost twice as large as that of the next three biggest emerging economies, India, Brazil and Russia, combined. Moreover, there is another crucial reason why China's integration into the world economy is today having a bigger global impact than other emerging economies, or than Japan did during its period of rapid growth from the mid-1950s onwards. Uniquely, China combines a vast supply of cheap labour with an economy that is (for its size) unusually open to the rest of the world, in terms of trade and foreign direct investment. The sum of its total exports and imports of goods and services amounts to around 75 per cent of China's GDP; in Japan, India and Brazil the figure is 25–30 per cent.[7]

China and the Supercycle

Suddenly China was exerting a huge influence beyond her shores. After years in the doldrums, commodity prices entered what excited traders decided was the beginning of a 'supercycle' in around 2004, driven by

China's hunger for raw materials and energy. Such cycles are relatively rare; the only two previous ones in modern times were in the late nineteenth/early twentieth centuries, and in the twenty-five to thirty years following the end of the Second World War. It remains to be seen whether this one has the staying power to last for the several decades necessary to qualify as a true supercycle. The omens in 2004, however, appeared to suggest it. From virtually nowhere, China came to account for a fifth of consumption of many industrial commodities, from alumina through to zinc and, perhaps more importantly, the lion's share of the rise in demand for these and other commodities. In 2002–3, for example, China accounted for more than 50 per cent of the rise in worldwide demand for cement, 60 per cent of the increase in alumina demand, nearly 50 per cent for aluminium, 90 per cent of the rise in copper consumption, 70 per cent of zinc, 50 per cent of iron ore and 80 per cent of steel.

When oil prices rose sharply from 2002 onwards, from around $20 a barrel to nearly $80 a barrel during the summer of 2006, many factors could be blamed, including the war in Iraq, supply disruptions in producing countries such as Venezuela and Nigeria, the impact of Hurricane Katrina on oil facilities on America's Gulf Coast, and the heightened risk of terrorist attacks in Middle East states and of insurgence in Saudi Arabia. But as well as these supply disruptions, both actual and feared, there was an important shift happening on the demand side. Until well into the 1990s China was not an oil importer of any consequence. Suddenly, however, by the first five years of the twenty-first century, Chinese oil demand had begun to exert a huge influence. Figures from the International Energy Agency show that global oil demand rose by 7.9 million barrels a day over the period 2000–2005. Of this, more than 2.4 million barrels a day – over 30 per cent of the increase – was accounted for by China. There were two reasons for China's thirst for oil. One was its rapid rate of economic growth; the other was the 'oil intensity' of that growth. Western economies have become, over the past three decades, gradually less sensitive to oil. The oil intensity of economic growth in the advanced economies averages 50 per cent, Organisation for Economic Co-operation and Development data shows, by which is meant that for every 1 per cent rise in gross domestic product there is a 0.5 per cent rise in demand for oil. In contrast, oil intensity for developing economies, including China, is about 120 per cent, each 1 per cent GDP increase requiring 1.2 per cent additional oil demand. The shift in the world economy towards China has had a momentous effect on the demand for oil and other commodities.

The China Price

China's economic power has not just been hard to ignore because of her weight in the global economy and the resulting impact on demand for scarce resources. 'The China price', according to *Business Week*, constitute 'the three scariest words' in US industry. Cut your price by 30 per cent or lose your customers. Nearly every manufacturer is vulnerable – from furniture to networking gear. It has not just been American industry, of course, which has been vulnerable to competition from low-cost Chinese manufacturers or, more to the point, the Chinese operations of multinational firms, many of them US-owned. Indeed, for Western-based industry, the China effect is a double whammy. China has bid up the price of raw materials while at the same time severely limiting the ability of companies to pass on cost increases. Chinese competition more usually has the effect of forcing price cuts, or forcing firms to give up the ghost. 'In general, it means 30 to 50 per cent less than what you can possibly make something for in the US,' wrote *Business Week*. 'In the worst cases it means below your cost of materials. Makers of apparel, footwear, electric appliances, and plastics products, which have been shutting US factories for decades, know well the futility of trying to match the China price.'[8] It gave the example of XCel Mold of Ohio, which bid $2.07 million to supply a set of plastic moulds to a US appliance maker but lost the business when a Chinese supplier bid $1.44 million. Mission-style beds made in China retail for $829, compared with $1,800 for a typical American-made model. Network and telecoms equipment firm 3Com's Chinese operation could make datacom switching exchanges for corporations with an $183,000 list price, against Cisco's US-made price of $245,000. Chinese suppliers have sold crepe streamers to US retailers for just 9 US cents a roll, below the production costs of Seaman Paper, one of America's biggest suppliers.

It is not only firms that have to face up to the cost of China's emergence. Workers in the advanced world have suffered a collective loss of bargaining power. It is no coincidence that China's entry into global markets has been accompanied by subdued growth in wages elsewhere. Employers can and do shift production. Richard Freeman of Harvard University, an expert in international labour markets, says the emergence of China, India and the former Soviet Union has effectively doubled the global labour force, with just under 1.5 billion new workers making their claim for a share of the action. Given that there has not been a commensurate increase in the supply of global capital, the effect has been to lower the capital–labour ratio to 55–60 per cent of what it was before. This may seem like an esoteric point but, as Freeman pointed out, it is highly significant: 'The capital/labour ratio is a critical determinant of the wages paid to workers and of the rewards to capital. The more capital each worker has, the higher will be their productivity and pay. A decline in the global capital/labour ratio shifts the balance of power in markets toward capital, as more workers compete for working with that capital.' As significant as the quantity of extra workers from China, India and elsewhere is their quality. The normal assumption, that economies like China are good only for low-value, low-cost production, is already being tested. By 2010 China will be producing more PhDs in science and engineering than America. 'Historically, advanced countries have innovated high-tech products that require high-wage educated workers and extensive R&D, while developing countries specialise in old manufacturing products,' added Freeman. 'The reason for this was that the advanced countries had a near monopoly on scientists and engineers and other highly educated workers. As China, India and other developing countries have increased their number of university graduates, this monopoly on high-tech innovative capacity has diminished. Today, most major multinationals have R&D centres in China or India, so that the locus of technological advance may shift … Certainly, the rate of technological catch-up will grow, reducing the lead of advanced countries over the lower wage developing countries.'[9]

These are big changes, which have already had political as well as economic consequences. The rich economies have faced competition before, and usually ended up as net gainers from the process. The effect of the 'China price' is both beneficial and damaging. It is an enormous boon to Western consumers, dramatically reducing the price of clothing, shoes and every kind of electronic gadget. But when those same consumers are wearing a different hat, as workers, they begin to worry where the next pay cheque is coming from. There will be more on that later. First it is worth asking the question: how did China come to be so economically powerful, and thus so influential, so quickly? The answer is that it only happened after a very long and bitter struggle, which is worth briefly revisiting.

China's Command Economy

The 1950s and 1960s were a golden age for the world economy. The recovery from the devastation of the Second World War, the bringing-down of trade barriers that had cemented the depression of the 1930s, and the determination to create a stable international financial system governed by the principles agreed by the Allies at Bretton Woods in New Hampshire in 1944, ensured strongly rising prosperity in the West. In China, however, it was a very different story. Almost the first act of China's new communist leadership after the 1949 revolution was to intervene – under pressure from Stalin – on behalf of North Korea in the Korean War, an intervention that resulted in three-quarters of a million Chinese casualties and left the country saddled with large debts to Moscow arising from the supply of Soviet arms. While the Korean War provided an important foreign policy distraction, domestically attention focused on land reform, that is, the redistribution of land from landlords and farm-owners to peasants. This displacement coincided with Mao Tse-tung's first reign of terror. Indeed, the two were often indistinguishable. According to Jung Chang and Jon Halliday: 'This nationwide campaign, which lasted a year, went hand in hand with the land reform in the newly occupied areas, where some two-thirds of China's population lived. Some 3 million perished, either by execution, mob violence, or suicide. Mao wanted the killings performed with maximum impact, and that meant having them carried out in public.'[10] The official view, then and now, was rather different. According to one current official website, 'farmers with little or no land were given land of their own, greatly arousing their enthusiasm for production'.[11]

China was tied to Russia by the Korean War and, increasingly, by economic policy. The first five-year plan under Mao, from the beginning of 1953 to 1957, took Stalin's blueprint. The aim was to achieve the transition from what remained of a mixed economy into a fully functioning socialist economy. Planners came over from Moscow to advise the Chinese government on how to achieve this. An army of Soviet engineers, technicians and scientists were on hand to supervise the installation of heavy industrial plant and equipment, itself mainly manufactured in the Soviet Union for export to its new, aggressively industrialising ideological soul mate. The plan's twin aims were to achieve a shift from primary production, particularly agriculture, into heavy industry, and to bring about near-complete state ownership of the means of production. All this was to be achieved alongside a high rate of economic growth. Initially, the prescription appeared to be working. We marvel at China's post-reform rate of economic growth of 9–10 per cent a year but this, surprisingly, was what was achieved under Mao's first five-year plan. Industrial production grew by 19 per cent a year, admittedly from a low base, but enough to see iron and steel, coal, cement and electricity generation industries established. Even agriculture, supposedly the poor relation, did relatively well, production increasing by 4.5 per cent annually – necessary to feed the growing population. Official Chinese accounts refer to this as a 'golden era' for farming. The collectivisation aims, meanwhile, were also achieved. By 1956, 67.5 per cent of industrial enterprises in China were state-owned, with the rest in public–private partnerships. More than 90 per cent of farms belonged to co-operatives.

This success on the surface did not, however, prevent disillusionment setting in well before the plan was completed. China's plan, as noted, was Stalinist, though Stalin himself died in March 1953, to be replaced by Nikita Khrushchev. In the Soviet Union, Stalin's plans, brutally enforced, had achieved the aim of producing enormous shifts from countryside to town and city, using rural workers as the engine of economic growth – the classic prescription for economic development. Mao's plan produced a rise in non-farm employment, mainly in the new heavy industries, from 36.5 million in 1953 to just below 41 million by 1957. But this was not enough to absorb the increase in the working-age population, which averaged at least 4 million a year. The planned restructuring of the economy was not happening, or at least not happening fast enough. China's rural population was continuing to grow rapidly, but agriculture, while raising its output, was not doing so quickly enough to stave off intermittent, and in some cases catastrophic, food shortages. Even in the 1950s some in China were critical of the Soviet-style approach adopted. Gu Zhun, an economist at the Economics Institute of the Chinese Academy of Sciences, pointed out in 1956 that the lack of any price or market mechanism in the plan was a fatal obstacle to economic efficiency, particularly in agriculture. He, however, was a voice in the wilderness, and labelled a 'bourgeois Rightist' for his trouble.[12]

The Great Leap Backward

In the late 1950s, with relations with Moscow cooling and the first Soviet-style plan being increasingly called into question, Mao launched his Great Leap Forward. From now on China would be subject to 'permanent revolution'. 'In making revolution one must strike while the iron is hot – one revolution must follow another, the revolution must continually advance,' he told the Supreme State Conference on 28 January 1958. China would catch up with Britain in steel output in fifteen years. Everything would move ahead at a faster pace, farm output as well as industrial production. To solve the problem of inadequate food supplies, Mao launched his *xiafang* 'down to the countryside' movement, dispatching thousands of ideologically sound technical experts into rural areas to amalgamate 750,000 agricultural co-operatives, by now called production brigades, into some 23,500 communes, each with around 5,000 households, or more than 20,000 individuals. Many combined agricultural production with primitive industrial activity, the famous backyard pig-iron furnaces that became a symbol, not of any leap forward, but of China's economic backwardness.

The idea was to exploit economies of scale, but the result was disastrous. Commune cadres, Mao's brutal enforcers, used every available method to try to get peasants to produce more, suspecting them of hiding their harvests and inflicting dreadful punishments, even death upon them. Paranoia was rife about the failure of the Great Leap Forward to deliver, Mao at one stage laying the blame on the humble sparrow as one of 'four pests' stealing grain and reducing production. But the results of his re-organisation, concealed at first by false official claims about the success of harvests, was a four-year famine, lasting from 1958 to 1961, in which an estimated 38 million people died.

Industry fared little better. By the end of 1958 1,639 arms-centred industrial projects were under construction, but only twenty-eight were producing, and many were never completed at all. As in the nineteenth century, when China had belatedly tried to catch up with the West, the quality of China's industrial output was dire:

> The breakneck speed he [Mao] imposed sabotaged quality and created a long-term problem that was to plague arms production throughout his reign. China ended up with planes that could not fly, tanks that would not

go in a straight line (on one occasion a tank swerved round and charged at watching VIPs) and ships that were almost a greater hazard to those who sailed in them than to China's enemies. When Mao decided to give Ho Chi Minh a helicopter, the manufacturers were so scared it might crash that they detained it at the border.[13]

Soon China was on her own. After a bitter and public dispute during 1959, Khrushchev withdrew all Russia's military and industrial experts from China, and cut off technical assistance. By then the failure of the Great Leap had cost Mao the chairmanship of the People's Republic, though he retained his position as Party chairman. This did not, however, prevent the launch of a second Great Leap, which focused on extending the commune principle to urban areas, in 1960. That too failed, and was abandoned in 1961.

Picking up the Pieces

Prominent among those who were tasked with salvaging the situation from the mess left by Mao's Great Leap was Deng Xiaoping, by then general secretary of the Chinese Communist Party, later the architect of China's genuine leap forward. Deng replaced the fanaticism and brutality of the Great Leap with pragmatism, a strategy based on gradually raising investment, valuing education and individual expertise. Pragmatism, he argued, would get better results in the end. 'It doesn't matter whether a cat is black or white so long as it catches mice' became his most quotable line, though he was inscrutable about its meaning. Deng, along with Liu Shaoqi, Mao's 1959 successor as chairman of the People's Republic, the economist Chen Yun and Peng Zhen, Beijing's mayor, set about reshaping the economy.

Liu, risking the anger of Mao, told a special conference of 7,000 senior Party officials in Beijing in January 1962 that 'there is not only no Great Leap Forward, but a great deal of falling backward', with tens of millions of people short of food, clothes and other essentials. He embarked with Deng and Chen's help, on a very different strategy. This time the priority was agriculture, with the country's most pressing need being to respond to the dire food shortages three years of falling production had brought about. Chen devised a strategy of investing heavily in agriculture, the state supplying new machinery. Chemical fertilisers were used extensively, often for the first time. The communes remained in place, but often individual farmers were allowed to lease land from them and effectively return to the way they had always operated, before the first five-year plan and, more notably, before the Great Leap Forward. From the wreckage of Mao's failed strategy agricultural output began to rise, eventually getting back to its 1957 level by 1965.

Liu's liberal approach also extended to industry, many 'Stalinist' state enterprises being closed down or abandoned before they had begun to produce. Thirty million workers, who had been recruited from rural areas to operate these new but hugely inefficient industrial plants, were sent back to the countryside. Free enterprise did not flourish but remaining industrial operations came to be run by managers, who were given production authority, rather than bureaucrats. New industries, including petrochemicals, were developed. This industrial recovery was, as J. A. G. Roberts notes, 'remarkable for two reasons: it was achieved at a time when China was technologically isolated, and when the development of nuclear weapons – China's first nuclear test took place in October 1964 – was absorbing high technology resources'.[14] Again risking Mao's ire, Liu and his colleagues had made room to increase state investment in agriculture and to restructure industry by cutting back on arms spending, cancelling some of Mao's pet projects, such as nuclear submarines, and drastically reducing the overseas aid that Mao had doled out liberally to win friends and influence leaders in developing countries. The economy, freed from its Stalinist yoke and run competently, enjoyed a renaissance lasting several years. But Mao was to ensure that it would not last.

Back to Square One

Any account of Mao's life inevitably dwells on the fact that, in terms of sheer brutality and lack of regard for human life, he ranked with Hitler and Stalin. He was also remarkably incompetent. Whenever Mao exerted control over the Chinese economy the results were disastrous, and the Cultural Revolution (1966–76) was no exception. During this period, according to one of the pre-eminent economists of the People's Republic, Jinglian Wu, 'market-oriented reform was politically unacceptable because of the obstacle of the ideological creed that administrative order is the only way to allocate resources under socialism'.[15] That must count as an understatement. The turmoil of the Cultural Revolution, and the economic damage it caused, meant that China suffered a lost decade of development. Mao's first failure, the Soviet-style planning of the 1950s, was to be repeated on a more dramatic scale. Indeed, the Cultural Revolution, or the Great Proletarian Cultural Revolution, to give its full name, had the specific aim of reversing what Mao and his followers saw as the 'bourgeois' and 'capitalist' reforms of Liu, Deng, Chen and the others. The Cultural Revolution was partly revenge for the snub Mao had received when he had been sidelined politically in the early 1960s, and partly an attempt to put China back on what he saw as the economic straight and narrow. Liu and Deng were the 'capitalist-roaders', who were turned into public enemies and purged from the leadership. Liu's persecution led to his early death in 1969, while Deng was paraded around the streets of Beijing wearing a dunce's cap.

To describe the Revolution in terms of its economic impact is, of course, to underplay it grotesquely. This was terror on a frightening scale, even the more so because it was brought about by the indoctrination of young people into becoming 'Red Guards' to rise up against their teachers and parents. The young became the ideologically pure, taking on their decadent elders. The violence was extreme, the disruption enormous, as tens of thousands of people were forced into internal exile while tens of millions were subject to attacks, mistreatment or wrongful imprisonment. Between 1966 and 1969 an estimated 500,000 died. Mao had unleashed the mob. No tradition was sacred. 'In summer 1966 Red Guards ravaged every city and town and some areas in the countryside,' write Jung Chang and Jon Halliday.

> Home, with books and anything associated with culture, became a
> dangerous place. Fearing that the Red Guards might burst in and torture
> them if "culture" was found in their possession, frightened citizens
> burned their own books or sold them as scrap paper, and destroyed their
> own art objects. Mao thus succeeded in wiping out culture from Chinese
> homes. Outside, he was also fulfilling his long-held goal of erasing
> China's past from the minds of his subjects. A large number of historical
> monuments, the most visible manifestation of the nation's civilization,
> which had so far survived Mao's loathing, were demolished. In Peking, of
> 6,843 monuments still standing in 1958, 4,922 were now obliterated.[16]

The turmoil on the streets provided the backdrop for Mao to seize political control and destroy his opponents (although in the case of Deng only temporarily). It also provided a re-run of the Great Leap Forward a decade earlier, although the main effect this time was on the country's recently strengthened industrial sector. The political activity of students and other activists severely disrupted production in the mines and factories. The requisitioning of trains to transport Red Guards around the country meant deliveries of goods and materials were curtailed. Most seriously of all, managers, engineers, technicians and scientists, who were accused like the political leadership of being 'capitalist-roaders', were deposed from their positions and forced into menial tasks. Predictably, industrial output slumped, dropping by a sixth in 1967. Imports of capital equipment were halted, depriving China of the latest technology, as the country turned inward. The closure of the universities meant the supply of highly educated scientists and engineers was halted. The atmosphere of suspicion and persecution provided an economic climate in which nobody was prepared to risk standing out from the crowd. Revolutionary committees, rather than managers, ran industrial enterprises. Mao, once more, had set China back years.

The economy stabilised by the early 1970s, though, largely thanks to a new drive intended to equip China with the defence capability needed both to achieve superpower status and to respond to the risk of war with the Soviet Union. Whether or not Mao ever believed in it, he used the Soviet threat to push through a big increase in military spending. More was spent on the nuclear weapons programme in the 1971–5 period than over the previous fifteen years. This was the era of Richard Nixon's historic February 1972 visit, which he called 'the week that changed the world', and which effectively guaranteed US support for China against Soviet aggression. The visit also gave China access to Western technology, particularly missile and aircraft technology, supposedly in exchange for more general access to the Chinese market. Not for the first time, however, that was to prove elusive.

Awakenings

For China's economy the early 1970s were in many ways a re-run of the aftermath of the Great Leap Forward. Even some of the characters were the same. Deng Xiaoping, apparently in a position of permanent exile from power for being China's number two 'capitalist-roader', was brought back into government by premier Zhou Enlai. Deng was made vice-premier in the spring of 1973, with responsibility for economic recovery, and quickly carved out a strategy based on the 'four modernisations', of agriculture, industry, defence and science and technology. The plan, presented by Zhou to the Fourth National People's Congress in January 1975, had echoes of the ambition of Mao's Great Leap Forward. The aim was to catch up with the industrial nations of the West by the start of the new millennium. It was, however, a false start. Zhou and Deng suffered constant sniping from the Gang of Four – Jiang Qing (Mao's wife), Zhang Chunqiao, Yao Wenyuan and Wang Hongwen – who described them as 'poisonous weeds' and continued to advocate a return to an economy devoid of incentives and private ownership. Deng stood in for Zhou when he became ill with cancer in the autumn of 1975 and appeared to be his natural successor when the premier died in January 1976. Pressure from the Gang of Four and their followers ensured he was passed over, however, and forced once more into political exile.

The result was, yet again, economic stagnation. The 'four modernisa-tions' programme was to reappear later, but never got off the ground in its first incarnation. By the time of Mao's death in September 1976, there was little reason for optimism. 'Ten years of the Great Cultural Revolution had driven the Chinese economy to the verge of collapse,' writes Jinglian Wu.[17] The fact that the mid-1970s were also a period of turbulence for the Western capitalist economies offered little comfort. The Chinese economy in the 1950s, 1960s and 1970s was characterised by wild lurches in policy, economic instability and an overwhelming lack of direction. The shift from Stalinist central planning, back to an emphasis on agriculture and through to the wasted years of the Cultural Revolution, all took their toll. This was a time, it should be recalled, when much of the rest of Asia was starting to stir. Japan, China's bitter enemy, grew at an average rate of 7 per cent a year for most of the 1950s, accelerating to more than 10 per cent during the period 1960–73. Assessing what was happening to China's growth rate over this period is more challenging. Even today there are serious doubts about the reliability of the country's economic data. Forming a judgement on the economy's performance during the Mao era, when there was even more of an incentive to exaggerate, is difficult. The Penn World Tables (maintained by the Center for International Comparisons at the University of Pennsylvania) offer one, often-quoted source. They paint a picture of extreme volatility for the Chinese economy over this period, big increases in output one year being followed by equally spectacular falls the next. Some of this is related to variations in the agricultural harvest, both because of climate and political decisions. Overall, however, they suggest that *per capita* GDP rose by 2.2 per cent a year during most of the 1950s, slipped to 1.6 per cent a year during the 1960s, and averaged 1.8 per cent during the 1970s. This was not only much slower than Japan, it was also significantly weaker than the industrialised world as a whole. For a developing economy, it was feeble in the extreme. When the communists took over in 1949, China had fallen behind the rest of the world. Three decades later it was even further behind. This was an economy crying out for genuine reform. The question was whether it would ever get it.

The Great Reformer

When Deng Xiaoping died on 19 February 1997 at the age of 92, three years after last being seen in public, the world was ready with its tributes. *Time* magazine, which made him its man of the year twice, in 1978 and 1985 (a rare honour), called him 'the last emperor'. CNN said he had 'set the People's Republic on a course of reform and liberalisation that would change the face of China and the world'.[18] Margaret Thatcher described him as 'a man of vision and leadership who profoundly changed the life of the Chinese people for the better'. For the *Washington Post* it was 'the end of an era for China. One of the last survivors of China's communist revolution, Deng had guided the country out of the chaos of the Cultural Revolution, flung open China's doors to the outside world and loosened the grip of central economic planning while insisting that the Communist Party's monopoly on power go unchallenged.'[19] This echoed the eulogy in Beijing's Great Hall of the People by President Jiang Zemin a few days later. Jiang, fighting back tears, pledged to continue to pursue the reform and modernisation agenda of his predecessor, of whom he said: 'The decision to take economic construction as the centre represents the most fundamental achievement made under Comrade Deng Xiaoping's leadership, in the effort to bring order out of chaos.' His state funeral was the biggest since that of Mao two decades earlier.

The only sour note was struck by those who thought Deng had sold out to capitalism, failed to keep the communist faith and brutally suppressed opposition within his own country. Thus, the International Committee of the Fourth International, in its obituary, was scathing. 'The career of Deng Xiaoping demonstrates the transformation of the Chinese Communist Party from an organisation based on the working class and fighting for its liberation from capitalism and imperialism into an organisation which is the principal instrument for the development of capitalism in China and the suppression of the working class,' its editorial board wrote. 'Deng Xiaoping, whose political awakening coincided with the May Fourth Movement of radicalized Chinese youth, will go down in history as the butcher of Chinese youth and workers at Tiananmen Square, mowed down by machine guns as they sang "The Internationale".'[20]

What nobody challenged was that in a decade and a half as effective leader of a quarter of the world's population, from the late 1970s to the early 1990s, Deng had profoundly changed China. A man whose earlier attempts to force through economic reform had been frustrated by domestic political opposition finally got his way, and with spectacular results. The modern Chinese miracle dates from 1978, the moment Deng was able to put his reform ideas into practice. Indeed, such is the difference of performance between the Deng and pre-Deng eras that it is almost as if he flicked a switch to turn on the extra economic power.

How did he do it? And how did he do it in a way that to the Communist Party machinery in Beijing, if not to the Fourth International, remained true to the principles of the People's Republic? He was, said the central government on his death, the 'Great Marxist, Great Proletarian Revolutionary, politician, militarist, diplomat; one of the main leaders of the Communist Party of China, the People's Liberation Army of China, the People's Republic of China; the great architect of China's socialist opening-up and modernised construction; the founder of Deng Xiaoping theory'.[21] Anybody who could achieve that, and win heartfelt praise from Margaret Thatcher, must have been something special.

Marxism and the Market

China's emergence started, as ever, on the land. Mao's legacy was a rural economy in which grinding poverty and hunger were the norm. 'In countless villages lived four-fifths of the hundreds of millions of Chinese, most of them in abject poverty,' one account described it. 'An entire family might share a single pair of trousers. If lucky, they might live in a small thatched roof hut with a hole at the top to let out the smoke from the open hearth fire. Peasants transported their ducks and geese to markets along rivers and ancient canals; there were few roads. This was not the Middle Ages, but China, circa 1976, the year Mao died. The country was in the depths, its people depressed and devoid of hope for their lives.'[22] Deng, purged from power by the Gang of Four in 1976, and rehabilitated in 1977, gradually emerged to become China's supreme leader, though without formal title. With his old ally, the economist Chen Yun, Deng's reform programme began with the handing-back of land to peasant farmers, and the introduction of new freedoms to sell surplus produce outside the state planning framework. Whether the effect was as they intended or not, it was spectacular.

The granting of new 'market' freedoms to rural families transformed Chinese agriculture, traditionally the economy's Achilles heel. Not only did rural reform lift tens of millions out of poverty – Deng ranks as the leader who lifted more people out of destitution than any other in the twentieth century, no mean achievement – but the example of agriculture provides a perfect illustration of his approach. Deng's declared aim was to preserve 'socialist agriculture'. The freedoms given to individual farmers to market their surplus produce were intended to provide a small incentive, but little more. Officially under Deng, farming was still intended to be organised in collectives, albeit small ones, not as family farms. But the incentives proved more powerful than anybody had reason to expect: Chinese grain production rose by a third in six years, reaching an all-time high of 407 million tonnes by 1984, and at the same time farmers diversified into other activities, including raising animals and making dairy products. At local level, meanwhile, farmers voted with their feet and turned themselves back into family units, an action to which Beijing turned a blind eye. The new units, the so-called household-contracting units, proved highly effective.

Suddenly, China's vast rural population started to experience a degree of prosperity unknown in the past. *Per capita* net incomes of rural households trebled between 1978 and 1985, rising to nearly Rmb 400, reaching Rmb 2,366 by 2001 (where Rmb is the renminbi, China's currency – worth roughly an eighth of a dollar in 2006). That has to be put into perspective – the 2001 level was still the equivalent of only $300 a year – but the direction of travel was unmistakable. Between 1978 and 2000 the gross value of the rural economy's output in money terms increased seventeen-fold.

It was not all plain sailing. The initial surge in output in the first half of the 1980s resulted in an unusual situation for China, a glut of grain. The government's response was to put in place a price-support system, official purchases being designed to ensure farmers were not penalised for their success. The rural problem was to return with a vengeance in the 1990s, when farmers were left behind by the rising prosperity of China's urban population. In March 2006 Wen Jiabao, the Chinese premier, announced a 14 per cent increase in rural funding and rescinded the agricultural tax, China's oldest, which had been collected from farmers for more than 2,600 years. The determination to build 'a new socialist countryside' was driven by the need to tackle 'the yawning gap between the city and the countryside', according to the Chinese government's own description.[23] Said Wen: 'We need to implement a policy of getting industry to support agriculture and cities to support the countryside, strengthen support for agriculture, rural areas and farmers, and continue making reforms in rural systems and innovations in rural institutions to bring about a rapid and significant change in the overall appearance of the countryside.'

These later problems aside, rising agricultural output killed two birds with one stone in a way that was crucial to China's rapid economic development. First, it produced the food surpluses that were in sharp contrast to the shortages and famines characteristic of the 1950s and 1960s. Rising farm output provided the bedrock of economic growth. Second, and as importantly, it allowed a surplus of people to move from rural areas to China's fast-expanding towns and cities. The increase in farm productivity meant that not so many people were needed to work the land.

The idea of the 'reservoir of cheap labour' as a key to economic development emanated from the great economist and Nobel laureate Sir Arthur Lewis, and has been much debated since. Few economists would argue that a shift in population from rural to urban areas is both a condition and a defining characteristic of economic development. It has certainly been integral to China's rapid growth. In 1980 China's rural population was 796 million, or 80.6 per cent of a national total of 987 million, while the urban population stood at 191 million. Ten years later, in 1990, the rural population had grown to 841 million but had fallen to 73.6 per cent of the total, the numbers living in urban areas having climbed to 302 million. This trend accelerated in the 1990s. By 2003, the latest year for which full population figures were available at time of writing, the rural population had dropped to 769 million, 59.5 per cent of a total of just under 1.3 billion. The growth in towns and cities, meanwhile, had accelerated, up by 222 million since 1990 to 524 million, more than two-fifths of the total. Half a century earlier nearly 90 per cent of the people of China lived in the countryside. The shift to urban living went hand in hand with economic development.

The Grand Opening

In January 1992, accompanied by his son and a daughter and a large team of advisers, the 87-year-old Deng Xiaoping, 'glowing with health and vigour' according to the *People's Daily*,[24] paid his second visit to Shenzhen in Guang-dong province, by then showing the rest of China the way with rapid indus-trialisation. The first, in 1984, had been to see the work in progress on the Shenzhen special economic zone (SEZ), which, like other such zones, was central to his vision of the modernisation and opening-up of China's economy. On his first visit Deng had toured Shenzhen in a minibus – later restored and preserved for posterity in the city's museum – and encountered a place only slowly being urbanised. Then there were still paddy fields, unmade roads and single-storey houses. This time there was something much closer to a properly functioning city, with skyscrapers sprouting up on every street corner. Shenzhen building contractors had established a reputation for being able to add three floors a day to the new office blocks. Over lunch at the revolving restaurant on the fifty-third floor of the National Trade Plaza, the leader was able to look out over the city he had created. Even he seemed surprised, but said he now had 'enhanced confidence' that his economic reform programme was working. He was also unworried that some people described Shenzhen and the other special economic zones as examples of red-blooded capitalism in red China. They were, he insisted, 'socialist' in nature as much as they were 'capitalist', foreign capital accounting for only a quarter of investment. Public ownership remained the mainstay of economic development, he told his audience, though nobody should be afraid of joint ventures with foreign companies.

Special economic zones were the embodiment of the 'open door' strategy embarked upon by Deng in 1978 when, in a momentous speech in September of that year, he argued for 'actively developing relations, including economic and cultural exchanges' with other countries. China, he said, 'could make use of capital from foreign countries and of their advanced technology and experience in business management'. China's 'closed-door policy' had inhibited the country's economic development and: 'If we isolate ourselves and close our doors again, it will be absolutely impossible for us to approach the level of the developed countries in fifty years'.[25] The first SEZs, officially described as 'regional export-oriented economies regulated mainly by market forces', were set up in August 1980, in Shenzhen, Zhuhai, Shantou and Xiamen. Goods imported by enterprises to be used in the zones were free of both tariffs and taxes. Otherwise, tariff and commercial tax rates were halved. Four years later fourteen coastal cities – Dalian, Ginhuangdao, Tianjin, Yantai, Qingdao, Lianyungang, Nantong, Shanghai, Ningbo, Wenzhou, Fuzhou, Guangzhou, Zhanjang and Beihai – were given similar status to the SEZs, with foreign-invested enterprises offered the same tax and tariff concessions. 'Open economic regions' followed a year later, including the Yangtze river delta, the Pearl river delta, the Xiamen–Zhangzhou–Quanzhou triangle, and the Jiaodong and Liaodong peninsulas.

The Pearl river delta, stretching from Guangzhou to Shenzhen, provided the most dramatic example of Deng's opening-up strategy at work. It was no accident that China's economic development occurred in mainland areas closest to Hong Kong, and Hong Kong businessmen were suddenly faced with a low-cost production location right on their doorstep. Early big investors included Jetta and Lee Kum Kee, respectively Hong Kong-based toy and oyster sauce manufacturers. They built large factories. They were followed by the multinationals, including Pepsi, Procter & Gamble, Mitsubishi and LG Electronics. Multinationals, last seen in China in any numbers in the 1930s, flooded back in the 1980s.

The 1992 visit to Shenzhen was not just a sentimental journey for Deng. His so-called 'Southern Inspection Tour' was intended to reinforce the economic reform message at a time when it was in danger of being submerged. The Tiananmen Square massacre of 4 June 1989 had cast a long shadow over Chinese politics and the economy. Shenzhen was a symbol of what the new China could achieve, *per capita* income in the city averaging $2,000 (more than five times the national average). The visit was intended to demonstrate to the people that there could be no turning back from the reform; indeed, it was necessary to press forward more energetically. He stayed for four days, visiting the new high-technology factories that were starting to compete with the world's best and urging local officials to be bold in pushing through further reforms. They should not, he told them, act like 'a woman with bound feet'. His remarks about socialism and capitalism, while on the face of it faithful to party orthodoxy, were intended to reinforce the new pragmatism that encouraged and rewarded entrepreneurs and established productive and profitable relationships with foreign capitalists. As if to underline that message, he even visited the newly opened Shenzhen stock exchange. 'There is no other option open to us,' Deng said of reform. 'If the economy cannot be boosted, over the long run we will lose people's support at home and be oppressed and bullied by other nations throughout the world. A continuation of such a situation will only lead to a collapse and disintegration of the Communist Party.'[26]

Trade Giant

The open-door strategy meant just that, establishing China as a location of choice for export-oriented industries, taking advantage of the country's low costs, while at the same time allowing imports of the latest technology, and in particular capital equipment. When Mao had tried to access foreign technology in the 1950s, he was limited to the best the Soviet Union had to offer, which often was not very good. Deng had no such hang-ups. He wanted to engage with the best the world had to offer, and he wanted to sell to that world. China was finally admitted to the World Trade Organisation (WTO) in December 2001, after years of knocking at the door. Long before that, however, it had made a huge impact on world trade. At the start of Deng's reform programme, in 1978, the economy was more or less closed. Exports and imports together accounted for less than 10 per cent of GDP, and the country's world trade share was just 0.6 per cent. The growth from that low point was extremely impressive. By 1990, exports and imports combined had risen to 30 per cent of GDP; by 2002 almost 50 per cent. This represented an opening-up on a dramatic scale, which would have been extraordinary if achieved by a small, capitalist economy such as Singapore, the Asian 'tiger' so much admired by Deng. For China to have done it, lumbering and state-controlled, was nothing short of amazing.

China had come to the exporting business late, long after Japan's sustained post-war export success had turned her economy into not only

Asia's dominant force but the second largest economy in the world. By 2004, however, China's export success outstripped that of Japan, exports from the People's Republic that year reaching $593 billion, compared with Japan's $565 billion. Only the United States ($819 billion) and Germany ($915 billion) ranked higher. China's share of world markets was 6.5 per cent, more than ten times its 'pre-opening' level just a quarter of a century before. Nor was it just a case of China selling low-cost, low-value products to the rest of the world. The Paris-based Organisation for Economic Co-operation and Development (OECD) reported at the end of 2005 that China had overtaken the United States the previous year to become the world's leading exporter of information and communications technology (ICT) goods such as mobile phones, laptop computers and digital cameras. China's ICT exports were valued at $180 billion, compared with America's $149 billion. Between 1996 and 2004 China's combined export–import trade in ICT goods had risen from $35 billion to $329 billion.[27]

China's export success did not come about by accident. Deng's strategy included not only the special economic zones and similar areas earmarked as export bases for Western multinationals, but a new exchange-rate regime. In 1994 the old dual exchange-rate system, with official and market rates of exchange, was merged into a single market rate, operated under a managed floating system. That managed float was to become highly controversial later – and the centre of diplomatic battles between Beijing and Washington – but it considerably helped to boost trade. So did the system of tax rebates on exports, again significantly extended after 1994. The Chinese authorities also moved to bring down formal trade barriers. In 1992 its average tariff rate on imports was more than 43 per cent. By the time of its WTO entry in 2001 it was 15 per cent and set to fall further.

Investment Magnet

Deng's visit to Shenzhen in 1992 was important for another reason. It signalled a new emphasis on attracting inward investment into China. While Deng on his tour played down the role of foreign capital, the reality was that China needed it. In October 1992 the Party Congress declared that China had a 'socialist market economy'. The following year there was a flood of foreign direct investment in China, more than in the previous fourteen years put together. Since then, China has been the magnet for direct investment from around the world, regularly attracting inflows of $50 billion or more annually, averaging ten times the amount of India. In 2002 China briefly overtook the United States as the biggest recipient of foreign direct investment (FDI), although it subsequently slipped back with the recovery of the global economy. Figures from the United Nations Conference on Trade & Development (UNCTAD) show that in 2005 China attracted $60.3 billion of FDI, compared with $106 billion for the US and $219 billion for Britain, though the latter figure was distorted by the merger of Royal Dutch & Shell. India attracted FDI of just $6 billion.

China's inward investment statistics have to be treated with a degree of caution. They show that the biggest source of foreign investment in China is not America, Europe or Japan, but Hong Kong. Over the period 1979–2005, the 'opening-up' era, more than 254,000 Hong Kong-financed investment projects were completed in China – more than 45 per cent of all such projects over the period, with a total value of $259.5 billion. Some of this is explained by so-called 'round-tripping', whereby Chinese business interests transfer money to Hong Kong and then invest it back in China to take advantage of the tax, tariff and other concessions available to foreign investors. Estimates vary, but a rough consensus estimate is that around a quarter of all FDI flows into China are accounted for by this phenomenon. That would still leave China as easily the leading developing country location for FDI. The other striking feature of the statistics is that a high proportion of the investment – around four-fifths – is from the Chinese diaspora, not just in Hong Kong but also overseas Chinese in Taiwan, Singapore and elsewhere in south-east Asia. Again, these figures may not tell the full story. There is plenty of evidence that American, Japanese and European multinationals, rather than investing directly, choose to do so through Asian subsidiaries, regional offices or front companies.

One man who has managed to ride the Chinese investment tide more than most is Li Ka-shing, said by *Forbes* magazine in 2006 to be the richest person of Chinese descent in the world. Born in Chaozhou in Guangdong province in 1928, he and his family fled the invading Japanese for Hong Kong in 1940. Beginning with a plastics factory in 1949, Li developed a business empire built around the Hutchinson Whampoa and Cheung Kong conglomerates. As well as operating in forty different countries, and being the world's largest operator of container terminals, his businesses dominate the Hong Kong economy, in real estate, mobile phones, retailing, electricity supply and other sectors. In March 2006 he revealed that he had investments worth more than 100 billion Hong Kong dollars, or $13.5 billion, in mainland China and planned to invest a lot more. Li, nick-named 'Superman' by newspapers in Hong Kong, said that 60 per cent of his worldwide land holdings were in China. His story is a fascinating one. Exiled from China at a young age but, like many exiled Chinese, showing his entrepreneurial ability elsewhere, he has been one of the champions and beneficiaries of the opening-up of the economy. In many ways, too, his business return to China means he has come full circle.

What's Good for Wal-Mart ...

Wal-Mart is a business phenomenon; the world's largest company is also, by a long way, its biggest retailer, with four times the turnover of its nearest rival. Wal-Mart's 'Every Day Low Prices' make it a magnet for American shoppers and, increasingly, for those in its subsidiaries around the world. It has 3,800 stores in the United States and 2,400 elsewhere, including Argentina, Brazil, Britain, Canada, China, Costa Rica, El Salvador, Germany, Guatemala, Honduras, Japan, Mexico, Nicaragua, Puerto Rico and South Korea. More than four-fifths of US households make at least one purchase from Wal-Mart each year and more than 138 million customers visit its outlets each week. Wal-Mart is also much criticised for its impact on local communities, driving small retailers out of business, and for squeezing suppliers, in many cases to the point where they are no longer viable. Its response is that it puts money back into all the communities in which it operates, making $200 million a year in charitable donations, and that its low prices – 17 to 20 per cent below rival supermarkets according to one study – are of particular benefit to low-income households.

The Wal-Mart story is, however, also a China story. Founded in 1962 with its first store in Rogers, Arkansas, it was listed on the New York stock exchange in 1979, a year after Deng signalled the opening-up of the Chinese economy. The rise of Wal-Mart and that of China are closely inter-twined. While Wal-Mart's public policy was 'Buy American', its founder Sam Walton knew that 'Every Day Low Prices' would mean sourcing supplies from outside America and, in particular, from the Far East. According to one account: 'Early in his company's spectacular expansion, "Mr Sam", as everyone called him, decided to reach across the Pacific and make imports a pillar of Wal-Mart's business model. Forcing his American suppliers to cut costs, stressing sales volume over high margins, and wowing customers by showcasing one super low-priced item in each category – all hinged on importing to find the cheapest prices.'[28] By the mid-1980s, while the company's official position was that only a tiny proportion of its sales were of imported products, the true picture was that it had risen to 40 per cent, mainly US-branded items from Asia. There was nothing new in this; American retailers had for years been buying products from the Far East, particularly clothing and electronic goods. What was different with Wal-Mart, in the end, was the scale of it.

Wal-Mart, a standard-bearer for red-blooded American capitalism, was reluctant to be seen to be trading directly with communist China, particularly in the years after the Tiananmen Square massacre. It therefore operated through the Hong Kong-based Pacific Resources Export Limited, effectively but not in legal terms a Wal-Mart subsidiary, which acted as its exclusive buying agent. By the early 1990s, the company's China strategy was in full swing. Other low-cost locations such as Taiwan were no longer in favour. China, and in particular places like Shenzhen, offered significant labour cost advantages and tax concessions. Wal-Mart developed its own-brand product lines, almost exclusively made in China. As the political relationship with China thawed, the company no longer felt the need to hide behind its buying agency. Within a few years Wal-Mart grew to become the biggest US importer from China, its annual purchases exceeding those of entire large economies such as Germany. For the retailer, sourcing production in China provided it with the low-cost goods that increased its market dominance. Wal-Mart was the embodiment of the 'China effect' on global inflation, its competitive prices (falling continuously in year-on-year terms for many products) helping maintain the era of low inflation that began in the early 1990s.

For China, meanwhile, Wal-Mart was the way in which Deng's new economic model worked. The diminutive leader may not have had cheap jeans and T-shirts in Texas superstores in mind when he embarked on his opening-up strategy. But that is what happened. As Professor Gary Gereffi of Duke University put it:

> Wal-Mart gets its economic power because it is a gateway to the US consumer. Wal-Mart is the largest retailer in the United States. It's the largest employer in the United States. The demand for Wal-Mart stores is

what provides China and other countries in Asia with their access to the·
most powerful capitalist economy in the world. So Wal-Mart is providing
a gateway into the American economy for overseas suppliers in China and
elsewhere, and it's doing it on a scale that is unprecedented.[29]

The relationship between China and the rest of the world is changing, as
we shall see. The investment flow has become a two-way one as Chinese
companies look outward and seek to establish their own joint ventures, or
take over Western firms. The first phase of China's development, however,
was to establish itself as a country where the rest of the world would
come to invest, buy goods, and make money. Deng did not mind whether
the cat was black or white as long as it caught mice. First, though, he had
to make sure there were mice to be caught. This he did, and with stunning success.

3

India Rising

'A moment comes, which comes but rarely in history, when we step out from the old to the new, when an age ends, and when the soul of a nation, long suppressed, finds utterance.'

Jawaharlal Nehru, 14 August 1947

'The forces in a capitalist society, if left unchecked, tend to make the rich richer and the poor poorer.'

Jawaharlal Nehru, 7 September 1958

Flavour of the Month

Every January the small Alpine town of Davos in Switzerland, famous as the setting of Thomas Mann's 1924 novel *The Magic Mountain*, is transformed from being a chic ski resort into the world's biggest business networking event. There, for three days, the Audi and Mercedes limousines ferry their powerful occupants the short distances between their hotels and the town's congress centre, where most of the formal events are held. The World Economic Forum, which has been held in Davos since the early 1970s (apart from 2002, soon after 9/11, when it was held in New York), has always been a place where the companies who fund it can meet and discuss ideas, be exposed to some new ways of thinking and – while the declared purpose is intellectual enrichment and improving the state of the world – do business. It has also, from the early days, attracted politicians; those who want an international platform and those who want to attract some of the hundreds of billions of dollars of capital global business has at its fingertips. Davos, for a few days in January, is where the American corporate world meets its opposite numbers in Europe, and where countries go to sell themselves as the business locations of the future. Amid the fur coats and the crunch of tyres and expensive shoes on gritted snow, important introductions are made and business decisions sealed.

The World Economic Forum's themes tend to reflect the economic fashions of the day. In the 1990s these included the collapse of communism in Russia and eastern Europe and the business opportunities this offered, jockeying for position with the dot.com boom. Terrorism thrust its way to the top of the agenda, of necessity, after the September 2001 attacks on America. If there was another big and persistent theme in the early twenty-first century, however, it was China. This was the new economic giant most multinational businesses were concerned with. Many had already invested there. Most were aware of India, but at best as a distant second to China, at worst as one of many competing developing economies, the target of a tiny fraction of the foreign direct investment flowing to the People's Republic.

So, in January 2006, India decided to put itself on the map. Zurich airport, the nearest international hub to Davos, had wall-to-wall posters advertising India as the 'world's fastest-growing free market democracy'. The same message had been painted, in bright letters, on the public buses in Davos itself. On arriving in their hotel rooms the delegates and journalists discovered gift packs of iPod shuffles pre-loaded with Indian music, together with pashminas. They also discovered invitations to a series of India-themed breakfasts, discussions and parties, including the gala 'soirée' that traditionally closes the forum. That, according to one description, was 'an Indian extravaganza, with a bevy of Indian beauties dancing to pulsating Hindi tunes against an electric blue Taj Mahal. The guests joined in the festivities. The impeccably dressed chairman of the Forum, Klaus Schwab, donned a colourful Indian turban and talked up the country's prospects.'[1] The catering was handled by specially flown-in Indian chefs, including Atul Kochhar, the first Indian to receive a Michelin star.

On the Map

The drive to put India on the world economic map, which cost a conservatively estimated $4 million, had begun two years earlier at the 2004 Davos forum. Nandan Nilekani, chief executive and president of the successful Indian software firm Infosys, was bemoaning with fellow businessmen from the subcontinent the fact that India hardly figured in the discussions at the meeting. The China story was in full swing, as were questions about Europe's future, but awareness of India, even discussion of its prospects, was minimal. They decided that India had to attain a prominence in line with its growing importance, and the 'India Everywhere' campaign was born, not just to generate publicity but also to ensure that Indian experts, and the theme of India's economic emergence, featured prominently in the forum's deliberations. It worked. One session was 'India and the World: Scenarios to 2025', another 'India's Life Science Revolution', yet another 'New Energy for India's Reforms'. 'The Emergence of India' also featured on the agenda, both as a formal session and in plenty of informal discussions. Backing up the contingent of leading business figures assembled by the Confederation of Indian Industry, including as co-chair of the forum Mukesh Ambani, chairman and managing director of Reliance Industries, India's largest private-sector conglomerate, were senior Indian politicians. Though Manmohan Singh, the prime minister, was detained in Delhi by the annual Republic Day celebrations, others were in attendance, notably P. Chidambaram, the finance minister, and Kamal Nath, the commerce minister. 'China has been the flavour so far, but India was seen as a breath of fresh air,' he said. 'I thought it would take much more effort, and a couple of Davos conferences, but it took just one summit.'[2]

The Indian delegation left Davos with plenty of warm words, and with a target of converting those words into at least a doubling of inward investment within two to three years. More than that, India had achieved critical mass. 'If we had done all this five years ago, people would have laughed,' said Rahul Bajaj, chairman of Indian two-wheeler manufacturer Bajaj Auto and a regular attendee of Davos summits. 'You can't advertise or promote a product which has bad quality, but in the last few years, Indian industry has come of age.' That was true but, perhaps even more than with China, it would have seemed unlikely even a decade or so before. Even as China was well on the road to rapid economic development, India was languishing, her economic failings apparently condemning her people to permanent poverty. How had India moved from that to become the emerging economic superpower presented to the world's business élite along with the *gluhwein* and fondue in the Swiss mountains in 2006?

Crisis

The face India presented to the world just fifteen years before its Davos triumph could hardly have been more different. That image was one of violence, political instability and economic failure. The news from India in 1991 was almost all negative. On 21 May 1991, campaigning during the country's general election, Rajiv Gandhi, the former prime minister, was assassinated in Sriperumbudur in Tamil Nadu by a female suicide bomber carrying a device concealed in a basket of flowers. His death at the age of forty-six, at the hands of Tamil militants (though conspiracy theorists have suggested otherwise) appeared to confirm the doomed nature of the Nehru–Gandhi dynasty. His mother Indira had been assassinated seven years earlier and his brother Sanjay had been killed in a plane crash in 1980. Rajiv, who became prime minister after his mother's shooting by her own Sikh bodyguards in 1984, and remained at the helm until 1989, had tried to reform both the Congress Party and India's economy, opening it up to foreign investment. His violent death, however, suggested to the outside world that the only way India was going was backwards.

Even before the assassination, the *San Francisco Chronicle* had described India as a country 'at war with itself'. Another American newspaper, the *Baltimore Sun*, described India as a 'dazed democracy' after the killing. Analysts were in agreement that the country faced a period of turmoil and further violence, with religious and caste differences returning to the fore. If India was trying to convince American corporations it was a suitable destination for their investments, it was failing. President George Bush senior summed up the mood when he said an assassination of this kind, in a democratic country, was 'appalling'. 'I just don't know what the world is coming to,' he said.

The backdrop to Rajiv's assassination, and indeed to the 1991 general election in India, was a full-scale economic and financial crisis. The Indian economy was in a fragile state, government spending having risen at a rate far faster than tax revenues were being generated to pay for it, particularly in the first half of the 1980s, when government outlays rose by more than 7.5 per cent a year. A chronic external imbalance, the result of years of export failure, was exacerbated by the rise in global oil prices that accompanied the first Gulf War (following Saddam Hussein's illegal invasion of Kuwait). India suffered from the classic problem of 'twin' deficits, with both the government's budget and the current account heavily in the red. Successive Indian governments and state authorities had run significant budget deficits, but by the early 1990s the combined central and state deficit had reached nearly 13 per cent of GDP. In ten years, government debt rose from 35 to more than 50 per cent of GDP, and debt interest payments doubled their share of government spending.

There was a parallel development in India's external accounts. A manageable trade deficit in the 1970s widened sharply in the 1980s, partly under the impact of the second global oil shock of 1979–80, but also as a result of declining export competitiveness and a growing appetite for imports. The current-account deficit, like the budget deficit, doubled to an annual average of $5.5 billion in the second half of the 1980s. India, without natural capital inflows – it was not a favoured destination for foreign direct investment – was forced to turn elsewhere. 'In order to meet these large and persistent current account deficits, large scale commercial borrowings were undertaken along with contraction of substantial short-term debt. This, in turn, aggravated the problem of external indebtedness,' development economist Nirupam Bajpai recorded in 1996.[3] By the end of the 1980s, when the burden of repaying debt to the International Monetary Fund (IMF) and commercial borrowers began to bite significantly, the Indian economy was vulnerable to an external shock. That duly arrived with the first Gulf War.

War in the Gulf, apart from nearly doubling India's oil bill – thereby adding to an already serious balance of payments problem – also hit the country's export earnings and, almost as importantly, foreign currency remittances from Indians working in Gulf states.

Selling the Rupee

The closeness of Indian's economic ties to the Middle East oil countries, useful in the good times, now provided a source of vulnerability. By early 1991, the rupee was under pressure and a full-scale financial crisis, similar to that which was to hit a number of Asian economies in 1997–8, was in full swing. One important difference, brought out in a later IMF analysis,[4] was that the Indian economy remained relatively closed in nature, its openness both to trade and international capital flows being limited. Even so, the IMF concluded, India suffered from the earlier over-valuation of the rupee, a collapse in investor confidence and an apparently intractable current-account deficit.

'The balance-of-payments came under severe strain from one liquidity crisis experienced in mid-January 1991 to another in late June 1991,' wrote Bajpai.[5] 'On both occasions, the foreign exchange reserves dropped significantly and the government had to resort to measures, such as using its stocks of gold to obtain foreign exchange, utilisation of special facilities of the IMF, and also emergency bilateral assistance from Japan and Germany among others.' India avoided the embarrassment of having to default on her international debts, but only just.

Before his untimely death, Rajiv pledged to tackle India's economic crisis if re-elected. His radical programme included a 10 per cent reduction in state spending and a withdrawal of the public sector from areas in which it did not need to operate, together with a slashing of the red tape Indian businesses found stultifying. The private sector would be allowed to compete in telecommunications, electricity, coal and other 'state' sectors. Something had to change, he said, to correct a situation in which inflation was running at 16 per cent and threatening to spiral out of control, the currency was collapsing – against the dollar it was on its way to losing a third of its value since the late 1970s – and the country had racked up $70 billion of foreign debt.

Something did change, and 1991 has come to be seen as a watershed year for the Indian economy – Rajiv's reforms were a success, though he would not be around to see his pledges through. As sometimes happens, countries can rise, phoenix-like, from the bleakest economic ashes. That was not, however, how it looked then, when the air was thick with condemnations of India's post-independence economic failings. It is worth briefly revisiting them, to examine why, until relatively recently, India did so badly.

Under the Influence of the LSE

When India achieved independence in August 1947 it could, in theory, have chosen any number of economic directions. With the yoke of colonial rule removed, the world could have been the new democracy's oyster. Sixty years later it was proclaiming itself as proudly free market, so why not then? The answer, of course, is that India's new prime minister, Jawaharlal Nehru, chose socialist economic planning. His model was not as rigid as that adopted a few years later by Mao in China but it drew heavily on the Fabian 'mixed economy' approach advocated by Harold Laski. Laski, professor of political science at the London School of Economics (LSE) from 1926 until his death in 1950, and a leading figure in both British Labour Party and Fabian Society circles, advocated a central role for the state in industrial ownership, notably the 'commanding heights' of energy, transport and basic industries, but also in economic planning. Unkind souls would say that Britain, having been forced to set India free, did its best to hobble it. Nehru, who once said that India's five biggest problems were 'land, water, cows, capital and babies',[6] was impatient for a rapid transformation of the economy. 'We have to think in terms of large schemes of social engineering, not petty reforms,' he claimed. The first five-year plan, published in 1950, ran from 1951 to 1956. Despite India's current commitment to a free market economy, the Planning Commission remains in existence, albeit with a reduced role. The tenth five-year plan, 2002–7, was in progress as this book was being written.

Nehru's aim was rapid industrialisation, combined with self-sufficiency in energy and food and the build-up of military power. Basic industries, under state control, were to be developed, including iron and steel, machine tools, chemicals and power generation. Irrigation projects were given priority to boost agriculture. The private sector, meanwhile, became subject to tough price controls and other forms of bureaucratic intervention. This represented the beginnings of the so-called 'licence Raj', or 'permit Raj' (sometimes even the 'licence–permit Raj'), under which businesses required bureaucratic approval to carry out their operations, and which helped give rise to India's endemic corruption. For Nehru, however, deeply suspicious of the motives of business, such controls were necessary. 'Never talk to me about profit,' he once said to J. R. D. Tata, the great Indian industrialist. 'It is a dirty word.' Critics have been merciless in their condemnation of both Nehru's economic policies and his antagonism towards free enterprise. 'This aversion to free enterprise can be attributed, in part, to a Brahmin's sense that money sullies the soul,' wrote the journalist Tunku Varadarajan.

Yet it was the product, largely, of a destructive fascination with Fabian socialism – that is, the non-revolutionary, British-born variety – and of a blind admiration for the Soviet system of centralised economic planning. Nehru, a sanctimonious snob who was never entirely able to treat his fellow Indians as equals, dragged his country down in the years after the British left. He imposed on India a complex of malfunctioning, state-run, industrial white elephants, all the while denying private entrepreneurs the right to seek investment from abroad, or to export without oppressive controls, or to import at will the materials and technology needed to establish competitive industries in India. Meanwhile, he neglected India's agriculture, forcing the country to rely on American food aid to feed itself while he blithely charted a pro-Soviet, anti-American foreign policy under the flimsy guise of nonalignment.[7]

Gurcharan Das's 2002 book *India Unbound*, which combines optimism about the country's future with harsh criticism of the policy failings of the Nehru–Gandhi era, argues that the early five-year plans failed on just about every level. One flaw was to adopt an inward-looking approach, based on import substitution, rather than seeking to exploit the export opportunities made available by the world economy's 'golden age' of the 1950s and 1960s. Another flaw was the unfettered expansion of the public sector, combined with the most over-regulated business sector in the world. India's closed-economy model, meanwhile, deprived the economy of much-needed foreign capital and technology, while the government's tight relationship with the trade unions 'pampered' organised labour and held back necessary productivity improvements. 'Ultimately, we paid a heavy price for our scepticism of the market's ability to allocate resources wisely,' writes Das.

> We did not trust profit to reflect economic efficiency. Neither did we think Indian entrepreneurs had the will or the resources to make the investments needed to transform the country rapidly. We felt that only the state could assume this role. We were under the spell of the Soviet economic miracle and this led to a bias towards heavy industry and against agriculture and light consumer industry. We assumed that India could not export and would always be short of foreign exchange. Therefore we had to depend on substituting imported products, especially capital goods. These assumptions turned out to be wrong. It was a failure both of ideology and management.[8]

Was There an Alternative?

To what extent are such criticisms only valid with the benefit of hindsight? The political climate in the late 1940s and early 1950s was, after all, very different from now. Nehru may have been seeking to carve out an economic course distinct from that of Britain, but in many respects it was following the same socialist route, the big expansion of state ownership under the Attlee government (1945–51) closely matching that in its former dependency. The only thing missing back in Britain was central planning but, if anything, this was seen as Attlee's failure. Planning was fashionable, Britain's experiment with it coming as late as the Wilson government of 1964–70, after its success had apparently been proved elsewhere in other mixed economies, notably France. Nehru, perhaps, was in the vanguard of economic fashion. Das concedes that 'socialism was attractive to any sensitive person' in the 1950s. Indian society was desperately unequal and still smarting from perceived colonial exploitation. The country's great industrialists and merchants were envied and despised in almost equal measure. A free-enterprise, free-market approach would have been seen by many as handing over the spoils of independence, after 200 years of waiting, to those who already had plenty.

Even India's business leaders appeared to accept that their freedoms would be seriously constrained in an independent India. Leading industrialists who got together in 1944 to sign up to the so-called Bombay Plan, including representatives of the Tata and Birla business dynasties, agreed that: 'Practically every aspect of economic life will have to be so rigorously controlled by government that individual liberty and freedom of enterprise will suffer a temporary eclipse.'[9] The plan, formally called 'A Brief Memorandum Outlining a Plan of Economic Development for India', has been the subject of later reinterpretation, and suggestions that its real purpose was to make the case for enterprise-driven Indian economic development. What was noted at the time, however, was the acceptance by the country's business establishment of central planning, state ownership of key industries and a limited role for foreign capital, not least to protect its own interests. Nehru may have got it wrong, but business colluded in his economic failings.

Voices of Dissent

There were, however, alternative views around. In 1955 and 1956 Milton Friedman wrote two notes about Indian economic policies after visiting the country. The first was a memorandum to the government. The second, which has emerged relatively recently, was tougher and more personal in its criticisms of India's planning process and of the technocrat responsible for seeing it through, Nehru's close adviser Professor Prasanta Chandra Mahalanobis. Friedman knew Mahalanobis, a statistician. He also knew, even before the end of the first five-year plan, that it was doomed to failure:

> The scheme of the Five Year Plan attributed to Mahalanobis faces two problems; one, that India needs heavy industry for economic development; and two, that development of heavy industry uses up large amounts of capital while providing only small employment. Based on these facts, Mahalanobis proposed to concentrate on heavy industry development on the one hand and to subsidize the hand production cottage industries on the other. The latter course would discriminate against the smaller manufacturers. In my opinion, the plan wastes both capital and labour and the Indians get only the worst of both efforts. If left to their own devices under a free enterprise system I believe the Indians would gravitate naturally towards the production of such items as bicycles, sewing machines, and radios. This trend is already apparent without any subsidy. The Indian cottage industry is already cloaked in the same popular sort of mist as is rural life in the US. There is an idea in both places that this life is typical and the backbone of their respective countries. Politically the Indian cottage industry problem is akin to the American farm problem ... I found many supporters for the heavy industry phase of the Plan but almost no one (among the technical civil servants) who really believes in the cottage industry aspects, aside from their political appeal.[10]

Another dissenting voice, who later became something of a hero among critics of Nehru's approach, and of free market economists outside India, was Professor B. R. (Bellikoth Ragunath) Shenoy. At a time when the great and the good of development economics were queuing up to endorse the Indian government's plans, including Gunnar Myrdal, Joan Robinson,

Nicholas Kaldor, Thomas Balogh, Ian Little, Oscar Lange and Paul Streeten, Shenoy stood out. His note of dissent on the second Nehru–Mahalanobis five-year plan of 1956, which went further in its socialism than the first, warned against the direction India was taking. 'State intervention should be concerned with the prevention of monopolies or quasi monopolies,' he wrote.

> Efficient management of business and industrial concerns in a competitive market economy is a highly specialized function and demands qualities which a civil servant is not required to, and in the ordinary course of his training may not, acquire. This function is best left to private entrepreneurs, in the prevailing socioeconomic order which is dominated by the market economy and the pricing system. I do not feel convinced of the economic importance of continuing the remnants of controls ... There are great advantages in allowing freedom to the economy, and to the price system in the use and distribution of the needs of production. I am unable to agree with my colleagues that a case exists for continuing what controls now remain. Steps should be taken to remove controls as early as may be possible.[11]

His was a lonely voice. Just as India's business establishment was prepared to go along with Nehru's central planning and socialist controls, so the majority of economists agreed that the second five-year plan was the best way forward. Not only was it the conventional wisdom that planning guaranteed progress, it was also a source of considerable national pride. Although the Indian planning process was heavily influenced by the Fabians, and by the Soviet experience, it was seen as a pioneering exercise in economic development, which was why so many experts flocked to Delhi to see it at work and encourage the process along. Almost without knowing it, Mahalonobis had developed a growth model that, according to Meghnad Desai (an LSE economist, but a critic of planning) was more sophisticated than anything available in the academic literature of the time. The serious policy debate, indeed, was not over the efficacy of planning – how else to manage an economy as big and unwieldy? – but over the level of public ownership of industry needed to support it. India was to make many more economic mistakes before seeing the error of her ways.

The Hindu Rate of Growth

India's economic performance during Nehru's time in office (1947–64), and for years afterwards, was memorably christened 'the Hindu rate of growth' by Professor Raj Krishna, an Indian economist. While the economies of east Asia were powering ahead, South Korea, Taiwan, Singapore, Malaysia and Hong Kong achieving average growth rates of 7, 8 or 9 per cent a year, India merely trundled along, growing by roughly 3.5 per cent a year between 1950 and 1980. This was not the kind of accelerated growth needed to close the gap with the rich countries; in fact it was broadly in line with what advanced economies were themselves achieving. Even Pakistan, with growth of about 4.5 per cent, did better. Not only that, but as detailed calculations by one-time Indian government adviser Arvind Virmani have demonstrated, the performance got progressively worse rather than better. Growth over the period 1951–64 averaged nearly 4.5 per cent a year, but slipped below 3 per cent in the post-Nehru period, 1965–79. *Per capita* GDP, rising by just over 2 per cent a year in the earlier period, stagnated from the mid-1960s to the late 1970s, barely growing at all. The Nehru era was characterised by rapid growth in government spending (nearly 7 per cent annually) and in a doubling of public investment, but zero growth in exports, fully justifying the criticisms of Das and others. The later period saw state spending grow more slowly and exports do a little better, but overall economic growth was decisively weaker than in other developing countries and the advanced economies.

The Nehru and immediate post-Nehru eras differed in other ways. In the former there was confidence and enthusiasm, and a genuine belief that socialist planning could bring lasting prosperity. Later, the chickens came home to roost, and hopes of a brighter future began to fade. As Virmani puts it:

> In the first phase lasting till about 1964–5 the leadership was infused
> with moral righteousness and developmental enthusiasm based on the
> philosophical background of Fabian socialism and the experience of
> Soviet state socialism. The best and brightest development economists in
> the world journeyed to India to advise on how to accelerate development
> and growth and some of them even worked in the Indian government
> or the Planning Commission to convert ideas into practical policy. In the
> second sub-phase starting from 1965–6 and ending in 1979–80, both the

moral fervour and the academic certainties gradually seeped away. The policies were driven more by immediate crisis and political expediency than by economic logic.[12]

Mouths to Feed

Nehru, who died in 1964, was succeeded as prime minister two years later by his daughter, Indira (whose married name of Gandhi she shared, purely by coincidence, with India's greatest modern prophet). The country remained trapped in the 'Hindu rate of growth' during her initial period in office, which ran from 1966 to 1977, and was also affected by social and political instability. In the mid-1970s she called a nineteen-month state of emergency, a device that enabled her to cling to office when found guilty of electoral fraud. The state of emergency, enforced with staggering brutality by her son Sanjay, had been preceded by social unrest driven by high unemployment and sharply rising prices. The economy was in a poor state to face the global turbulence of the 1970s, and it soon showed.

Though the 'Hindu rate of growth' was disappointing, many Indians, encouraged by their government to do so, preferred to contrast it with the immediate pre-independence period. In the thirty years before independence, India's economy had grown by just 0.7 per cent a year on average, admittedly badly hampered by the effects of two world wars. *Per capita* incomes were more than 10 per cent lower in real terms in 1946 than they had been in 1917. Anything, it seemed, was better than the stagnation of the final days of British rule. That, however, was scant comfort to India's poor. Modest economic growth in the post-independence era coincided with big increases in population. India's population of around 347 million in 1947 had virtually doubled to 683 million by 1981 (rising further to more than one billion by the end of the twentieth century). This meant a lot of hungry mouths to feed, and a lot of jobs to create if mass unemployment was to be averted. Neither famine nor high unemployment was averted and the condition of the majority of Indians remained one of grinding poverty. The proportion of Indians officially living in poverty remained unchanged, at around 55 per cent, in the three decades after independence.

This was the India the world came to know, a country of rapidly rising population – averaging more than 2 per cent a year from the early 1960s onwards – and increasingly desperate family planning policies. The hoped-for virtuous circle of economic development, in which rising prosperity led to changes in social behaviour – large families no longer being seen as necessary – never arrived. The death rate declined as cholera, smallpox and leprosy were either controlled or eradicated (though infant mortality was still as high as 122 per 1,000 under-fives in the early 1990s), but the birth rate remained high. In the 1950s, under Nehru, India became the first developing country to adopt explicit family-planning policies in pursuit of the goal of population control, though initially just through the provision of birth-control advice. In the 1960s, population control was made part of the economic planning process, with targets set for male sterilisation through vasectomies and for a near-halving of the birth rate from 41 to 23 per 1,000 within ten years. The 1976 National Population Policy, adopted during the state of emergency, warned of the 'vicious circle' of rapid population growth and called for a 'direct assault' on the problem. A surge in the number of vasectomies resulted – many of them forced on unwilling men – but the impact on the birth rate, and on population growth, was limited. Having failed to restrict population increases to suit the modest economic growth rate, India's pressing need was to achieve stronger, sustained economic growth to match the requirements of her fast-rising population. Only gradually did the penny drop.

State of Corruption

The lasting legacy of the Nehru era, even more than slow growth, was corruption. Long after India had cast off the poor economic performance of the three decades following independence, the country continued to be hampered by widespread, corroding corruption at national and local level. Professor Jagdish Bhagwati, the noted Columbia-based Indian economist, has described the system of regulation and red tape put in place in support of the planning process as 'a Kafkaesque expansion of import, production and investment controls via a restrictive licensing system known then as "permit Raj", so that competition and innovation were stifled'.[13] Mark Tully, the former BBC South Asia editor, described in his book *India in Slow Motion*, co-written with Gillian Wright, not only his deep love for the country but his despair at the profound and damaging effects of corruption. In India bureaucrats are corrupt because they are allowed to be, and because the system of regulation has encouraged them to be. Atal Behari Vajpayee, then prime minister, said in 1999 that 'corruption has become a low risk and high reward activity'. Tully describes the system that has developed since the 1950s as 'a peculiarly Indian form of bad governance' and 'a brake slowing down a country with enormous but unrealized potential'.[14]

The high watermark of Indian corruption probably occurred after Nehru, and during his daughter Indira Gandhi's first period in office. When the government itself was found guilty of fraud, and responded by declaring a state of emergency, as Gandhi's did, the lack of moral leadership from the top was tantamount to an open invitation to every public servant to milk the system. Many gratefully accepted it. Tully writes of the 'neta-babu Raj', the nexus between the civil servants (babus) and the politicians (netas), who scratch each other's backs and 'join hands to share the spoils of office'. Worse even than having to pay bribes to get things done is the fact that in India bad governance means that corruption is intertwined with inefficiency. He cites a non-resident Indian industrialist, who says: 'I would prefer to invest in my own country but I go to East Asia instead because there I certainly have to pay but I know I'll get my money's worth. In India the system is so complicated and everything takes so long and you never know whether you'll get what you paid for in the end.'[15] The Indian elephant, he writes, is shackled by this 'neta-babu Raj', and nobody has a strong incentive to change it:

> It is because India's archaic, complicated, inefficient system of
> government allows money to be diverted, rules to be disobeyed and
> procedures to be subverted that neither the netas nor the babus have
> shown interest in reforming it. Perhaps it would be taking this theory too
> far to suggest that politicians have deliberately opened up other fronts
> to take Indians' minds off good governance, but it is certainly true that
> caste and communalism, as religion-based politics are known in India,
> have crowded that issue out. It might have been, though, that economic
> policies, and especially the removal of poverty, would have been the most
> hotly debated subjects in elections after the reforms started, because
> there was evidence that economic liberalization was only benefiting the
> middle and upper classes, but even three general elections since then
> have, as usual, been dominated by issues of caste and communalism.[16]

There have been steps to bear down on bureaucratic red tape and corruption, as we shall see. More than half a century after the 'licence Raj' became central to the Indian system, however, the attitudes and practices it ushered in continue to have a limiting effect on the country's economic growth. The World Economic Forum (WEF), in a survey conducted for its 2005 India Economic Summit, found widespread business concern about corruption and red tape. The WEFs *Global Competitiveness Report 2005* found that India ranked 72nd out of 117 countries (where 1 is the best and 117 the worst), for 'irregular payments to officials associated with imports and exports', 75th for 'irregular payments in tax collections', and 83rd for 'irregular payments in public utilities'.[17] An inefficient bureaucracy and corruption ranked as the second and third most important factors when it came to the problems of doing business in India. Transparency International, in its annual Corruption Perceptions Index for 2005, ranked India 88th, alongside Armenia, Benin, Bosnia and Herzegovina, Gabon, Iran, Mali, Moldova and Tanzania. India, it said, was one of seventy countries in which corruption was rampant. A survey it carried out of 5,000 Indians found that paying bribes was routine, with the police, together with health and education officials, the worst offenders. Corruption, it appears, is so deeply ingrained that it is expected.

Even where corruption was not the problem – which was rare – the bureaucratic framework established in the 1950s and subsequently built on, was often a story of good intentions either misdirected or simply badly carried out. Those who the rules were intended to help were hindered, the efforts to engineer the desired economic outcomes, as so often, ending in failure. One example was the system of so-called small-scale reservations, described by Joydeep Mukherji as 'the most peculiar and uniquely Indian form of bad regulation'.[18] The aim was simple. Small enterprises would be protected from competition by their being given the exclusive right to manufacture and market a long list of products. That way, it was thought, small-scale firms (defined by their level of investment in plant and equipment) would thrive, and their employees prosper. In fact, as Mukherji points out, the effect was to condemn small enterprises to staying small, restricting economic development: 'The policy, designed to create lots of small, labour-intensive companies, has instead blocked the development of labour-intensive manufacturing in India. It denies companies the opportunity to gain economies of scale, expand output, and improve efficiency in order to be able to export.'

Start of a New Era

Most accounts of India's recent economic history split the modern, post-independence era into two distinct periods. There is the pre-reform period, 1947–91, when the country is crippled by over-regulation and corruption, but also by a misguided belief in the ability of the state to direct the economy. Then there is the post-1991 period when, as a result of a confidence-shattering economic and financial crisis, the politicians are finally forced to institute a change of direction, and success ensues. The pre-reform and post-reform story is neat and convenient in the telling, and is also rather helpful to the Indian case, particularly when its record and prospects are contrasted with those of China. Why has China grown so rapidly and for so long, becoming significantly richer than India in the process? Because, the answer goes, it started first. China's reforms date from 1978, India's from thirteen years later, so it is not surprising that there is a gap. But, like the tortoise and the hare of fable, India's later and slower start may turn out to be an advantage in the long run. Similarly, India's failure so far to attract more than a fraction of the foreign direct investment flowing into China may simply be a timing issue.

The question of India versus China will be tackled later in this book. There is, however, a serious problem about using 1991 as the year when the Indian economy cast off its 'Hindu rate of growth' and acquired a new dynamism and energy. For, while the pre-1991 economy was one that was dangerously unbalanced and over-dependent on borrowings from abroad – the factors that tipped it into crisis – it was no longer subject to weak growth. Bradford DeLong, a Berkeley-based American economist, cites IMF data that shows that India's average growth rate of GDP in the 1980s was 5.9 per cent, and that *per capita* GDP rose by an average of 3.8 per cent a year. It remains true that growth accelerated in the 1990s, to an average of 6.2 per cent a year (4.4 per cent for *per capita* GDP). But the break with the past, and from the subdued 3.5 per cent rate of growth of the thirty years after independence, is unmistakable. DeLong asks: 'What are the sources of India's recent acceleration in economic growth? Conventional wisdom traces them to policy reforms at the start of the 1990s. Yet the aggregate growth data tells us that the acceleration of economic growth began earlier, in the early or mid-1980s, long before the exchange crisis of 1991 and the shift of the government of Narasimha Rao and Manmohan Singh toward neoliberal economic reforms.'[19]

Other authors have questioned the new conventional wisdom about the timing of India's growth revival. Arvind Virmani describes the later, faster growth rate as the 'Bharatiya' (or Indian) rate of growth, contrasting it with the 'socialist' growth rate that preceded it. He places the change even earlier than DeLong, in 1980–81. So what happened to produce the change? After all, in 1980–81, the Nehru–Gandhi dynasty still had nearly a decade to run. Virmani attributes the onset of the new era to a belated acceptance by the Indian political establishment of the need for change. 'The Bharatiya growth phase has been characterised by recognition of the harmful effects of industrial and other controls on distribution, production, and investment and the need to remove the distortions created by government policy on industry and exports,' he writes. But that change was by no means universal: 'There was much more gradual and hesitating recognition of the problem of government and public sector failure.'[20]

The Gandhi Reforms

In January 1980, three years after being swept from power on a wave of national repulsion about the country's state of emergency and her own questionable ethics, the 62-year-old Indira Gandhi won an impressive landslide victory, gaining more than 350 seats in India's 525-seat lower house, the Lok Sabha. Though she campaigned on a ticket of banishing poverty and restoring law and order, winning strong support in rural areas, there was little to suggest the new Mrs Gandhi would be very different from the old one or, for that matter, that the economy would perform any differently than in the past. The language, however, changed. Suddenly the government was no longer hostile to business, introduced a modest relaxation on production quotas for manufacturers and on import barriers for capital equipment, and appeared ready to work with the private sector. For a prime minister who had inherited a deep suspicion of business from her father, this was a significant change.

'The trigger for India's economic growth was an attitudinal shift on the part of the national government in 1980 in favor of private business,' wrote Dani Rodrik and Arvind Subramanian, in a study for the IMF.

Until that time, the rhetoric of the reigning Congress Party had been all about socialism and pro-poor policies. When Indira Gandhi returned to power in 1980, she realigned herself politically with the organized private sector and dropped her previous rhetoric. The national government's attitude toward business went from being outright hostile to supportive. Indira Gandhi's switch was further reinforced, in a more explicit manner, by Rajiv Gandhi, following his rise to power in 1984. This, in our view, was the key change that unleashed the animal spirits of the Indian private sector in the early 1980s.[21]

Other researchers concur with this. Arvind Virmani argues that the effect of her shift to a more pro-business stance was amplified, as was the impact of her relatively modest liberalising reforms, because of their provenance. Their credibility was enhanced because they came from the same Indira Gandhi who had been instrumental in placing restrictions on business in the first place: 'As she was perceived to have learnt from her own experience, the changes were more credible to both potential beneficiaries and losers.'[22] Bradford DeLong concludes that the change in attitudes and the beginnings of reform go a long way towards explaining why growth suddenly accelerated: 'If you look for a single structural break, you look at the last years of Indira Gandhi's rule and at Rajiv Gandhi's administration, the years when economic reform and economic liberalization became ideologically respectable within the Indian government and policies that a development-seeking government ought to pursue to some degree.'[23]

Not everybody accepts such explanations. Gurcharan Das, in *India Unbound*, provides first-hand evidence that Mrs Gandhi's pro-business attitudes did not go very deep. In March 1981, as the 38-year-old managing director of Richardson Hindustan, he was invited to an industry–government business roundtable, which included breakfast with the prime minister. In the prime minister's garden she 'looked charming, surrounded by spring flowers' in a white cotton saree, and after a short speech took questions from the assembled businessmen. When nobody appeared willing to throw her a testing question, Das himself did, asking firstly about the still-restrictive licensing regime, and then about the high taxes and duties on imports. Then an American businessman stood up and asked why foreign companies were restricted to minority stakes in Indian-based operations, thus deterring multinationals from investing. In response to each question Mrs Gandhi brushed aside the implied criticisms, saying that in each case the policies were necessary to protect India's interests. 'With great charm, on the spring morning, amidst shining marigolds, Mrs Gandhi had attempted to preserve three myths of the *ancien règime* – the value of licensing, the importance of high taxes and the need to limit foreign investment,' Das recounts.[24]

What about Rajiv Gandhi, elected, following the assassination of his mother, by an even more convincing majority? In the December 1984 election he won 415 seats in the lower house and, on the face of it, had a mandate for thoroughgoing reforms. He, unlike his mother, was at home with businessmen and committed himself to deregulation, import liberalisation and access to foreign technology. The first budget of the new regime offered reductions in marginal tax rates, tariff reductions, a switch to more transparent import controls (replacing quotas with tariffs), giving larger firms the freedom to grow by relaxing tough anti-trust laws, and easing the licensing restrictions on manufacturing industry. In his first year alone, tariffs on imports of capital goods were reduced by more than half, taxes on export products were cut sharply and the number of industries subject to so-called capacity licensing (limiting the ability of individual firms to grow) was reduced from seventy-seven in 1984 to just twenty-seven in 1988. Yet the reforms did not go as far or as fast as many had hoped and expected, given Rajiv's position of political strength. According to Bradford Delong:

> Factions within the Congress Party seemed not to believe that their
> interests were bound up with the success of their leader and his policies,
> but were instead threatened by the potential backlash against an
> administration that was concerned with the prosperity of the rich rather
> than alleviating poverty ... Thus the reform plans carried out under Rajiv
> Gandhi were hesitant, and less bold than one would have expected given
> the rhetoric of its initial speeches.[25]

Rajiv faced opposition from rural interests, who saw little benefit from the country's improved economic performance, and from within his own Congress Party, much of which appeared wedded to the Nehru model of public-sector provision. Despite its legendary inefficiency, the public sector emerged largely unscathed from the Rajiv era. Privatisation, which could have worked well in India (as it was to do in Britain in the 1980s), was eschewed. The opening-up of the Indian economy to foreign competition, meanwhile, was opposed by another powerful interest group: big business. There were reforms, though probably not far-reaching enough to produce the step change in economic performance that occurred.

So what really happened? One view is that the Gandhi reforms, introduced by mother and son, made little difference. Instead, Indian growth in the 1980s was a product of two factors: a decline in the exchange rate, which provided a competitive boost, and what the economist T. N. Srinivasan has described as 'fiscal expansionism (financed by borrowing at home and abroad), leading to Latin American-style debt-led growth'.[26] The other view is that the Gandhi reforms, while modest, did indeed set India on a new path, and marked recognition, for the first time, of the central role of the private sector in generating economic development. Anti-business attitudes, a legacy of colonial rule and a product of inequalities of income, were put to one side. The truth is probably somewhere in between. India did begin to change in the 1980s. In 2006 Infosys, the highly successful Indian IT services giant, celebrated its twenty-fifth anniversary. Its birth in the early 1980s offers proof that something was stirring in that era. In 1981 seven experienced software professionals led by Narayana Murthy left Patni Computers, which sold American Data General computers in India, to set up on their own. From the start, however, Infosys based its business on overseas customers and, while the government was ostensibly more pro-enterprise during its early years, the company's history tells of battles with bureaucrats and red tape.

It is also true that, notwithstanding the fact that there was more of a spirit of enterprise around in India in the 1980s, macroeconomic policies were irresponsible and unsustainable. India borrowed too much and believed it could grow its way out of trouble. The 1991 crisis provided a rude awakening. It also gave a vital spur for the reforms needed to continue the job that had begun tentatively in the 1980s.

Rao and Singh

If Deng Xiaoping is credited for putting China on the path of true reform, that accolade in India, notwithstanding what occurred in the 1980s, goes to the 'double act' of Narasimha Rao and Manmohan Singh. On the face of it, neither fits the bill. There was little to suggest in advance that their actions would be as important to India as Deng's were for China, Margaret

Thatcher's for Britain, or even Ronald Reagan's in America. They were, in most respects, unlikely candidates to steer through radical economic reforms. P. V. (Pamulaparthi Venkata) Narasimha Rao viewed India's 1991 election almost as an interested spectator. A Congress Party veteran, originally from Andhra Pradesh, he was then approaching his seventieth birthday, and had already told Rajiv Gandhi of his intention to stand down from frontline politics. He had been in semi-retirement for eighteen months and had packed up his large collection of books in preparation for a life of contemplation in Hyderabad. Not only did he think he had served his time but he had little admiration for Rajiv's style of leadership. An anonymous article in the Indian magazine *Mainstream* following the Congress Party's 1989 defeat, under the byline 'Congressman', was highly critical of the 1984–9 government headed by Rajiv, which it said had been brash and divisive. It later emerged that Rao was the anonymous author. After Rajiv's assassination he was not the favourite to succeed him as Congress leader, Arjun Singh and Sharad Pawar being more commonly mentioned. He emerged though, as is often the case, as a compromise candidate, a 'safe pair of hands'. His political philosophy appeared to be 'anything for a quiet life'. 'When I don't make a decision, it's not that I don't think about it,' he once said. 'I think about it and make a decision not to make a decision.' 'Inaction is also action,' he said. Unlike in 1984, when Rajiv swept to power in the wake of his mother's assassination, there was no wave of voter sympathy following Rajiv's own killing. Although Congress gained nearly 50 seats compared with 1989, its parliamentary representation in the lower house, 244, was barely more than half that achieved by Rajiv in 1984. The political hand Rao was delivered by the electorate – with the Congress Party being able to form only a minority government – was thus far from ideal, though he insisted that politics was 'the art of the possible'.

An equally unlikely reformer, on the face of it, was the man Rao chose as his finance minister and right-hand man, Manmohan Singh. Singh, born in west Punjab in 1932, had spent his career as an academic, bureaucrat and international economic diplomat. His academic credentials were impeccable. After study in India, he gained a first-class honours degree in economics from Cambridge in 1957, followed a few years later by an Oxford doctorate. As a young economist he had written a book, *India's Export Trends and Prospects for Self-Sustained Growth*, implicitly criticising the government's inward-looking economic policies. But then he entered government service, working as an economist in the commerce and finance ministries, the latter as chief economic adviser, before being appointed governor of the Reserve Bank of India, the central bank, from 1982 to 1985. He then became deputy chairman of the Planning Commission (a promotion) and, in 1987, was posted to Geneva as secretary-general of the South Commission. At a time when the requirement might have been thought to be for a sharp-elbowed politician, used to playing the game, Rao opted for a mild-mannered and unerringly polite economist. Elected to India's upper house of parliament, the Rajya Sabha, only in 1991 (to this day he has never had a seat in the lower house), he was a political *ingénu*. Rao, however, knew what he was doing. He wanted a finance minister who knew India's economic problems from the inside, and had an expert's authority, but who was not part of the dealmaking, compromising tradition of Indian politics.

Rao later became embroiled in a bribery scandal and was sentenced in 2000 to a three-year prison term, though he never served time and his conviction was later quashed. Though his minority government lasted for five years, until 1996, and though it saw India embark on a new economic path, his period in office was marred by the destruction of the Babri mosque in Ayodhar by Hindu militants in December 1992, which was followed by the deaths of 2,000 people in inter-communal rioting. After his own death in 2004, his achievement in pushing through reforms from a position of political weakness won him only grudging praise. Many preferred to focus on Singh as the real architect of change. Partly this was because of Rao's soporific speech-making style and dull, austere personality; on a visit to London, where he unveiled a waxwork of himself at Madame Tussaud's, one journalist joked that the waxwork looked livelier. When, after his period in office, he wrote a novel, *The Insider*, containing sex scenes, there was considerable shock, though he was father to eight children. Rao, too, always appeared to go out of his way to understate the importance and novelty of the reforms he was overseeing. In his first speech as prime minister, he emphasised that his task was to implement Rajiv's programme 'to the hilt'. His policies, he said later, were 'part of a long process of liberalisation'.

The New India

Rao may have played down the impact of his reforms, but to most political and economic analysts they were highly significant. Politically, the post-1991 era represented a clear break with 1947–91, when Indian politics was dominated by the Nehru–Gandhi dynasty. In economic terms, while India's growth performance in the 1990s was not markedly different from that in the 1980s, it was more clearly driven by reform and liberalisation. That, as noted above, may be the way India chooses to present herself to the world. But if it implies that the reform process was painless, that would be misleading. Rao and Singh faced opposition and sometimes had to backtrack. One early tussle with conservative elements in the Congress Party came as early as July 1991, when Singh's proposal to reduce the fertiliser subsidies, the effect of which would have been to push up prices by 40 per cent, faced such opposition that he offered his resignation. That was not accepted by Rao. He did, however, reduce the price increase to 30 per cent and exempted small farmers from it, to secure grudging approval from the party. Arjun Singh, a strong candidate for the party leadership following Rajiv's death, became a critic, defending India's planning tradition and warning that economic reforms had to be of clear benefit to 'the common man'. The period 1991–3, now seen as the time when India finally severed links with her slow-growth past, and put the 'Hindu rate of growth' to rest, was a politically challenging one.

In the end, however, Rao succeeded, because there was no obvious alternative to the reform programme. The Indian economy, it should be remembered, was effectively bankrupt when he took over, with a public-sector deficit of nearly 11 per cent of GDP and external debt of $69 billion, a third of it owed to private creditors. Part of the reform process, therefore, was crisis management; the immediate impact of which was to slow the economy sharply. Growth, which touched more than 10 per cent in the late 1980s, when the economy was clearly overheating, slowed to just over 1 per cent in the early 1990s. The reforms themselves fell into two broad categories: liberalisation of external trade and capital flows, and de-regulation of the domestic economy. On the face of it, an economy facing an external debt crisis should not be removing barriers to trade. Rao and Singh recognised, however, that India's balance of payments problems were a function of a failed import-substitution strategy. India was highly protectionist. Data from the World Trade Organisation (WTO) show that the highest tariff rate in 1991 was 355 per cent, and the average more than 100 per cent. On top of these very high tariffs there were quantitative (volume) limits on imports. The Rao–Singh reforms slashed tariffs, bringing down the weighted average to between 25 and 30 per cent. In addition to opening up the Indian economy to imports, the government signalled that it was setting in train a new export-led policy. To help the process along, and ease the immediate balance of payments problems, the rupee was devalued by 22 per cent against the dollar. Rao and Singh also took a leaf out of Deng's book. China's export success had been built on foreign investment; now India was to try a similar medicine.

A new 'open door' policy on inward investment was part of a package of industrial reforms announced by Rao on 24 July 1991. The importance he attached to it was underlined by the fact that, as well as his prime ministerial duties, he took charge of the industry brief. The 40 per cent limit on foreign-equity investment was abolished, with the Reserve Bank of India empowered to grant automatic approval for 51 per cent foreign investment in thirty-four industries. Further liberalisation followed, enabling higher proportions of foreign investment – up to 100 per cent in certain sectors and in the newly created Special Economic Zones, a direct steal from the Chinese. As significant was what Rao announced on 24 July for domestic industry. As the political economist Arvind Panagariya puts it: 'With a single stroke, the "Statement of Industrial Policy, July 24, 1991", frequently called the New Industrial Policy, did away with investment licensing and myriad entry restrictions on MRTP firms (firms that fell under the Monopolies and Restrictive Trade Practices Act). It also ended public-sector monopoly in many sectors.'[27] It was called the New Industrial Policy with good reason. Out went 'public sector knows best' attitudes; public-sector monopolies being confined to narrow areas of security and national strategy. Now only nuclear energy and the railways fall into those categories. Out also went the idea that the Indian economy should always be subject to tight bureaucratic control. The 1991 reforms did not turn India overnight into a freebooting capitalist economy, but it did mean that parts of the licence Raj began at that point to pass into history.

Singh, quoting Victor Hugo in a famous speech to parliament a month after becoming finance minister, said: 'No power on earth can stop an idea whose time has come.' The vision, as he explained a decade later, was a bold one:

I sincerely believed that if we did the things that I was saying to Parliament that they should do, no power on earth could stop the realization of this idea. So the dream was that we were in crisis, we should undertake basic structural changes. Out of that will emerge a new India, an India where there will be no poverty; the freedom from poverty, ignorance, and disease. You get that with India becoming a major global player in the world economy. That was the vision that inspired our economic reforms.[28]

Political Backlash

One of the criticisms of India, certainly in comparison with China, is its lack of single-mindedness. Some would say this is the natural consequence of democracy versus authoritarianism. Others would argue it reflects deep ambivalence within India about the process of reform, its effects and the fact that the benefits were not more widely spread. In 1996, five years after the crisis from which the economy had staged a phoenix-like recovery, the government that delivered that recovery might have expected to have been rewarded at the polls. Ahead of the May 1996 election, Narasimha Rao warned voters that backing the rival Hindu-nationalist Bharatiya Janata Party (BJP) would wreck the economic miracle and take the country back to the uncertainties of a few years earlier. The BJP, publicly sceptical about the economic liberalisation process and critical of the effects of globalisation, would, if elected, take India 'the way of the former Soviet Union and Yugoslavia', he warned. The 1996 election saw a typically messy Indian outcome, with the BJP, despite Rao's dire warnings, emerging as the largest party. But the government, led by Atal Bihari Vajpayee, lasted for less than a fortnight, unable to secure parliamentary support in a confidence vote. Its failure did not, however, let the Congress Party back in. Instead, for two years, the country was ruled by the thirteen-party United Front coalition, initially under H. D. Deve Gowda, chief minister of Karnataka state in southern India, and leader of the tiny Janata Dal Party. The coalition, perhaps surprisingly, did not turn its back on globalisation – the new government was keen to emphasise its enthusiasm for foreign investment – or reform. Gowda chose as his finance minister P. Chidambaram, who had served as commerce minister under Rao, but had left the Congress Party in 1996. The Harvard-educated Chidambaram, who later set up his own party, was finance minister again (after a period out of office) when India presented itself to the world in Davos in 2006.

Indian voters may not have succeeded in blocking reform in 1996, but they made another effort two years later when the United Front, by now under I. K. Gujral, lost the support of Congress (not part of the coalition but a key parliamentary powerbroker), forcing an election. Again, the result in 1998 was messy, with the BJP emerging comfortably as the largest party, but without enough seats, even with its allies, to form a majority. Vajpayee, the BJP leader, tried again to form a government, however, and this time he succeeded, remaining in power until 2004. Ahead of the 1998 election that saw it achieve power, the BJP took an economic policy position that was strongly nationalist, based on the principle of *swadeshi* (self-reliance). Its 1998 election manifesto strongly suggested that a BJP government would reverse some of the opening-up of the economy and envisaged only a limited role for foreign investment. 'The economy of India has come under tremendous pressure because of misguided tariff reductions and an uneven playing field for the Indian industry,' it said. 'It is clear that foreign capital will be only of little value to the national economy, though crucial to some sectors like infrastructure …While the declared agenda [of every nation] is free trade, the undeclared, but actual agenda is economic nationalism. India too must follow its own national agenda. This spirit is *swadeshi*.'[29]

Again, however, Indian voters got liberalisation whether they wanted it or not. As David Arulanantham has written, 'the BJP comprises a pragmatic pro-capitalist wing and an ideological wing opposed to foreign involvement in the economy. As a result, the party employed economic nationalism to energise its activist base while it was in opposition. After winning the election, the pragmatic wing captured power within the party and implemented its agenda, reflecting the views of India's emerging middle class.'[30] The BJP, under Prime Minister Vajpayee, abandoned its opposition to the WTO process, reduced import duties, reduced the barriers to foreign ownership and redefined *swadeshi* as competing effectively in the global economy. Vajpayee, however, found himself on the losing side in the May 2004 election, an upset that was described as the biggest since independence in 1947 and thus even bigger than Rao's defeat in 1996. The BJP had been expected to coast home on the back of the economy's success but Vajpayee's coalition ended up with barely a third of Lok Sabha seats, well behind Congress (now led by Sonia Gandhi) and its allies. Was this because of the impossibility of reconciling the two wings of the BJP, economic nationalists and globalisers? Or was it just another straight vote against globalisation and reform? Plenty thought the latter. 'The BJP raised the slogan of development, but the people found there was no real development on the ground,' said Kuldip Nayar, a political columnist and a member of the upper house of parliament. 'This is a verdict against globalisation. Now the next government will have to think how to employ more hands than machines.'[31]

Fits and Starts

While Indian governments struggled to establish a relationship between liberalising reforms and political popularity, the reform process itself was criticised from another standpoint. This was that it did not go far or fast enough. Gurcharan Das reflects the views of many in business when he writes that reform in India has been a case of 'two steps forward, one step backwards'. India's politicians, even when they have been reformist in their actions, have often been cautious to the point of timidity in their rhetoric. For Das, this signifies a half-hearted attitude towards liberalisation. 'When the crisis receded and reforms slowed, the truth came out, revealing the true character of India's policymakers,' he wrote.

> Barring a few exceptions, no one in the political class – bureaucrats or politicians – was truly enthusiastic about the changes. There had been no radical change in personnel. Without a change in people, the planners of yesterday became the liberalizers of tomorrow. The prime minister did not have the courage to close down redundant ministries. There was no national soul-searching about the causes of our disease. The nation did not internalize the drastic need for restructuring. Hence the policymakers could not defend themselves against the cries for protection which rose after the reforms, cleverly dressed up as complaints about the inequities of liberalization. They had not publicly admitted that the Nehru–Indira Gandhi path had failed.[32]

It takes time, of course. The more people that benefit from India's rising prosperity – the growing middle class and the increasingly influential business lobby – the more that reform becomes the natural state of things. And while India's politicians may not have had the fire in the belly of the world's great reforming politicians, at least liberalisation did not become a political football, to be reversed with each change of government. For some, indeed, the slow but steady approach was preferable; the Indian elephant may have chosen to travel at a gentler pace than its great rival China, but the race would be a long one, and who was to say that India's would not be more sustainable in the long run? That is a question for later in the book. In the meantime, however, there were – and are – serious questions about whether India had done enough to ensure that the momentum was maintained.

Everybody who looks at the Indian economy comes to two immediate conclusions. The first is that, in terms of growth and the ability to attract inward investment, India's performance has so far been inferior to China. The second conclusion is that there was a decided slowdown in growth after the immediate post-1991 spurt. Not only that, but post-reform India still had serious problems, when it came to the 'twin' deficits – current account and budget deficits. Montek Ahluwalia, reviewing the performance of the Indian economy ten years after the 1991 watershed, noted that economic growth slowed from 6.7 per cent in the first five years after the reforms to 5.4 per cent in the following five, a slowdown some blamed, though not very convincingly, on the Asian financial crisis of 1997–8. Growth fell short of the 7.5 per cent target the government had set for the later period and the performance on other measures was unconvincing. The new emphasis on export-led growth, for example, resulted in only a fractional increase in India's share of world markets by the end of the 1990s. For Ahluwalia, deputy chairman of India's Planning Commission, the problem was not that the reform process was gradualist but that its targets were often vague and uncertain. 'Critics often blame the delays in implementation and failure to act in certain areas to the choice of gradualism as a strategy,' he wrote.

> However, gradualism implies a clear definition of the goal and a deliberate choice of extending the time taken to reach it, in order to ease the pain of transition. This is not what happened in all areas. The goals were often indicated only as a broad direction, with the precise end point and the pace of transition left unstated to minimise opposition – and possibly also to allow room to retreat if necessary. This reduced politically divisive controversy, and enabled a consensus of sorts to evolve, but it also meant that the consensus at each point represented a compromise, with many

interested groups joining only because they believed that reforms would not go 'too far'. The result was a process of change that was not so much gradualist as fitful and opportunistic.[33]

Growth, however, is a great economic healer. By the end of 2006, when India had achieved three consecutive years of growth averaging 8 per cent, some of the earlier doubts had faded, and talk of a new official growth target of 10 per cent no longer seemed fanciful. Perhaps it had just taken longer than those impatient for change had allowed for. Perhaps, too, there was political method in the softly softly approach towards reform. Liberalisation by stealth, in the case of India, may have been a more successful strategy. The current-account deficit, once apparently an intractable problem, moved into surplus for three successive years from 2001–2 onwards, before being dragged back into deficit by rising global oil prices. This was a long way, however, from the crisis-triggering problem of 1991. There was still a problem when it came to the country's fiscal position. The combined budget deficit of national and state governments was no longer in double figures as a percentage of GDP but, even after a period in which strong economic growth has boosted tax revenues, it was 7–8 per cent of GDP in 2006. The doubts, however, had faded. India, it appeared, had embarked on a new growth phase that put both the 1980s and 1990s in the shade. That was the buzz in the cool alpine air in Davos in January 2006, followed swiftly by a question. Could India keep it up?

4

China Roars, the World Listens

'If GE's strategy of investment in China is wrong, it represents a loss of a billion dollars, perhaps a couple of billion dollars. If it is right, it is the future of this company for the next century.'

Jack Welch, former chairman and chief executive officer, General Electric

'The timing does not matter, but we in the West do need to prepare ourselves, particularly our young people, for a powerful and exciting re-emergence of China on the world scene. The first of the ancient, historic powers to return to glory.'

Sir John Bond, former group chairman, HSBC

Five-ringed Circus

In July 2001, in a controversial decision, the International Olympic Committee (IOC) awarded China the 2008 summer games. Beijing beat off competition from Toronto, Paris, Istanbul and Osaka and, perhaps more importantly, stiff opposition from groups protesting about the country's human rights record. Critics said the award of the games to China, given its brutal treatment of dissidents – notably the outlawed Falun Gong spiritual movement – was the equivalent of holding the 1936 event in Berlin when the Nazis were in power. There are said to be 80 million Christians in China, though most do not shout about it, outnumbering members of the Chinese Communist Party. A group of organisations – Reporters Without

Borders, Solidarity China and the Committee for the Support of Tibetan People – had called on the IOC to reject Beijing's candidature. They said: 'There are enough democratic countries to avoid giving one of the last and most violent dictatorships in the world the privilege of organising the most prestigious festival of sport.' But the IOC, which said 'a Beijing Games would leave a unique legacy to China and to sports', was unmoved. Eight years earlier, China had missed out on the 2000 games, which were awarded to Sydney. Its turn had come.

The IOC does not make its decisions for economic reasons, but its awards of the games are often heavy with economic symbolism. In 1964, when Tokyo hosted the summer Olympics it appeared to be an endorsement of Japan's emergence as one of the miracle economies of the 1950s and 1960s. South Korea, which modelled its economic development on Japan, hosted the games in Seoul in 1988 and, again, this was widely seen as the equivalent of an economic coming-out ceremony. Even in 2001, when the China story was much less of a part of the conventional wisdom than it is now, some saw the economic implications. Laura D'Andrea Tyson, formerly chairman of Bill Clinton's Council of Economic Advisers, saw the games as part of the opening-up of China, like membership of the World Trade Organisation. It would benefit the average Chinese citizen economically, and put pressure on Beijing to clean up its act on human rights. 'Paradoxically, hosting the games is likely to be a boon for China's citizenry and a headache for their leaders,' she wrote. 'Preparation for the games will require infrastructure and environmental upgrading that will improve the lives of millions of Chinese. Indeed, these investments will be so large that they may well add nearly half a percentage point to China's annual growth rate over the next several years.'[1]

Showcase

Certainly, if one of the aims of the IOC was to spur Beijing into building itself a twenty-first century infrastructure, and not solely for sports, the award of the games worked. The budget for the 2008 games, including new venues, the modernisation of the city (including slum clearance) and infrastructure, was put at $38 billion. The comparable working figure for the 2012 games in London is $16 billion, though it is likely to rise. Beijing's new international airport, intended to be designed, built and operated in the space of four years, would be bigger than London's Heathrow, currently the world's busiest international airport. The new Beijing international airport, designed by the architect Lord (Norman) Foster, would be capable of handling 53 million passengers a year and, according to Foster, would be 'the gateway to the city. It is advanced not only technologically, but also in terms of passenger experience, operational efficiency and sustainability. It will be welcoming and uplifting; a symbol of place, its soaring aerodynamic roof and dragon-like form will celebrate the thrill and poetry of flight and evoke traditional Chinese colours and symbols.'[2] Architects are prone to this kind of imagery, but few who have seen the transformation of Beijing in the run-up to the Olympics are left unmoved. Look beyond the builders' dust and you will see a city that is dressing to impress in a spectacular way. Beijing is a big, crowded, overwhelming city, with open space at a premium. But the planners are pulling out all the stops to put on a show. *Business Week* described the new buildings, including controversial Dutch architect Rem Koolhaas's new headquarters for Central China TV, resembling 'nothing so much as a skyscraper tumbling into a somersault', and the Olympic stadium itself as 'China's new architectural wonders'. Deyan Sudjic, the architectural journalist, saw China as using the Olympics 'as the chance to make a defiant and unmistakeable statement that the country has taken its place in the modern world'. He described in 2005 the contrast with China in the early 1990s. 'A city that, until 1990, had no central business district, and little need of it, now has a cluster of glass towers that look like rejects from Singapore or Rotterdam,' he wrote. 'And these, in turn, are now being replaced and overshadowed by a new crop of taller, slicker towers, the product of the international caravan of architectural gunslingers that has arrived in town to take part in this construction free-fire zone. Rem Koolhaas, Jacques Herzog, Zaha Hadid, Jean Nouvel and Will Alsop are all building, or trying to build here.'[3]

The reconstruction of Beijing for the 2008 Olympics says much about the way modern China operates. The city's Olympic district, once the home to tens of thousands of low-income people, had been cleared of its occupants and flattened to make way for the new showcase for the world, centred on a futuristic nest-like stadium, designed by Jacques Herzog and Pierre de Meuron, who turned a former power station into London's Tate Modern gallery. The mobilisation of huge numbers of construction workers – 40,000 on the airport alone – is testimony to China's huge resources of labour, but also its ability to pick up and dump people at will. The target is to have Beijing a construction-free zone for a year before the Olympics. 'There will be nothing for them to do,' Sudjic wrote.[4] 'They will be shipped back to their distant villages, and two centuries back in time, leaving the glossy new city they have built to the party élite and the foreigners. The new Beijing will be a hugely impressive demonstration of China's newfound status as an economic superpower. But it will also serve to highlight the fault line that divides the country's rich and poor.' The authorities, meanwhile, determined to present the best possible face to the world, have ordered the shutdown of factories for the duration of the games, and the removal of most of Beijing's 2 million cars from the streets. The city's legendary smog, which rises up like a grey-yellow mist in the early morning, will be put on hold – or at least that is the plan. Visitors expecting to encounter the dirty, smoggy city they have heard about will be treated to something much cleaner and greener. The capital's citizens, too, are being exhorted to be on their best behaviour. The 'Basic Reader in Civility and Etiquette', sent to millions of homes two years before the games, provides detailed guidance. Among the advice is that 'pyjamas should not be worn in public areas'. Only in China, perhaps, could this happen.

In Goldman Sachs, China Trusts

In November 2001, two months after the 9/11 attacks on America, when people were thinking about one way that the world was changing in the light of Islamic terrorism, Goldman Sachs offered another. In a report called 'Building Better Global Economic BRICs', the investment bank focused on the four big emerging economies, Brazil, Russia, India and China, the so-called BRICs. Jim O'Neill, the author and the bank's global head of economic research, noted that while the combined weight of these four economies was small in terms of gross domestic product – less than 8 per cent of the global economy – that weight increased dramatically when the figures were analysed in a different way. Purchasing power parity (PPP) is a concept used by economists to make international comparisons when market exchange rates are very different from what they should be. The idea is simple: use an exchange rate which means that buying a basket of goods and services costs roughly the same wherever in the world it is bought. On this basis, O'Neill pointed out, the combined weight of the four BRICs in 2000 was not 8 per cent but more than 23 per cent. And, whichever way you looked at it, China was becoming a dominant force. It accounted for more than 12.5 per cent of the world economy on the adjusted basis, that is, more than the three other BRICs combined. On this same PPP basis, the Chinese economy was half as big again as Japan, and thus ranked as the world's second largest economy, behind only America.

The Group of Seven (G7) – the US, Japan, Germany, Britain, France, Canada and Italy – is effectively the world economy's steering committee. Since the oil crises of the 1970s, it has made pronouncements that move global financial markets, in some cases backing up those pronouncements with policy action. According to O'Neill, however, by 2001 its member-ship had become badly skewed. 'We think China deserves to be in the G7 and, under some scenarios, so do others – certainly Brazil, Russia and India relative to Canada,' he wrote.[5] Global economic governance would be better operated through a new grouping, the G9, he added, consist-ing of the four BRICs, the US, Japan, Germany, 'Euroland' (the members of the single currency) and Britain. He also offered a tantalising glimpse of the size of economy China might become in the space of a decade. By 2011, even on a conventional basis – ignoring PPP – an extrapolation of China's growth suggested that her economy would overhaul those of both France and Britain. On plausible assumptions, it was possible that China would by then even have left Germany (the world's third largest economy on conventional measures) in her wake. O'Neill acknowledged that size alone did not necessarily guarantee admission to the world's economic élite, China's political model being a barrier. But nonetheless, China was fast becoming too big to be left out.

The China Growth Story

At the end of 2005 China's National Bureau of Statistics announced big changes in its estimates for the country's gross domestic product in 2004. A new economic census, which provided more accurate data for the fast-growing private-sector service sector, paved the way for an upward revi-sion of GDP. The Chinese authorities had suddenly discovered nearly 17 per cent of additional economic output, in telecommunications, retailing and real estate, and also in a range of low-level service industries such as the restaurant trade and garages. The effect was to push China's 2004 GDP significantly above Italy (then the sixth largest economy in the world) and pave the way for it to overtake both France and Britain once full figures for 2005 were available. The figures, not for the first time, put the spotlight on the Chinese economy, but they also raised the question of how China was managing to achieve such sustained economic success. Was this just a bigger version of the Asian growth story, a story that had seen miracle transformations in first Japan, then Singapore, Taiwan, Hong Kong and South Korea – the tiger economies? In some respects China has indeed followed the Asian model, which is why some economists argue there is nothing special about the China story apart from the country's sheer size and its huge population. There are, though, other unique features about China it is worth briefly describing.

Asian Parallels

By the end of 2005, when the Chinese authorities revised the GDP data, China had achieved twenty-seven years of rapid economic growth, at a rate averaging about 9.5 per cent a year. How unusual is this? Between 1962 and 1989, during its purple patch, Taiwan grew by 9.4 per cent a year, while Singapore achieved an average growth rate of nearly 9 per cent a year during its most rapid expansion, from 1967 to 1993. More typical 'miracle' rates of growth rate for the Asian economies are between 7 and 8 per cent a year. On a straight statistical reading, however, two things set China apart. One is the rapid increase in its *per capita* GDP levels. By 2005, China's *per capita* GDP, in constant prices, was more than six times its 1978 level. Having started from a low base, progress had been extraordinarily rapid; the typical achievement over twenty-five to thirty years for Japan and the Asian tigers had been to raise *per capita* GDP by between four and five times. The other key feature was that at this stage of their development the other Asian economies had for various reasons begun to slow down to a more sedate rate of expansion. Just over halfway through the first decade of the twenty-first century there is no sign of this happening to China.

China's growth miracle is easy to caricature as a product of unsustainable levels of investment, largely driven by the opening-up of the economy to foreign capital. Some have questioned, indeed, whether China should not have grown faster than it has, given investment rates of between 40 and 50 per cent of GDP, more than the smaller Asian economies during their purple patches. The China story, in fact, is a little more complicated than that. It is, first and foremost, the product of the successful privatisation of a state-run economy that has occurred in a gradual way and which has further to run. Compared with the instability that followed the collapse of central planning in the former Soviet Union, and the emergence of 'cowboy' capitalism there, China's controlled change has been a model of economic management. State-owned enterprises, formerly bloated, bankrupt and inefficient, have been halved in number, while those that remain have sold off non-core activities, become 'corporatised' (managed and run like quoted companies) to improve the way they are run and have achieved impressive efficiency gains. Even without any other changes, this scaling-back of inefficient state enterprises and the rapid improvement in the running of remaining ones would have generated big economic gains.

The caricature also ignores the fact that China has achieved strong rates of productivity growth, partly as a result of greater efficiency within organisations and partly because of the shift of workers from low-productivity agriculture to higher-productivity industry and services. Since the onset of the reforms in the late 1970s, about a fifth of China's working population has left the land. Labour productivity has increased sharply, and so has the productive use of capital. Combining the two gives total factor productivity. During the 1990s the International Monetary Fund estimated that productivity gains were contributing more than investment to Chinese growth. Updated estimates published in 2005 by Goldman Sachs suggested that productivity and investment were the biggest contributors to Chinese growth, and were roughly equal in importance.[6]

China's levels of educational attainment are often exaggerated, but there is no doubt that the equipping of workers with basic literacy and numeracy skills has been one of the country's great advantages, which shone through even when all else was failing. The mass-literacy strategy of the 1950s – the basic literacy campaign – had begun to pay dividends by the mid-1970s, by which time China had an adult literacy rate of 66 per cent, compared with just 36 per cent in India. It was reinforced by the Law of Compulsory Education of 1986, which had as its goal that from the age of six all children should receive at least nine years of education. Adult education has also been an important element in raising ability levels, through radio, television, part-time courses at universities and other institutions, and courses taught at people's places of work. The so-called 'delayed generation', whose education was disrupted during the

Cultural Revolution, have been a particular focus. By the mid-1990s adult literacy rates were just over 80 per cent in China, compared with 50 per cent in India. Education is important in its own right, but it has created something approaching a virtuous economic circle for China, allowing the country to sell itself more effectively as a location for foreign firms and making it easier for workers to adjust to the requirements of a rapidly changing economy. By 2025, it is said, there will be more English speakers in China than native English speakers in the rest of the world. There is much more to the China story, in other words, than just high rates of investment. Walk around a Chinese city and you are likely to be accosted by young people wanting to practise their English, or so they say. Mind you, the easiest way of getting lost in China can be to get into a taxi. Even with the address written out in Chinese characters, the journey can be an adventure.

How Big, How Fast?

While Goldman Sachs's 2001 report set the scene, its focus – on whether fast-emerging large economies such as China should become part of key international groupings like the G7 – was relatively narrow. Such matters are of great importance for followers of international economic diplomacy, but they do not set the world alight. Another report by the firm two years later did, however, change the way many people thought about China, and to a lesser extent India, Brazil and Russia. 'Dreaming With BRICs: The Path to 2050' was written by Dominic Wilson and Roopa Purushothaman under O'Neill's supervision. As its title suggests, the aim was ambitious. It was to look forward not just a few years but right through to the middle of the century. The report gave an insight into the size and potential of the new economies, and the projections for China were particularly dramatic. Even without the helping hand offered by purchasing power parity (PPP), it was clear that China was going to get very big, very quickly. The forecasts, presented in conventionally measured GDP, pointed to China quickly overtaking France and Britain, followed by Germany before 2010, Japan in about 2016 and the United States around 2041. Well before the middle of the century, in other words, China would stand proud as the world's biggest economy. For those accustomed to seeing the world in terms of the North Atlantic axis, plus Japan, this was a big change, the more so because Goldman Sachs had India not too far behind.

Aware of being accused of naïve extrapolation, the authors carefully laid out their assumptions. China was not assumed to be capable of growing at 9.5 per cent a year indefinitely, or even the 8 per cent rate it was recording at the time of the report. As they put it:

> As countries develop ... growth rates tend to slow towards developed country levels. In Japan and Germany, very rapid growth in the 1960s and 1970s gave way to more moderate growth in the 1980s and 1990s. This is why simple extrapolation gives silly answers over long time frames. As a crude example, assuming that China's GDP continues to grow at its current 8 per cent a year over the next three decades would lead to the prediction that China's economy would be three times larger than the US by 2030 in US dollar terms, and 25 times larger by 2050.[7]

Instead, thanks to the expected convergence with rich countries' growth rates, China's apparently breakneck expansion was expected to settle down to something more normal. Thus, by 2020, the economy would be growing by about 5 per cent annually, and by the 2040s the rate of expansion would be nearer to 3.5 per cent. The huge rates of investment that have driven the Chinese economy in recent years would come down to the Asian average of 30 per cent of GDP by 2015. It also made the assumption that one of the by-products of rapid economic growth in China and the other BRICs economies would be that their currencies would also appreciate. In broad terms, about one-third of the rise of China in comparison with the existing advanced economies would be explained by a rising renminbi, which would be expected to rise to four times its value by the middle of the century, with about two-thirds of the rise explained purely by economic growth. Such assumptions may seem bold, particularly in the context of the bitter dispute between Washington and Beijing over whether and by how much China should allow her currency to rise. It is, however, a plausible assumption based on the experience of earlier 'emergers' such as Japan, Korea, and even America.

The Goldman projections set many people thinking. China's path from communist backwater to the world's biggest economy was occurring at an extraordinary rate. In China itself the projections were seized upon with enthusiasm. Elsewhere they provoked mixed reactions, including scepticism, alarm and fear of environmental catastrophe. The authors themselves lodged the important caveat that each of the BRICs economies needed to work at keeping their development on track, and that bad policy or bad luck could derail any or all of them. That was an important health warning, given the shaky record of long-term economic projections. Even the firm's 'stress test' of its projections, an analysis of how well the model would have done in the past, did not entirely remove the doubts. But hidden in the detail was one particularly intriguing fact. If the Goldman Sachs numbers turn out to be right, by 2050 China's GDP *per capita*, in constant dollars (2003 prices), will be more than $31,000, nearly thirty-seven times its level in the year 2000. China is going to get rich very quickly, apparently offering mouth-watering opportunities to companies supplying its markets. Even by then, however, China's *per capita* GDP would be less than 40 per cent of projected American levels and significantly smaller than Britain, Japan, Germany, France and Italy. The biggest economy in the world will still be, in relative terms, only a middle-income country, with living standards below those in the West. China, it seems, is set to travel a long way in a very short time. But having done so, the journey will only have partially been completed.

Saving for That Rainy Day

Projections like this are important but they fail to capture the full flavour of China's likely development. That China is an economic curiosity is not in doubt. A rapidly developing economy – an emerging nation – should not be a creditor to the rest of the world. Yet that is what China, with a saving rate averaging around a quarter of household income, has been in recent years. Accumulated household savings in China are the equivalent of at least $1,250 billion, on conservative estimates. Why do the Chinese save so much out of relatively modest incomes when many citizens in much richer countries, such as America and Britain, have low or negligible saving rates? One explanation, favoured by most economists, is that Chinese people are driven by a powerful precautionary motive to save. Such is the scale of poverty and, even to those with rising incomes, the recent memory of poverty that there is a powerful incentive to put money away for the inevitable rainy day. Add to this the fact that, for a communist country (or perhaps because it is a communist country), provision of even basic safety net support in China is minimal. Most people lack any form of health cover, so they are forced to save for medical emergencies or treatment. Pensions, similarly, are not available to most workers via the state or company schemes. Much spending on education, in which the Chinese take great pride, is also self-financed (private education is 2 per cent of GDP; the state sector only slightly larger, at 3 per cent). But the system can play harsh tricks. Many Chinese parents find, to their chagrin, that their expensively educated offspring cannot find work. More than 4 million Chinese students graduated in 2006 but there were jobs for fewer than half of them. Some of the saddest stories are of 'returnee' students, sent to overseas universities at great expense, only to find that there is no job for them when they return from Britain and America. In response to this, the British government has relaxed its rules, allowing Chinese graduates to stay in the UK for a year to pick up some job experience.

The Biggest Market in the World

In March 2006, addressing the National People's Congress, prime minister Wen Jinbao promised to tackle China's bias towards saving and let consumer spending off the leash. Signalling a determination to shift the balance of Chinese growth towards the consumer, he said: 'We will address people's concerns that increasing consumption will make them unable later to meet basic living needs.' In part, low spending reflects generational differences, older people being much more reluctant to spend. There is also, in some areas, a lack of consumer infrastructure. Outside the cities and larger towns, shops remain primitive. For many Chinese people, household electricity is a novelty, and for many others, particularly in rural areas – though a diminishing number – it has yet to arrive.

Though Chinese people save, they also spend once they have got into the habit. But the impression of them as immature consumers, ready to be seduced by products designed by Western companies for Western markets, almost like primitives ready to exchange precious commodities for shiny beads, is wide of the mark. While China's rural population continues to experience low living standards and insecurity, this is not the case for the young and growing urban population. When the New Economist blog ran a piece asking whether China's people could afford the goods produced in its own factories, it got this response from a contributor signing himself simply Chang:

I am from a middle-class (Chinese standard) family in a north-eastern city, not so affluent compared to Beijing or Shanghai. We have two TV sets, desktop PC, audio system, fridge, DVD player… you name it. My dad is one of the 'cool dads', he bought a digital video recorder and laptop last year. My parents just bought a retirement apartment in southern China (in cash, Chinese people are not used to mortgages yet). I have never worked and am still in school working on my PhD, thus I contributed nothing to my family.[8]

The figures suggest he was not exaggerating. The OECD, in its 2005 report on China, quoted statistics suggesting that for every 100 Chinese households there are 46 refrigerators, 94 colour television sets, 12 personal computers, 28 air conditioners and 59 washing machines. As early as 1993 China had the biggest television 'population' in the world (230 million sets), according to the Chicago-based Museum of Broadcast Communications. By 2005 there were more television sets, colour and black and white, than there were Chinese households, allowing for the fact that some families own more than one and that in many farm communities a flickering black and white set is as good as it gets. Official figures in February 2006 said the number of mobile phone users in China had risen to more than 400 million – equivalent to nearly a third of the population – and that they were sending 34 billion text messages a month.

Despite this evidence of growing consumer prosperity, there is a long way to go. Economic development follows certain patterns; as countries grow richer the proportion of individual spending by households on necessities gradually declines, to be replaced by higher expenditure on luxuries. That is happening in China, though only gradually. As recently as 1997, nearly half of household spending was on food. Six years later that had come down to 40 per cent.

Even Wal-Mart is growing richer thanks to spending by Chinese consumers. There is a neat circularity in the world's biggest retailer, which owes so much of its success to sourcing production in China, tapping into the market. Wal-Mart's first Chinese supermarket was opened in Shenzhen in 1996. Ten years later it had fifty-six stores in mainland China and had already seen some differences between its customers there and those in its 3,700 stores in America. The Chinese have smaller homes and prefer fresh rather than frozen produce, so shop between three and four times each week, in contrast to the weekly or fortnightly 'big shop' typical of its American customers. Wal-Mart, however, is a long way from conquering China. It has been accused of being slower than some of its international competitors. Even among foreign supermarket groups, the French retailer Carrefour had by 2006 opened four times as many outlets as the US giant, with Britain's Tesco also catching up fast. So far, though, all foreign retailers together have only captured a fraction of the Chinese food market, which is dominated by local retailing groups such as WuMart (sounds familiar) or Lianhua, as well as millions of small shops and street sellers. Sales of imported goods are, however, growing rapidly, including Western branded products. China was the seventh largest retail market in the world in 2005 according to the Retail Forward consulting group, and it will become a lot bigger, overtaking Italy and France before 2010.

Looking for Luxury

For foreign firms who have had their fingers burned in China in the past, one of the most attractive features of the Chinese market is that the country's rapidly growing middle class favours Western brands. Branded goods meet the aspirations of China's increasingly sophisticated urban population in a way locally produced goods do not. 'In other markets brands measure quality and help people make choices,' said Doris Ho, principal consultant at Sprout Brands, an Asian branding consultancy.[9] 'Brands in China are status enhancers.' Foreign brands are seen as being of higher quality and more desirable, with the exception of food, where consumers tend to stick with what they know. German-made cars, Japanese-branded electronics and French, Italian and US fashion names appeal to China's new breed of shoppers. Even in food, Western brands such as Taco Bell, Pizza Hut, KFC and McDonald's (which is adding more than a hundred a year to the 700 restaurants it had opened by 2006), have made serious inroads.

It is in luxury goods that some of the most enticing prospects lie, which is why counterfeiting is rife. In December 2005 several luxury brands, including Chanel, Prada, Burberry, Gucci and LVMH, won a legal action against a Beijing shopping mall owner whose stores were selling fake versions of their products. The appetite of the country's newly wealthy for imported luxury products is considerable, and growing. In 2005, sales of 'high-end' fashion products, accessories and other luxury goods topped $2 billion, or 12 per cent of the global market. In this respect as well as others, China is rapidly catching up with Japan, in recent times the most important global market for luxury products. The China Association of Branding Strategy estimated in 2005 that 175 million people of the country's population of 1,300 million could afford to purchase at least some luxury goods, a number it expects to increase to 250 million by 2010. This segment of the population has incomes of $30,000 a year and upwards, at least twenty times the national average. Many Chinese are poor, and will remain so for the foreseeable future (as will be discussed below), but there is also fast-rising prosperity for some.

How big is the potential for what the Norwegian–American sociologist and economist Thorstein Veblen, in identifying the new leisure class of the late nineteenth century, famously called 'conspicuous consumption'? International accountancy firm Ernst & Young, in a September 2005 report, 'China: The New Lap of Luxury', predicted that the luxury goods market in China would grow by 20 per cent annually over the period 2005–8, then increase by 10 per cent a year until 2015. By that time, according to its projections, China would account for nearly a third of global demand for luxury goods, matching Japan and well ahead of any other country. There was, it said, 'enormous potential' for growth.[10]

By 2015, too, China will have opened up in another respect. Increasing numbers of Chinese people will be using their newfound wealth to take holidays in other parts of the world. Outward tourism, virtually unheard of a generation ago, will grow rapidly. The Economist Intelligence Unit predicts that there will be 100 million Chinese tourists visiting other parts of the world by 2015, compared with less than 30 million in 2004.

Will China Take to the Road?

In April 2005, after visiting the Shanghai motor show, Bob Lutz, the vice-chairman of General Motors (GM), was upbeat. 'The Shanghai show is rapidly turning into an absolutely world-class event, with most of the world's automakers taking part,' he wrote on GM's company blog.

> There's no longer anything about the show that has the slightest smattering of less than first-class production, especially in terms of the elegance of the stands, and the elegance of the facility that houses the show … When you look at the country, anybody who says the future of China is overblown or over-hyped just doesn't get it. If anything, it's

under-hyped. We have no conception of what that place is going to be like in ten years, and beyond. Shanghai and its surrounding province alone will have hundreds of millions of people with enough income to buy cars. And that's just one part of China. They're in the process of building 50,000 miles of interstate freeways, north–south and east–west routes, and it's likely that cities will spring up at the nodal points where the highways meet, as the nation shifts from largely agrarian to largely industrial. Picture America's industrial revolution replicated on a scale of a billion and a half people. In ten years, China will be, by far, the world's largest automobile market. Ignore it at your peril.[11]

Few motor manufacturers, in fact, are ignoring China. With private car sales of three million in 2005, out of total sales of 5 million – small in relation to the size of population, but nevertheless the third largest market in the world behind America and Japan – the global auto industry sees huge potential in China, just as environmentalists worry about the impact on the planet of a growing car population on the country's roads. On this, as with many things, China starts from a low base. In 2005 there were about fifteen cars for every 1,000 people in China, compared with more than 500 in the United States. The nightmare, for the global environment and demand on the world's energy resources, would be a rise in Chinese car ownership towards American levels. Could this ever happen? China's emergence as a car nation was confirmed by Shanghai's deal with Formula One, which has turned motor racing into a vast money-spinning operation. The inaugural Chinese grand prix took place in September 2004 in Shanghai on a custom-built $300-million track, with a commitment to run the race for at least a further six years. The first race, won by the Brazilian Rubens Barrichello in a Ferrari, was attended by a crowd of 150,000, each paying, by Chinese standards, a king's ransom for tickets, with the average price equivalent to a month's wages for a manual worker.

Car buyers in China tend to be young, with a median age of 35, and they also tend to favour foreign brands such as General Motors' Chevrolet (GM has the biggest share of the market) and Volkswagen, though niche models like BMW's British-manufactured Mini also do well. In one respect, at least, China is not following America's path. Cars tend to be small-engined, 'compact' models. In its March 2006 budget, the Chinese government reinforced this trend by sharply raising the tax on cars with engines of two litres or more, while cutting the rate on vehicles with smaller engine sizes. But in other respects there are similarities with the American approach. In a re-run of the golden age of motoring in America, China is rapidly building the roads to allow its citizens to take to them. The motorway network at the end of 2004 was 34,000 kilometres, twice its length four years earlier (the first motorway was not built until the 1980s), and the second biggest such network in the world, behind only America.

China's motorists are discovering the freedom of the road, but at a price. Tolls are the norm on the motorway network; the 1,100-kilometre journey from Beijing to Shanghai attracting toll charges equivalent to $60. That means freight drivers, whose ludicrously overloaded lorries belching noxious diesel smoke are a common sight, often prefer to use the old roads to avoid the tolls. Perhaps because of the tolls, many private car owners appear reluctant to venture too far afield. 'Curiously, however, the car remains largely a tool for short-distance travel, usually to the office and back', reported the *Economist*.

> The motorway network has so far failed to transform travel and leisure habits. Steve Bale of BatesAsia, an advertising firm, says that last year fewer than 20 per cent of car owners used their vehicles to travel out of the city at the weekend. Hitting the open road and following it wherever it leads is not, it seems, a particularly inspiring notion to the Chinese car owner ... China's media love to talk of an emerging 'car culture' in China. Yet in the popular imagination there is no equivalent yet of a Route 66. Map-reading is a skill few have mastered (detailed topographical maps are classified as state secrets). Group travel is preferred in a country where a bewildering variety of cuisines, dialects and cultures can make independent travel daunting.[12]

By 2050, Chinese car ownership could rise to about two-thirds of current American levels on a *per capita* basis, according to Goldman Sachs.[13] That will be a lot of cars – more than 500 million. But even with a tiny fraction of that number of cars, the strains are emerging in China's cities, as are the pressures on global oil supplies. The traffic is bad most hours in the day in Beijing and Shanghai and the other big urban centres, to the point where the authorities are keen to encourage car owners off the road, in a message that will sound familiar to people living in London or New York. In April 2004, the *China Daily* reported with approval the story of Li Qian, who had abandoned her car commute in her 'mid-size Buick' from the Tiantongyuan district of northern Beijing in favour of the metro. While owning a car and driving it to work was the dream for millions of Chinese people, it said, Li Qian and at least twenty of her acquaintances had found it stressful and impractical. 'Now she relies on the light rail every weekday to get to downtown Beijing, where she works as an archive specialist at a law firm,' the newspaper reported.[14] 'With the four-car train departing Lishuiqiao Station every 10 minutes during rush hours, it takes Li just 25 minutes to arrive at her office in the Jianguomen business zone. Traffic officials hope the light rail will not only make the morning commute easier, but also help ease congestion on city roads.' The propagandist tone reflects the uncertainty of the Chinese authorities about allowing a car-owning middle class to develop. On the one hand it will provide a market for China's domestic car industry, which also has big export ambitions. DaimlerChrysler is planning a new small Chinese-built car to sell to the US market. Chinese car-makers Hafei and Chery have already begun to export, selling to Latin America, Africa and the Middle East. But how many cars can China itself take? The *China Daily* article quoted a senior official of the Ministry of Land Resources (MLR), who warned that rising car use would make the country dangerously reliant on oil imports. 'Petroleum is not only for driving, it is a basic production material of modern industrial society,' said Zhang Dawei, director of the MLR's strategic research centre. 'How can we sacrifice basic needs of food, clothing and shelter for transportation only?'

These are the kind of growth strains that will come increasingly to the fore. It is where China's huge population becomes more of a curse than a blessing. China's population is unevenly distributed but its average density – 134 people per square kilometre – compares with under 30 in the United States. The question of whether China can sustain growth that will take it towards a US-style economy, and American levels of consumption, is a key one. How rapidly it is able to do so will depend partly on events, and partly on its ability to embrace and harness technology to its advantage. And of all the worries in the West about China, perhaps the most powerful is that its size will be combined with ruthlessly efficient technological progress. The fear is that the technology advantage of the advanced industrial countries, in other words, will rapidly disappear.

Space Adventure

In October 2003, from the Jiuquan launch site in the Gobi desert, Yang Liwei was blasted into space aboard the *Shenzhou V* spacecraft. The 38-year-old astronaut, a fighter pilot, completed fourteen orbits in twenty-one hours before coming back to earth in Mongolia, and had no doubt about the importance of what he was doing. China's first manned space-flight would, he said, 'gain honour for the People's Liberation Army and for the Chinese nation'. 'I will not disappoint the motherland,' he added. China's manned space programme, first conceived as long ago as 1966, when the space race between the Soviet Union and the United States was in full swing, had finally achieved its goal.

Two years later, in October 2005, two astronauts were launched from the same spot in *Shenzhou VI* and orbited the earth for five days. The Chinese authorities declared their ambition of establishing a space station within five years, followed by a moon landing. The symbolism was deliberate and clear. Just as America and Russia had used space flight to demonstrate their superpower status, so China – only the third country in the world to have an independent manned space programme – was following suit. No matter that the Shenzhou craft used relatively old technology, based on the Russian Soyuz programme; the manned flights were a powerful demonstration of China's capabilities and, perhaps as importantly, her potential.

A Technology Superpower?

In 2004 China's exports of information and communication technology (ICT), including mobile phones, laptop computers, digital cameras and other equipment, rose by nearly half to $180 billion. More significantly, as noted above, China became for the first time a bigger exporter of ICT equipment than America, which shipped $149 billion of such products overseas that year. That same year, in December, Lenovo, one of China's leading computer manufacturers, announced plans to buy IBM's personal computer division for $1.75 billion. The sale was a logical one for IBM, which had lost $1 billion trying to compete in the PC market between 2001 and 2004. The purchase was also logical for Lenovo, giving it an opportunity to cash in on IBM's long-established name, which offered a quicker route to customers in the West than building its own brand reputation. It worked for at least one buyer. I bought a Lenovo laptop during

2006. Without the IBM deal, the name would have been unknown to me, and not trusted. But the deal, which eventually went through after months of scrutiny by the US authorities, also underlined the changing nature of the world's relationship with China. No longer was it just a place where low-cost products such as clothing and toys were made or assembled for consumers in Europe and America, Chinese companies were capable of high-technology production, and of owning technology brands. The suspicions ran deep in America, and not just about the potential loss of technological superiority. In March 2006 the US State Department cancelled an order to install Lenovo–IBM personal computers on its secure network linking Washington with its embassies around the world. The move came after the US–China Economic and Security Review Commission, a panel appointed by Congress, warned that China aggressively spied on America and that the Chinese-supplied PCs would make it easier for it to do so.

The question of China's technology status is important. The more advanced China becomes, the bigger the competitive threat. The numbers certainly look impressive. A third of China's exports are categorised as 'high technology'. US official figures suggest some $40 billion of America's trade deficit with China is down to imports of what are described as 'advanced technology products'. A 2005 report, *The Emerging Chinese Advanced Technology Superstate* by Ernest Preeg, tracked the rapid development of China's technology investment, production and trade, together with a tripling in a decade of the number of university graduates being produced each year, and a 20 per cent annual increase in research and development (R & D) spending. Preeg predicted China would be a technology superpower by 2015 and bemoaned 'the lack of national purpose in responding to a rapidly changing world, driven by the development and application of wide-ranging new technologies on a global scale'.[15]

Or Technologically Limited?

On the face of it, the main question about China's emergence as a technology superpower is not whether, but when? Some argue, however, that China flatters to deceive. Authors from two leading US think tanks, the Center for Strategic and International Studies (CSIS) and the Institute for International Economics (IIE), certainly think so. In their joint 2006 book, *China: The Balance Sheet*, they question the extent of China's technological emergence, arguing that 'the data that are used to support the hypothesis that China is rapidly emerging as a high technology superstate are flawed'.[16] They point out that, while China awards four times as many undergraduate engineering degrees as the United States, when it comes to master's degrees and doctorates China produces only 50 per cent more annually. Most of these engineering graduates, in addition, are civil or electrical engineers, bound for the country's huge infrastructure programme. The quality of China's graduate output is also open to question, with the McKinsey Global Institute suggesting that only 10 per cent of the country's engineering and IT graduates are capable of competing with their peers in other countries. As for the rapid increase in Chinese high-technology R & D, this is from a low base; Chinese R & D spending is only a tenth of that in America. The CSIS/IIE authors are also sceptical about the nature of China's technology exports, pointing out that very few of them could be described as 'leading edge' technology. The biggest category of Chinese technology exports to America, they point out, are notebook computers, followed by monitors, TVs, mobile phones and DVD players. The pattern of production and export for all these is typical – a foreign company, from Taiwan, Japan or America itself, shifts production to China to take advantage of low assembly costs. 'More than half of all China's exports, and almost 90 per cent of its exports of electronic and information technology products, are produced by foreign-owned factories where interaction with domestic firms appears somewhat limited,' the book notes. 'Increasingly these firms are wholly foreign-owned, which makes them much less inclined than joint ventures to share technology.[17]

The authors quote the experience of George J. Gilboy, a senior manager since the mid-1990s at a major multinational firm in Beijing and a research affiliate at the Center for International Studies at the Massachusetts Institute of Technology (MIT). His experience on the ground has left him distinctly underwhelmed about Chinese technological and management know-how.

Gilboy painted a picture of haphazard technological development in China and plays down China's status and potential. 'Rather than thinking of China as yet another Asian technological and economic "giant", it may be more useful to regard it, like Brazil or India, as a "normal" emerging industrial power,' he wrote.

Thanks to the interaction of political structure and industrial culture,

China's twenty-first-century technological and economic landscape looks like a pattern of 'nodes without roads' – a few poorly connected centres of technological success. Burdened by these peculiarities, China has yet to lay the domestic institutional foundations for becoming a technological and economic superpower. Without structural political reforms, its ability to indigenize, develop, and diffuse technology will remain limited. And most of its industrial firms will struggle to realize exiguous margins at the lower reaches of global industrial production chains.[18]

Maybe China is deliberately moving slowly, so as not to cause too much alarm. Professor Jon Sigurdson of the Stockholm School of Economics, in a presentation for Demos, the British think tank, pointed out that China's technological ambitions are for a gradual build-up in power, not a sudden and spectacular rise.[19] Thus, while China will be the world's largest semi-conductor market by 2008, surpassing America and Japan, its official strategy is merely to be in the front rank of developing countries by 2010, to be a medium-ranking technological power by 2020 and to be among the world's technological giants – in other words a superpower – by 2049. Those goals may be unduly modest. Sigurdson noted that China's cost advantage relative to countries such as Finland and Germany is greater in technology products than in conventional manufacturing. He also observed that, while China is indeed weak when it comes to the level of patent activity, it is expanding rapidly in design capability and is increasingly strong in terms of flexibility; time to market. The lesson is not to exaggerate Chinese technological prowess but not to sweep it aside either.

China Lifts Millions out of Poverty

In October 2005 Paul Wolfowitz, the former Bush administration hawk nominated by the US president to run the World Bank, paid his first visit to China, starting in the poor western province of Gansu. There he visited several of the bank's projects, aimed at improving the lot of the mainly rural population. But he also paid tribute to his Chinese hosts and said he was anxious to learn from them. 'East Asia has experienced the greatest increase in wealth for the largest number of people in the shortest time in the history of mankind,' he said.[20] 'It is an incredible fact, and of course, without this growth in China, it wouldn't have happened. Since 1980,

China accounted for 75 per cent of poverty reduction in the developing world.' China, he pointed out, had lifted more than 400 million out of poverty since the reform process began in the late 1970s, leapfrogging *per capita* income levels of many other poor countries (including India and Pakistan) in the process. 'How did China do it?' he asked. 'I want the World Bank to be able to do more to help other countries learn, too, so that elsewhere in the world we can see more progress made to improve the lives of the poor.' He had good reason to ask the question. During the 1990s the number of people in the world living in absolute poverty – defined as on less than a dollar a day – fell from 1.29 to 1.17 billion. In the absence of China, however, not only would the reduction in east Asian poverty never have happened but overall global poverty numbers would have risen.

How indeed did China achieve such a dramatic reduction in poverty? Partly because, as is often said, a rising economic tide lifts all boats. Mainly because, many would argue, China's poor have benefited from the opening-up of the economy to the outside world; so that they are the beneficiaries of globalisation. The picture, in fact, is a little more complicated than that. The United Nations Development Programme, in its 2005 report on China, praised China's 'considerable progress' in human development on almost all measures.[21] Its ranking on the basis of the UN's overall human development index had risen continuously over twenty years and stood at 85th (out of 177). While still classified as a low-income country, China's achievements in literacy and life expectancy had placed it among the rank of middle-income countries, with primary-school enrolment above the average for developing countries and literacy levels equivalent to those in middle-income countries such as Poland, Hungary and the Czech Republic. Moreover, there was no single province or autonomous region within China which fell into the low human development category. The number of people living in absolute poverty in rural areas had dropped in a quarter of a century from 250 million to just over 26 million.

Unequal Footing

But, and there has to be a but, much of the poverty reduction in rural areas occurred in the early 1980s, under the impact of Deng's agricultural reforms – the market freedoms that resulted in a sharp increase in farm output, and so in countryside incomes between 1980 and 1984. The opening-up of China to the outside world in the 1990s, following

Deng's 'southern tour' in 1992, had rather less positive effects. In the 1990s, according to the UNDP, the reduction in poverty slowed because of rising income inequalities. China became, along the way, a highly unequal country. Measured by the Gini coefficient, the best statistical measure of income inequality, China's rose by 50 per cent between 1982 and 2002. Inequalities in China are about twice the level in Sweden and significantly more than in India. Most surprising of all, China is a more unequal society than the United States. This, of course, is what many see as China's Achilles heel: whether the authorities can contain discontent when inequalities are growing sharply in what is still a poor country ostensibly run on communist lines. The scale of political unrest in China is difficult to assess accurately, though Beijing admitted to nearly 90,000 'public order disturbances', mainly in rural areas, in 2005. They are, according to human geographer Joshua Muldavin,

> a result of widening gaps between rich and poor, and between urban and rural areas, and between the rapidly growing industrial east and the stagnating agricultural hinterlands. Guangdong – a booming epicentre of foreign direct investment, with thousands of new factories of global as well as Chinese corporations – embodies these inequalities most intensely. It is not surprising that the province has become a focus of resistance to development as peasant lands are overrun with industries. Peasant land loss is a time bomb for the state. While avoiding full land privatization and, until recently, massive landlessness of the rural majority, Beijing still allows unregulated rural land development for new industries and infrastructure. Land seized from peasants reduces their minimal subsistence base, leaving them with what is called 'two-mouth' lands insufficient to feed most families, thus forcing members of many households to join China's 200 million migrants in search of work across the country.[22]

Because Many Remain Poor

In the past the Chinese people have suffered from a lack of economic development and, during the Mao era, from spectacular policy failures and the cruel and inhuman official response to them. But economic success has also had its downside, and the victims of China's rapid development are well known. Those left behind in rural areas tend to be the less well educated – four times as many as in the cities have received no formal education – and, despite Deng's reforms, are often asset-poor. Of the poorest 10 per cent of the population in ownership of property, three-quarters are in rural areas. The rewards of China's success, moreover, have accrued disproportionately to men. In this notoriously male-dominated society, women operate under considerable disadvantages. Illiteracy and semi-literacy among women outnumbers that among men by 2.6 to 1. Women are poorly represented in white-collar and professional jobs, and have been first in the queue when it comes to large-scale layoffs by failing organisations. Many workers of both sexes in China struggle, however, with extreme insecurity.

The UNDP report noted the country's 'unfair and insecure' labour market, with 40 million made unemployed by enterprise restructurings and 140 million rural migrant workers seeking jobs in the cities and coastal areas. For employees of China's state-owned enterprises (SOEs), recent years have been anything but secure. The downside of the greater efficiency described above has been large-scale labour shedding. In November 1993 the 14th Central Committee of the Chinese Communist Party adopted 'The Decision on Issues Regarding the Establishment of a Socialist Market Economic System'. A month later the National People's Congress passed the 'Company Law of the People's Republic of China'. These, notwithstanding their ponderous titles, transformed the way SOEs work. No longer would they be operated for the benefit of the state and their employees. The aim was to turn them into properly run enterprises, with corporate structures and outside shareholders. This was taking the market economy into the heart of the Chinese system. The effect was dramatic. In 1995 there were over 300,000 state-controlled companies in China (SOEs and companies controlled by the state). By 2005 this had dropped to under 150,000, through a mixture of closures, sales and consolidation. The effect of this on workers, particularly in the industrial sector, was dramatic. In the five years from 1998 to 2003, for example, employment in state-controlled industrial companies dropped by 16 million, or 40 per cent. The labour-shedding in collective enterprises controlled by local government was even more pronounced: around 60 per cent. Indeed, the work force has borne the brunt of restructuring. The OECD, in its 2005 survey of China, noted that the consequence was a sharp improvement in output per worker. China, however, needed it. At the start of the restructuring process in

1995, labour productivity in China's state-controlled manufacturing sector was just 4 per cent of US levels.

While China's growth rate of 9 or 10 per cent a year is enough to have economists worrying about overheating, it is insufficient to mop up the supply of workers in search of higher-paid urban jobs. Official figures suggested urban unemployment was 8.4 million in 2005. Unofficial estimates suggest a figure at least three times that. Life for workers on the fringes of the Chinese economic miracle is grim in the extreme. The Hukou household registration system means they are deprived of access to education, healthcare and China's rudimentary social-security system. This discrimination goes deep; one survey found that only one in eight of the children of migrant workers were enrolled in schools. The workers themselves are often savagely exploited by employers, with lower wages and benefits and harsher working conditions than their city-born counterparts.

Still a Sweatshop Economy?

What do you get when millions of migrant workers flood into China's towns and cities who lack basic rights or even the awareness that they have any, but are willing to work for tiny wages? When, waiting to meet them are firms manufacturing products for multinationals at minimum cost, the answer appears obvious: exploitation on a grand scale. China has certainly been a sweatshop economy. Many would say it still is. Part of its economic advantage derives from the fact that labour costs across the board are a fraction of those in the advanced economies. Trade unions in the West, faced with large-scale job losses as a result of competition from China, argue that the country's poor labour standards add to its ability to undercut advanced-economy prices. John Sweeney, president of the American Federation of Labor and Congress of Industrial Organizations (AFL–CIO), which represents more than fifty national and international unions, wrote to George W. Bush in April 2006, ahead of President Hu Jintao's visit to Washington:

> Labour conditions in China are not improving. Thousands of Chinese
> miners lose their lives every year in accidents caused by carelessness and
> greed. Chinese construction workers, who have financed the skyscrapers
> of the Chinese economic miracle with their sweat and blood, cannot
> collect the billions of yuan in back pay that they are owed. And hundreds

of thousands of migrant workers continue to be forced to work inhuman hours at wages that fall below even Chinese minimum wages. A key factor in the persistence of these conditions is certainly the suppression of free and democratic trade unions.

An AFL–CIO petition in 2004 suggested that China's denial of safe working conditions for workers, its use of forced labour and suppression of trade unions lowered wages by between 47 and 86 per cent 'on conservative assumptions'. If China did not violate workers' rights, it said, the price of the country's manufactured exports would rise sharply, pricing hundreds of thousands of American workers back into jobs.[23]

Whether or not this is wishful thinking – and there is an element of that – few would dispute that there is a problem when it comes to worker exploitation in China. Robert Rosoff, director of the China Working Group, writing for the US–China Business Council, dwelt on the undeniable attractions of doing business in China; its cost advantages in a range of sectors, including clothing, footwear and toys, and its growing consumer market. But, he also pointed out, 'terrible labour rights' continued to exist.[24] The 1995 Labour Law of the People's Republic of China sets out the legal requirements on employers and provides for a maximum working week (in theory, forty hours), safety conditions, locally negotiated minimum wages, child labour and disputes procedures. 'In practice, however, the rights of Chinese workers are routinely violated,' Rosoff wrote.

Workers are often required to work far more than 40 hours a week, have few days off, are paid below the minimum wage, and are not paid required overtime. Improper deductions from wages are common. Some Chinese workers must pay a large sum of money as a 'deposit' to their employer, and they may have to pay a 'recruitment fee' in order to be hired. These payments can prevent workers from leaving jobs where their rights are violated. Physical abuse of workers, and dangerous working conditions, are also common.

Violations are so commonplace they could be presumed to exist in all factories, he suggested, though among foreign-owned plants the worst offenders tend to be those owned by Hong Kong Chinese, Taiwanese and South Korean firms. As for domestically owned factories, the worst conditions are in those which are smaller and privately owned. But Rosoff did not absolve American, European and Japanese firms from responsibility. The financial incentive for subcontractors to cut costs was powerful, and often driven by their customers in the West. 'Western companies' sourcing practices can contribute to the problem when, for example, large orders are made with short deadlines, the lowest possible prices are demanded, and orders are changed at the last minute,' he added. 'Factory owners are afraid to lose business if they refuse orders, even if they have to violate the law to complete an order.'

Model Factories

Is China getting any better? In August 2005 the National Labor Committee, a US anti-sweatshop pressure group, produced video evidence of the conditions under which workers producing children's books for the Walt Disney Company were operating. The video showed injured employees from the Hung Hing and Nord Race factories in China, their bandaged hands and faces said to have been caused by using unsafe equipment. Workers in the factories reported heat, oppressive conditions, long hours and a scant regard by managers for their safety. Disney's response was to ask Verité, a Massachusetts-based, non-profit-making audit and research organisation, to investigate. On Verité's advice, Disney insisted on improved working conditions and ceased trading with two factories which refused to comply. Verité has since the mid-1990s undertaken hundreds of factory audits on behalf of multinational corporations. Usually, as in the case of Disney, it is because the firm is under pressure from trade unions, consumer groups or pressure groups such as the National Labor Committee or the Clean Clothes Campaign.

Each summer since 1998 Verité has also held a China suppliers' conference, designed to promote best practice. At its 2005 conference, held in Beijing, it provided a case study of a 'model' Chinese supplier, the Shanghai Changjiang Clothing Adornment Co., which produces gloves, hats, scarves and headbands for a wide range of international customers. The firm, established in 1993, had been subject to outside audits on behalf of multinationals keen to underline their social responsibility from the early days. Initially, according to Verité, these audits merely ensured no child labour was employed and that fire safety regulations were observed. Low pay and long working hours went unchallenged. By the late 1990s though, these too had become subject to regular audits. Years of dealing with bureaucrats and the pressure to meet centrally set targets had, however, given Chinese managers an almost instinctive cunning when it comes to dealing with inspections. Shanghai Changjiang, like many other factories of its kind, found ways of getting round the external audits, notably by the use of a double book-keeping system – one of the commonest ways of avoiding close scrutiny. One set of books, often a complete set of records including the entire payroll system, appears to suggest the factory is complying fully with all local and national labour laws. The other, the genuine set, reflects the hours and pay the workers actually receive. But Shanghai Changjiang came good, scrapping its double book-keeping system, apparently because of the desire of its management to be genuinely socially compliant, not cook the books to make it appear so. The story shows what can be done, but also how hard it can be for outsiders to determine what is really happening. Often Western customers have little genuine idea of factory conditions in China. Just as royalty gets used to the smell of fresh paint – every new place they visit has just been given a facelift – so China's factories put their best face on for outside inspections.

Outside pressure will gradually reduce the exploitation, but so will internal economic forces within China. In January 2006 the BBC reported the story of Huang Xin Xu, a 20-year-old working for the Singaporean electronics company Flextronics in Shanghai for less than $150 a month. Having come to Shanghai from Hunan province in central China, she was about to go home for the Chinese New Year holiday and was not planning to return. While she would not be regarded as among the most exploited Chinese workers, neither the lifestyle – sharing a dormitory with seven other girls – nor the pay in high-price Shanghai was sufficient enticement to stay. 'Living in Shanghai costs a lot more than living in my home town, so the company would have to pay higher wages to keep me here for longer,' she told the BBC.[25] Many firms operating on China's east coast report high staff turnover and poor retention rates – staff turnover ranges from an acceptable 5 per cent to a hugely inefficient 50 per cent annually. Professor Ding Jon Hong, head of the Population Institute at east China's Normal University, carried out a survey of 800,000 migrant workers in Shanghai. 'Most migrant workers, when they first arrive in Shanghai, work in factories,' he said. 'When they have made enough money, they will either take that money home to build a house, get married and return to farming or they will set up their own small businesses here in the city because it pays better. If the factories want to keep this second group of people they will have to offer them more money.'[26]

This raises important questions about China's long-term competitiveness. It also suggests that economic progress will gradually bring an end to worker exploitation, just as it has lifted hundreds of millions of Chinese out of poverty already. No country can get rich on a permanent basis by ruthlessly exploiting its own people. But many countries get away with doing it for a very long time.

People Movers

One of the apparent puzzles about China is why with such rapid economic development on their doorsteps so many of its people are prepared to risk life and limb in order to find grim, low-paid jobs in America, Europe and elsewhere. Each year tens of thousands of Chinese, probably many times more, leave the country on rust-bucket ships and in the back of container lorries on tortuous journeys organised by 'snakehead' or other criminal gangs. In March 2006 Cheng Chui Ping, otherwise known as Sister Ping, was sentenced in a New York court to thirty-five years in prison for leading an illegal Chinese people-smuggling operation. The court was told that Ping's operation had begun in the early 1980s with the smuggling of a few villagers at a time, usually on planes to the United States from Hong Kong. Later, however, she graduated to using ships, her human cargo being locked in the hold for months on end, with little food and often only two sips of water a day. Each illegal worker paid between $25,000 and $45,000 for their trip, usually out of their subsequent earnings in America, payment being enforced by brutal thugs. The trips were extremely hazardous. On one occasion fourteen of the migrants were drowned transferring from a cargo ship to a smaller landing craft in stormy seas. Another time, in June 1993, the *Golden Venture*, one of the cargo ships used by Ping, was intentionally grounded off Queens, New York, when the landing craft failed to show. The 'illegals' were told to swim for the shore in the inhospitable waters of the Atlantic. Ten died in doing so. According to the Federal Bureau of Investigation:

> She amassed great wealth by exploiting the yearnings of her often
> impoverished countrymen to come to America. People of limited means

paid exorbitant sums for passage to this country under deplorable conditions. Some of those people lost their lives in the process. When her crimes were exposed, she fled the US with as much determination as her victims had shown in getting here. Only a truly international law enforcement effort secured Sister Ping's capture and return to face justice.[27]

Intriguingly, her 35-year sentence comprised five years for people smuggling, ten years for 'trafficking in ransom proceeds' and twenty for money laundering – financial crimes mean more than people crimes, it appears.

Operations like Ping's are sadly only too common. That same month of March 2006 Lin Liang Ren was sentenced to fourteen years in prison, and two Chinese accomplices received lesser sentences, for running a people-smuggling operation to Britain which resulted in the tragic deaths of at least twenty-one Chinese cockle pickers in Morecambe Bay, off the Lancashire coast. On a cold February night in 2004 Lin Liang Ren took a gang of thirty illegal workers down to the treacherous sands of the bay, on a night when experienced local cocklers stayed away because of high winds and dangerous tides. Some of the Chinese workers had never seen the sea before, the court was told, let alone gathered cockles from dangerous waters. The party was engulfed as the waters came in. Some were carrying mobile phones and called loved ones in China to say goodbye, trapped as they were by the rising tide and the grip of the sand. Twenty-three of them never returned; two of the bodies were never recovered. The story that emerged was of poor Chinese living thirty to a modest terraced house and being ruthlessly exploited. The cocklers, mainly from Fujian province in south-eastern China, died owing most of the £20,000 each the snakehead gangs had charged them for their passage.

A Journey Too Far

The grim toll of Chinese migrant workers seeking a better life elsewhere has been rising. Three years before the Chinese cocklers perished in Morecambe Bay, Perry Wacker, a Dutch lorry driver, was sentenced at Dover to fourteen years in prison and his co-conspirator Ying Guo received a six-year sentence, for their part in a smuggling operation that led to the deaths of fifty-eight Chinese migrants. In the summer of 2000 Wacker had hidden sixty people in a container on the back of his lorry, concealing them under boxes of tomatoes bound for Britain from Europe. To avoid detection on the five-hour ferry journey from Zeebrugge, Belgium, to the UK and ensure the Chinese were not heard by customs and immigration officials, he had shut the air vents. The result was a horrific death by suffocation for all but two of them. When customs officers opened the container at Dover they were expecting to find cigarettes or alcohol. Instead they were confronted by the most appalling scene and evidence of the migrants' frantic but futile efforts to escape.

Why do the migrants do it? In one respect they are maintaining a pattern established over decades, if not centuries. But, as Frank Pieke of Oxford University argues, the nature of Chinese migration changed in the 1980s and 1990s. The opening-up of the Chinese economy to outside influences and investment, its exposure to the forces of globalisation, was accompanied by an increase in the number of Chinese seeking opportunities elsewhere. The new migrants came from areas of China which had long sent people to Europe, such as southern Zhejiang. But they also came from places which had no previous history of overseas migration, for example Sanming in western Fujian. 'Mass migration not only provided cheap labour for the restaurants and shops owned by the established Chinese communities in western Europe, but also inserted a dynamism and appetite for expansion that led to the exploration of new economic niches,' wrote Pieke.[28] The demand was there, often from already established Chinese migrants who had prospered, moved up the social scale but still needed a supply of cheap, pliant labour to run their businesses. The change, evident in the tragedy of the cockle pickers, was that increasingly illegal workers sought work outside the tight-knit Chinese communities, though often through Chinese go-betweens. In both America and Europe, anywhere where there is a demand for cheap labour – in construction, or seasonal farm work such as fruit-picking – illegal Chinese workers can be found. As for the motivation of the 'illegals' to travel and work in other countries, the simple answer is economics. A low wage in Britain or America is still a king's ransom in China.

After the Dover container tragedy, the House of Commons Home Affairs Committee conducted an investigation. One adviser to the Chinese community neatly summed up both the motivation and the plight of the illegal workers:

There is a severe shortage of labour in the UK Chinese food industry. Earnings in China are 1/20th of those in the UK. Chinese immigration trafficking is the result of the government's refusal to admit a controlled flow of legal immigration. Economic migrants are forced to become asylum seekers. A Chinese snakehead is the head of a smuggling ring, part of a triad. A triad is an underworld gang whose activities are wide and varied, they include loan-sharking, illegal gaming, prostitution, extortion and smuggling ... Snakeheads are active also in London and other cities in the world. The current cost of coming to the UK is in excess of 200,000 RMB ($25,000), equivalent to at least thirty years' savings in China for an average migrant. Those who cannot raise the money from relatives and friends have to borrow from loan sharks or snakeheads, in which case a guarantor is involved. Interest is currently 2 to 2.5 per cent per month compound. Punishment for non-repayment is severe. Beatings and maiming are common.[29]

In other words, they come for economic reasons; they stay because they have to. One day, perhaps, China's economy will be successful enough to remove the incentive for migration, ending this grim trade. That day, however, is some way away.

China's Pull on the Developing World

Migration is one way that China makes a big impact on the rest of the world, as does its contribution to global economic growth. The China effect, however, extends much further. Increasingly, China's rapid emergence is having a significant impact, for both good and ill, on the developing world. China is both a huge customer for the commodity exports of developing countries and a competitor that threatens to undercut their own exports of manufactured goods. Whether this nets out to a beneficial effect or not depends on the balance of these factors. Even countries that benefit through higher prices from Chinese commodity demand may find their development constrained. Rather than moving up the value chain into manufacturing and services, the China effect may mean there is little incentive for them to do so. It is beyond doubt that China is a growing factor, particularly in Africa.

In 2005 sub-Saharan Africa grew by more than 5 per cent, its best economic performance for three decades. The explanation lay not with development aid from the West or the opening-up of advanced country markets to African products. Africa had China to thank. 'The Chinese are investing in Africa and getting results, while the G8 are putting in huge amounts of money, and they don't see very much,' said Sahr Johnny, Sierra Leone's ambassador to Beijing. 'They just come and do it. We don't start to hold meetings about environmental impact assessment, human rights, bad governance and good governance. I'm not saying that's right, I'm just saying Chinese investment is succeeding because they don't set high benchmarks.'[30]

China's interest in Africa has been driven by her thirst for oil, although it extends into other areas as well. Some 700 Chinese companies already operate across the African continent. During 2005 they invested more than $200 million, mainly in projects associated with oil exploration and development. In January 2006 the China National Offshore Oil Corporation (CNOOC) announced it was spending $2.27 billion to acquire a 45 per cent stake in a Nigerian offshore oil field. China buys oil from a range of African countries, including Sudan (more than half of the country's production), Chad, Nigeria, Angola, Algeria, Gabon and Equatorial Guinea. Nearly 30 per cent of China's oil imports came from sub-Saharan Africa in 2005. China has also invested in hotels and other tourist facilities, mining and infrastructure, including roads, bridges and dams. Chinese companies mine diamonds in Sierra Leone, copper in Zambia and cobalt in the Democratic Republic of Congo. Timber in Mozambique, Gabon and Equatorial Guinea is logged by Chinese operators and shipped back to meet the huge demand in the construction industry back home. Chinese farmers have been seconded to Nigeria to teach the locals how to improve crop yields for cassava, which China imports in large quantities.

In Freetown, the capital of Sierra Leone, said by the United Nations to be Africa's poorest country, the Chinese presence is visible, with the construction of a new military headquarters, sports stadium, government offices and a new parliament building. Angola, which exports 25 per cent of its oil output to China, has benefited from $2 billion of loans from Beijing, which is being used to fund Chinese-built railways, roads, schools, hospitals and lay a fibre-optic network. China will also train Angolan telecommunications workers; all in return for a guarantee of future oil supplies.

This is not the first time China has been active in Africa. In the 1960s

Mao Tse-Tung tried to use Chinese influence and money to persuade the leaders of former colonies to follow his Maoist line, but failed. This time it is different. Beijing is less interested in spreading ideology than in pursuing the country's commercial interests; ensuring it has adequate supplies of energy and raw materials and developing the kind of loyalties and dependence that should mean future markets for Chinese goods.

Bolstering the Corrupt

China's trade with Africa has already grown rapidly, the share of sub-Saharan Africa's exports going to China increasing more than twenty-fold between 1990 and 2004. China–Africa trade is closing fast on trade between America and Africa. But, as with everything to do with China, the economic relationship with Africa is a two-way street, involving both pros and cons. One worry is that China's lack of ethical standards helps bolster corrupt regimes. 'China refuses to join in Western rebuke of African corruption and human rights abuses,' wrote Vivienne Walt for *Fortune*. 'Much like the militant Islamic officials in Tehran – another of China's key oil suppliers – many African leaders regard China as a balance to Western meddling. Heavily dependent on its Sudanese oil imports, China last year used its permanent seat on the UN Security Council to block genocide charges against Sudan for the massacres in Darfur.'[31] China's blind eye has extended to supplying Zimbabwe with fighter planes and troop carriers, and even to donating a roof for the palatial $9-million new home of Robert Mugabe, its president, which was built by Chinese construction workers. No African countries, or leaders, appear off limits or beyond the pale to China.

That is one worry about China's impact on Africa, but there are plenty of others. Professor Raphie Kaplinsky and colleagues, in research published by the University of Sussex's Institute of Development Studies (IDS) in 2006, note that Chinese competition, particularly in clothing and furniture, has badly hit local industries in Lesotho, Swaziland, Madagascar, Kenya and South Africa. For workers in these countries, whose main advantage has been low labour costs, the effect of Chinese competition has been to generate unemployment and nip emerging African manufacturing industries in the bud. Nigeria is a beneficiary of Chinese oil demand, but its trade unions blame Chinese imports for the loss of 350,000 manufacturing jobs. In Ethiopia, a third of small-scale shoe manufacturers have been forced out of business and a similar proportion have had to downsize their operations. The IDS authors also note that China's apparently positive contribution via commodity demand, bringing higher prices to the producers, may not be all it seems. 'Poorly handled, a resource boom can easily become a resource curse,' they write. Chinese companies are able to invest in fragile states in Africa because in many cases they are pushing the long-term goals of the Chinese government, notably to secure supplies of natural resources, in a way that would be difficult for commercial firms. The danger is that these lucrative resource contracts have the effect of propping up corrupt regimes:

> In the 1960s in particular, the very large surpluses that some African economies could earn from exporting agricultural commodities stimulated kleptocratic governance and undermined the legitimacy of newly-independent regimes. Since the 1970s, world market prices for most agricultural exports have declined substantially, and this form of kleptocracy has declined considerably. However, recent research shows that rents derived from the extraction of 'point resources' (oil, gas, diamonds and minerals) have, since the 1970s, clearly encouraged authoritarian rule, high military expenditure, corruption and violence.[32]

Does China Move the Goalposts on Globalisation?

There is a wider point about China's impact on poor countries. The pro-globalisation argument is that free trade brings benefits to rich and poor countries alike. Countries that close themselves off from global markets tend to suffer; they remain economic backwaters. A highly influential study by Jeffrey Sachs and Andrew Warner came up with the striking result that over the period 1970 to 1989, 'open' developing economies grew by an average of 4.5 per cent a year, closed economies by 0.7 per cent.[33]

It is hard to overstate the importance of the view that free trade boosts economic growth, particularly for poor countries. It forms the basis of policy recommendations from the OECD, IMF and World Bank. When the G8 announced debt write-downs and aid assistance for Africa at Gleneagles in July 2005, the sentiment expressed by Tony Blair and the other world leaders was that much more could be done to help Africa through trade liberalisation. That meant, among other things, African access to the protected and subsidised agricultural markets of Europe, America and Japan. In fact, while such access might help African farmers, support for the general proposition that 'openness' is the key to prosperity is weaker than it seems. Francisco Rodriguez and Dani Rodrik, in a paper they described as 'A Sceptic's Guide' to the evidence on trade policy and growth, suggested that previous researchers had been generous in attributing growth to openness. 'We find little evidence that open trade policies – in the sense of lower tariff and non-tariff barriers to trade – are significantly associated with economic growth,' they concluded.[34]

This is an important issue. One key aspect of it is whether China, with its sheer size and the extent of its influence, changes the arguments in favour of globalisation. Michael Meacher, a former UK Secretary of State for International Development, argues that China's emergence is both a threat to the rich countries and a block on the development of the poor. 'The share of global income of the poorest fifth of the world has actually halved since 1960 to a paltry 1.1 per cent today,' he wrote.

> World inequality has grown drastically. The richest countries now have 125 times higher GDP per head than the 20 poorest countries. The main reason for this impoverishment is that a global economy has locked developing countries into the role of primary producer of basic commodities, forced to open up their markets to transnational competition that they cannot resist as the price of receiving the investment they cannot do without. What is needed is the right for the poorest countries to erect tariff walls to protect their infant industries at least until they are strong enough to meet the full force of international competition.[35]

Raphie Kaplinsky, in his 2005 book *Globalization, Poverty and Inequality*, argues that China's development has thrown up a whole category of 'squeezed' economies, including much of Latin America, central Asia and Africa; economies that do not benefit from the open-market policies advocated by the so-called Washington Consensus – the approach to development advocated by the World Bank and the International Monetary Fund. The optimal response of these squeezed economies to the challenge from China may be rather different. 'These economies will experience decreasing returns from competing in external markets because of China's increasingly successful participation in these major markets,' he writes. 'Consequently, in addition to maintaining the capacity to promote production through active and selective innovation and investment policies, some form of selective disengagement may be required from the global economy for these economies, notably selective protection against imports.'[36]

If there is a case for poor countries to protect themselves against Chinese competition, what about their wealthier counterparts? That raises questions about how long the rest of the world will be prepared to tolerate China's rise. Is there anything special about China which bolsters the case for protectionism in comparison with, say, the rise of Japan? One factor, plainly, is China's size. Another is the nature of the economy. A country whose enterprises are supported and only able to compete as a result of loans from a bankrupt, state-backed banking system is competing unfairly. While the banking system is now being cleaned up, and the problem of 'non-performing' loans is being tackled, it is certainly the case that much past lending was not on a commercial basis. Such financial arrangements would, for example, immediately fall foul of European Union rules on illegal state aid. Add in the doubts about labour standards in China and the case for 'selective disengagement' from a globalised world it increasingly dominates appears stronger. China, to some, has suckered the world into seeing it as a permanent source of low-cost goods, benefiting Western consumers and making the task of policymakers easier by keeping a lid on inflation. The long-term effects of China's emergence may, however, be much less benign, doing more harm than good. China, whose modern-day economy is in many respects a product of globalisation, could be responsible for bringing about globalisation's decline by having called into question the conventional wisdom about the benefits of openness. In a worst-case scenario China could end up partly destroying the global economy on which it thrives. There will be more on this later in the book. In the meantime, it is time to go back to India.

5

India's Networked Economy

'India has a fantastic pool of software professionals. The world needs to benefit from this.'

Bill Gates, chairman, Microsoft

'India has evolved into one of the world's leading technology centres.'

Craig Barrett, chairman, Intel Corporation

'Through the wisdom of its government leaders and the entrepreneurship of its private sector, India has risen to become a major force in the global economy.'

John Chambers, president and chief executive officer, Cisco Systems

Flattening the World

For Thomas Friedman, the *New York Times* columnist, the moment of revelation – that flash of inspiration – came during a conversation with Nandan Nilekani, chief executive and president of Infosys, one of India's highly successful growth companies. Infosys has in a quarter of a century come from nothing to be a significant global force in software, IT services and consultancy. Friedman was visiting the firm's Microsoft-style campus in Bangalore, the city that has become the hub of India's information technology industry, its Silicon Valley. As Friedman passed through the gates of Infosys's campus, the appropriately named Electronics City, leaving the poverty, grind and traffic chaos of Bangalore behind him, he moved from the economically backward into an environment that on any continent would be regarded as unmistakably twenty-first century. He was greeted, as all visitors to the campus are, by the sight of manicured lawns, gleaming modern buildings, even a huge swimming pool. There was a large food court, a company store selling Infosys-branded merchandise, and an enormous gym for the use of the firm's 16,000 on-site employees (out of a global workforce of more than 52,000). The campus's modernity was evidenced by the fact that its oldest building, the Heritage Building, which stands apart from the most recent glass and steel structures, and is of mainly brick construction, was completed as recently as 1994. In Electronics City, what they describe as 'heritage' is rather different from the rest of India.

It was on the Bangalore campus that Friedman, travelling with a television crew, was waiting to record an interview when Nilekani told him: 'The playing field is being levelled.' What he meant was that IT and the massive global investments that had brought down the cost and convenience of long-distance communications had created a new world in which companies operating in countries like India could compete directly and successfully with the most successful businesses, and their skilled workers, in the rest of the world. For Friedman the levelling of the playing field of which Nilekani spoke meant that, as he called his book, 'the world is flat'. 'Clearly, it is now possible for more people than ever to compete in real time with more other people on more different kinds of work from more different corners of the planet and on a more equal footing than at any previous time in the history of the world – using computers, e-mail, networks, teleconferencing, and dynamic new software,' Friedman wrote. 'That is what Nandan was telling me. That was what I discovered on my journey to India and beyond.'[1]

Nilekani is a persuasive advocate, on behalf of both Infosys and his country. When I met him he had one ear on the questions I was putting to him and one eye on the Blackberry in his hand, firing off responses to e-mails, every inch the modern high-tech executive. His pride in the firm he co-founded is palpable. 'We are proud that we have been able to create a global company out of India,' he said. The significance of Infosys was that it had developed in the way it had, under the yoke of India's legendary bureaucracy and outside the subcontinent's normal boundaries.

Enterprise in India had usually been associated with huge public-sector organisations – the product of the Nehru era – multinationals, or long-established family firms; the great Indian business dynasties such as Birla and Tata. The seven software engineers who set up Infosys in 1981 broke the mould. It was, said Nilekani, 'the democratisation of business: 'We introduced a new model of company.' Infosys's success, and India's future prosperity, will be based, he argues, on 'soft power', which is reflected not just in the growth of certain types of business, but in the burgeoning international appeal of its music and cinema. India is the world's second biggest market for mobile phones and by 2010 will have an IT industry with annual exports of $50 billion (this at a time when Infosys's turnover had doubled to $2 billion in the space of two years). The next ten years, he predicted, will see changes as spectacular as the past decade, with India at the forefront of them. Technological devices will become smaller, more powerful and more mobile, and with improved connectivity. India, moreover, will be at the forefront of this new technological revolution. There can be no turning back for technology, and there can be no turning back for India. Economic growth rates of 10 per cent are perfectly possible, he suggested, and are probably needed to meet the expectations of the population and mop up a labour force expanding at between 10 and 12 million a year. 'The engine has left the station and the train is chugging along,' said Nilekani. 'But we have to de-regulate further; we have to have more flexibility. We have to design public policies that are humane and equitable, reforms with a human face. We cannot tell a group of people that prosperity will come along but they have to wait for ten years. We have to have a rate of growth that will give us an adequate rate of job creation.'[2]

India's Outsourcing Boom

If there is one sector that embodies India's economic transformation, its drive for modernity, it is information technology. Ask somebody in the West what they think of when they think of India and these days the answer is as likely to involve IT, or one of the services made possible by it. The call-centre worker or the distant voice on the telephone manning the IT helpdesk, or the salesman selling you a Dell personal computer, is for many people the image of modern India. India has become the outsourcing or 'offshoring' capital of the world, the place Western businesses have chosen when relocating back office or other functions – business process outsourcing (BPO), as it is known. The motivation for doing so is usually, though not always, to save costs. It can involve the transfer of payroll administration, accounting work, basic research and, most notoriously, call-centre operations. IT-enabled services (ITES) are, like BPO, often functions that firms used to carry out in-house but are now contracted out to another company. Examples would include data analysis and data mining. In both cases, these are huge and rapidly growing markets in an IT era, and India has commanding market shares in each of them.

Beginning in 1999, India's National Association of Software and Service Companies (Nasscom), the representative body for the IT software and services industry in India, has commissioned McKinsey, the management consultants, to report every three years on the development of the Indian IT sector, its prospects and its place in the world. The 2005 Nasscom–McKinsey Report confirmed India's continued success in these areas. India, it said, had a 65 per cent share of the market in ITES, or 'offshore' IT. When it came to BPO, India's global market share was nearly as impressive, at 48 per cent. Moreover, there was enormous potential for further growth in these markets, according to McKinsey's estimates. A business process outsourcing market worth $11.5 billion in 2005 had the potential to grow to at least ten times that size. The combined market for outsourcing and IT services would eventually hit $300 billion, it predicted, reaching $110 billion by 2010, with India claiming at least a 50 per cent share. That would confirm the IT sector as the jewel in India's economic crown, contributing at least 1 per cent a year to the country's overall growth rate, nearly half of export growth and, by the end of the decade, employing 2.3 million people directly and 6.5 million indirectly.[3]

It looks like a gilded prospect and it is, it should be said, built on a formidable record of achievement. India's IT sector has grown from almost nothing in the space of a relatively short time; Texas Instruments made the first IT investment in Bangalore as recently as 1984. The country's comparative advantage in IT could have turned into a disadvantage at the end of the 1990s, with the bursting of the dot.com bubble. In fact, it went from strength to strength, capitalising on the push by businesses, having spent a lot of money to protect themselves from the so-called millennium bug (unnecessarily, as it turned out), to start saving money by using IT more intelligently. In the four years to 2004 India's 'offshoring' sector tripled its turnover to nearly $13 billion. For an economy always desperate for overseas earnings, this booming sector has been invaluable, contributing 95 per cent of India's service-sector foreign-exchange inflows in the early years of the twenty-first century. An Indian economy that has always been somewhat closed has benefited from spectacular, export-led growth in one sector at least.

New Names at the Top

That success is reflected in the rise of individual companies. In 1992, the year after the second and most significant stage of India's reform programme had begun, the ten biggest companies on the Mumbai stock exchange were all in traditional sectors – the State Bank of India, Tata Iron and Steel, ITC Ltd, Reliance Industries, Hindustan Lever, Tata Engineering and Locomotive, the Associated Cement Company, Century Textiles, Grasim Industries and Tata Tea. By 2006, four firms whose rise was directly related to the IT, outsourcing and telecommunications boom – Tata Consultancy Services, Infosys, Wipro and Bharti Airtel – were in the top ten, along with the Oil and Natural Gas Corporation, the National Thermal Power Corporation and the Indian Oil Corporation. Only Reliance, ITC and Hindustan Lever survived from fourteen years earlier at the top of the list of the very largest firms by market capitalisation, a reflection of the rapidly changing economy.

There is another contribution the IT industry makes to the Indian economy. Expatriate Indians have been successful across the world in a wide variety of fields, many proving to be formidable businessmen when free from the stifling bureaucracy that characterised their home country in the past. There is probably no other sector, however, in which Indian expatriates have had more impact in modern times than in IT. The success of Indians in Silicon Valley, in Europe and elsewhere has resulted in significant flows of remittances back to the mother country, making a substantial contribution to foreign-exchange inflows.

India's IT Advantage

Why do certain countries prosper in some industries and sectors and not others? Why is India so successful in IT? Economists analyse this in terms of comparative advantage. India does not have a comparative advantage when it comes to the production and export of, say, luxury cars or fine wine, though it has both a car industry and its own wine makers. But India has an unmistakable comparative advantage in software and IT services, which has become a symbol of the 'new' India. Part of that advantage, like China's in manufacturing, is down to labour costs. Indian call-centre workers typically earn between 10 and 15 per cent of their advanced country counterpart's salaries, though wages in India are rising at a faster rate than in most Western economies. Even adjusting for purchasing power parity, an Indian IT professional is paid only about a third of his or her European counterpart, and an even smaller proportion of what the equivalent job in America pays. The offshoring boom would not have happened, however, without another key trend – the fall in global telecommunications costs. This really did make the world smaller and flatter, and allowed outsourcing to happen on a scale that would not otherwise have been possible. Between 2001 and 2004 peak call rates between India and America fell from 60 rupees an hour to 10, while those between India and Britain dropped from 48 rupees to 6. This reflected not only increased competition in international telecommunications services, but also – and more importantly – big investments in the infrastructure needed to provide fast and reliable connections. The offshoring boom is a product of the digital and broadband age.

There is nothing in any of this, however, which answers the question: Why India? The explanation for India's advantage appears to be twofold. First, many Indians appear to be unusually good at IT, their skills reinforced by the education system; and second, the success of an official strategy of prioritising the sector – a throwback to old-style planning. Sir Keith Whitson, until 2003 chief executive of HSBC (a bank which has successful outsourced operations), caused controversy when he said of Indian call-centre staff: 'They're quicker at answering the phone, highly numerate and keen to come to work every day. Staff are hugely enthusiastic about their jobs, they dress well. A lot have degrees.'[4] He was reflecting what many see as the principle reason for India's IT success, its human capital. At the élite level this has been associated most notably with the seven Indian institutes of technology (IITs). These institutes, in Kharakpur, Mumbai, Madras, Kanpur, Delhi, Guwahati and Roorkee, began to be established soon after independence in 1947, with the aim of providing educational excellence in science, technology and engineering, using the model of the Massachusetts Institute of Technology (MIT). In this, they have been a success; in 2005 *The Times Higher Educational Supplement* ranked the IITs as the third best educational institutions for technology in the world, behind only MIT and the California Institute of Technology. For many years, however, they were criticised for providing talent that benefited, not the Indian economy, but other more advanced economies. India, in other words, exported its brightest and best to seek their fortunes elsewhere, particularly on America's west coast.

Some, however, stayed. Notable graduates include, not only N. R. Narayana Murthy, the chairman and founder of Infosys (as well as Nandan Nilekani, co-founder and current chief executive), but also Arun Sarin, who rose to become chief executive of Vodafone, Vinod Khosla, co-founder of Sun Microsystems, Rajat Gupta, managing director of McKinsey, and Lord (Kumar) Bhattacharrya, founder of the Warwick Business School. At one stage three-quarters of IIT graduates formed part of a significant Indian 'brain drain'. In April 2005 the US House of Representatives passed a resolution praising the contribution of Indians in general, and IIT graduates in particular, for their 'economic innovation' and for 'helping to advance and enrich American society'.[5]

Diaspora

The brain drain has been reduced. One of the measures of the turnaround in the Indian economy is that India's technology élite no longer regard the best career opportunities as outside their own country. Less than a third now go abroad following undergraduate or postgraduate courses. The brain drain of the past, however, contributed to India's later success in attracting outsourcing business. There are 1.7 million people of Indian descent in the United States, and their contribution to the economy has been substantial, from small 'mom and pop' local stores (think of the iconic Apu – full name Apu Nahasapeemapetilon – proprietor of the Kwik-E-Mart in *The Simpsons*) to the top of big corporations. Academics of Indian birth or descent hold some of the most prestigious university posts in America. But it is in Silicon Valley, where 200,000 Indians live, that their contribution has been biggest. An Indian created the Pentium chip (Vinod Dham) and Hotmail (Sabeer Bhatia). A third of the engineers in Silicon Valley are Indians, and 40 per cent of start-ups are by Indian entrepreneurs. One in every fourteen firms has an Indian chief executive. This, in turn, is now feeding back. Not only have some who have achieved success in California returned home to ply their trade in Bangalore and other centres, but they have provided an important conduit through which business is directed back to India. Organisations like the Silicon Valley Indian Professionals Association (SIPA) have focused increasingly on providing information and contacts for American firms thinking of outsourcing. The same pattern is repeated, albeit on a lesser scale, elsewhere in America, and in Europe and Asia. The diaspora, having been criticised in the past for turning its back on India, has been in the forefront of its revival.

So, in this instance, has been government policy. The IT industry was one of the earliest beneficiaries of the post-1991 economic reforms, notably the liberalisation of the telecommunications industry from 1994 onwards, the welcoming of foreign direct investment and technology in IT, and the establishment of a National Venture Fund for the IT and software industry. Successive governments have worked closely with Nasscom, the industry body, to ensure the removal of obstacles to the growth of the outsourcing sector, and the industry as a whole. Or, when the industry has just wanted to be left alone to grow, the government has generally done so. Perhaps most importantly, the industry's very newness has been a significant plus. Older industries come to be shackled by red tape and stifling bureaucracy. The longer they have been around, the more the bureaucrats have found ways of making life more difficult. IT does not have to deal with this red-tape legacy.

Bangalore Blues

Nowhere has the changing nature of India's economy been more keenly felt than in Bangalore. In the 1980s it was known as a quiet hillside southern city with lush greenery, a population of some 3 million and 300,000 cars. It had a reputation as something of a backwater, with a high proportion of elderly people, a place in which to grow old gracefully. From the 1920s it had been developed as a 'Garden City', with open spaces and attractive buildings. Bangalore also had a successful industrial and commercial history, developing as a manufacturing and research base for the state-owned aerospace and defence industries in the period after independence. In 1972 the Indian Space Research Organisation was established in Bangalore. This turned out to have been a momentous decision for the city, for it was this high-technology bias that made it a natural location for the IT industry, initially for multinationals but also for India's new generation of firms. Both Infosys and Wipro chose to base themselves in the city. Thus a city in the south of India, modernised and developed under British rule as a colonial centre, with railway, telegraph and postal links, and the first in the country to have electricity, became India's Silicon Valley. Indeed, on some measures, employment in Bangalore's three technology parks – Software Technology Parks India (STPI), International Tech Parks Ltd, and Electronics City – and in surrounding areas exceeds that in Silicon Valley itself.

Rapid development has its costs, however, and in many ways Bangalore's struggle to cope with economic success is a microcosm of India as a whole. The city's population having grown to 6.5 million and, perhaps as significantly, its car population to 2.3 million, Bangalore streets, which have not kept pace, are frequently gridlocked. Jonathan Kaminsky, reporting on the 'other' Silicon Valley for the *San Francisco Chronicle*, encountered Shwetal Mehta, who had moved from America to the 'back office of the world' to lead the expansion of a small software-services company:

> The managing director of Cyberwerx, who is Indian-born and US-bred, does not regret coming here. But the drawbacks are considerable. For one, the power at his downtown office goes out at least twice a day, necessitating a costly backup generator. And because of Bangalore's choked, narrow roads, he says, his three-mile commute to work, which used to take 10 minutes, now pushes an hour each way. Mehta is in many ways emblematic of the information technology sector in Bangalore. As an Indian, he's proud of the city's emergence as a global power. But as an executive, he's fed up with its growing pains and with the government's seeming inability to deal with them. Bangalore's jam-packed streets, rolling power outages, rising salaries and deteriorating quality of life – and the emergence of smaller, cheaper Indian cities competing aggressively for investment – mean that the city that has claimed so many Bay Area tech jobs is now in danger of becoming a victim of its own success.[6]

Bangalore, home to 1,700 software firms and more than 300,000 IT workers, and responsible for two-fifths of India's IT services and outsourcing work, is creaking under the strain, to the point where its future as a high-technology centre is under threat. Mercer, the human-resources firm, ranks cities worldwide for quality of life, a survey carried out mainly for multinationals to assist them with location decisions (but which also makes great copy for journalists). Its 2006 ranking of 215 world cities placed Bangalore in 153rd place – not good for a Garden City, though no Indian city scores well. Delhi and Mumbai were in joint 150th place, Chennai 160th. The Garden City, with many open spaces claimed for offices or shopping developments and the urban sprawl extending well into its green belt, is in any case becoming a distant memory. More troublingly, Bangalore's infrastructure problems appear to go well beyond mere bureaucratic delays. Serious flooding during 2005, caused by a failure to invest in new drainage capacity, exposed deep tensions between the business community and the city and state authorities. The Karnataka state government, in whose jurisdiction Bangalore lies, has been accused by the city's businesses of standing in the way of progress by dragging its feet on infrastructure: not just drains, but a long-delayed international airport, new roads and a metro system. The effect is to damage Bangalore and India's reputation, notably in American boardrooms. According to one US account:

The high-tech firms in Bangalore produce $7 billion in software exports yearly, or 35 percent of India's total exports. But amazingly, little is being done to modernize Bangalore's dilapidated streets, drainage system and power grid. That's because the coalition government that runs Karnataka – a union of the Janata Dal (or Secular) Party and the Congress Party – is actively feuding with the city's business community. Some analysts say the government is more concerned with pandering to rural voters than responding to the frustrations of wealthy business people. Similar conflicts are playing out in other parts of India as politicians try to balance the concerns of rural constituents with the pressing need to improve the rickety infrastructure of fast-growing cities.[7]

Bangalore's infrastructure problems will not mean it loses its status as India's Silicon Valley in the foreseeable future, though it has resulted in a number of high-profile investment decisions going against the city, mainly in favour of Hyderabad in Andhra Pradesh, which has a similar size of population (6 million) and also boasts a strong reputation in science and technology. Hyderabad's IT ambitions, and indeed its success, are reflected in the fact that some in the city call it 'Cyberabad', or India's second Silicon Valley. During 2006 a planned $3 billion semiconductor plant, nicknamed Fab City, was switched from Bangalore to Hyderabad, and Honeywell announced its new research and development centre would be built there. Even the local champions, Infosys and Wipro, have been expanding in other cities, while Siemens said in February 2006 that it would not be expanding further in Bangalore because of the 'total chaos' afflicting the city's roads and power supplies.

Call Centres – Coming Home?

When companies relocate operations to other cities, it is Bangalore's loss, but not India's. Is there a threat to India's IT and outsourcing success, which could undermine the economy more generally? One threat is that India's dominance of the outsourcing market will be challenged by other countries and continents, which can combine low labour costs with technology and (English) language skills. In a speech in June 2006, Peter Ryan, call centre and outsourcing analyst for Datamonitor, a market-analysis firm, predicted that the most rapid growth in call-centre work outsourced from Western economies in the following few years would occur in Africa, not India. 'They provide excellent language capabilities and agent sophistication and are on a par with most other popular outsourcing destinations,' he said.[8] Egypt produces 200,000 graduates a year, 80,000 with IT and engineering degrees. Other well-placed African countries include Botswana, Ghana and Kenya. The ION Group, a consultancy, reported in 2005 that South Africa was superior to India in call-handling quality, technological infrastructure and language skills. Morocco and Tunisia have been successful in attracting call-centre work from France, as part of a francophone network against which India – with the exception of the old French enclave of Pondicherry – cannot compete. The threat to India from Africa is not yet significant, and starts from a very low base, though it could grow. More immediate may be the threat from countries such as the Philippines, Malaysia, Vietnam and eastern European members of the European Union, including Hungary and Poland. Tied to this is another potential threat, that of a commercial and political backlash.

It is a testimony to India's success in attracting outsourcing business that it becomes a story when it does not, or when the flow is in the opposite direction. In June 2006, Powergen, the British energy firm, announced it was closing its Indian call centres and would create up to 1,000 jobs in

Bedford, Bolton, Leicester, Nottingham and Rayleigh, all in the UK. The firm, which had had a large number of complaints from customers about the Indian centres, said it was responding to improve customer service. 'Offshore call centres may have their place for certain industries,' said Nick Horler, Powergen's managing director. 'However, we believe that we can best achieve industry-leading customer service by operating solely in the UK. When customers contact us they need to be confident that their query will be fully resolved quickly.'[9] Powergen's move had been anticipated by Abbey, the Spanish-owned UK-based bank, which in 2005 announced it was returning its call-centre work to Britain, having moved 1,000 jobs to Bangalore two years earlier. Delta, the US airline, closed its Indian call centre in 2004, returning the work to America, while Dell, the computer firm, also transferred some of its Indian operations back to the United States. India's call-centre industry suffered a blow during 2005 when three employees were arrested for allegedly siphoning off $300,000 from the accounts of Citibank customers. The sporadic return of call-centre work to its country of origin appears to have much more to do with customer unhappiness than fears about the security of accounts managed in India. One survey, carried out by the online pollsters YouGov for the British bank Alliance & Leicester, showed that 81 per cent of the 4,000 people surveyed would not be happy to have their financial accounts or other services handled by an overseas call centre. The biggest drawback, cited by nearly 90 per cent of respondents, was in problems of communication, defined as 'language, culture and general understanding of my circumstances'.[10]

Indian call centres have worked hard to iron out such problems. Potential staff whose accents are deemed to be 'too Indian' to talk to foreign customers are weeded out during the training process and either not employed or confined to back-office work. Staff are also encouraged to emerge themselves in the 'culture' of the country where the customers are located, whether it is baseball and movies in the case of America, or football and soap operas where Britain is concerned. One call-centre employee, Aniket Mahajan, a 23-year-old male graduate, describes the process. 'The accent training is hard work but fun,' he says. 'We are taught the basics first, the alphabet and single words. Once we have a grasp of the accent we watch English soaps such as *EastEnders* and *Coronation Street*. We learn about the differences in culture, too. Our trainers play films set in Britain – *My Fair Lady* and *Notting Hill* are favourites.'[11] By

Indian standards call-centre staff get paid well; some are encouraged to use Western 'stage' names while on duty to put customers at ease, and to engage in small talk before getting down to business. Shifts are arranged to fit in with customer hours; Mahajan's usual shift began at four in the afternoon, Indian-time, and finished at 1.30 in the morning. The downside for customers of dealing with Indian call centres is the feeling of distance, often reinforced, despite huge improvements, by poor-quality telephone connections. Newspapers running campaigns against this type of outsourcing have found a ready market among readers complaining about a lack of awareness among call-centre staff of the basics of dealing with customers, including an inability to spell common names and place names. In India, meanwhile, the call-centre staff are often on the receiving end of appalling abuse, some of it racist in nature, which they are under instruction not to react to. Staff turnover in Indian call centres is high – typically two-fifths of employees move on each year – and can be as high as 60 to 70 per cent, with customer abuse and low levels of job satisfaction often being blamed. That does not mean call-centre workers are necessarily leaving the industry; competition for qualified workers in Bangalore and elsewhere is intense, and many get poached.

The ultimate outsourcing reversal, perhaps, came with an announcement in the summer of 2006 by ICICI OneSource, the Mumbai-based company which has been at the forefront of business process outsourcing to India. It announced that it was planning to set up call centres and other outsourcing operations in Northern Ireland, thereby creating 1,000 jobs over two years.[12] Financial assistance from the UK government through Invest Northern Ireland had a hand in the decision but so too, according to Peter Hain, the Northern Ireland Secretary, did the province's claim to be 'the most competitive near shore option for companies seeking a base to service Western European markets'. The announcement was significant for two reasons. It showed that Indian companies are increasingly looking beyond India to expand, of which more below. But it also underlined the shortcomings of India for some kinds of outsourcing work. When British companies advertise 'UK-only call centres', as National Westminster, a subsidiary of Royal Bank of Scotland, does, firms hoping to pick up this kind of business have to respond.

The Outsourcing Backlash

Champions of India's economy, and its outsourcing industry, would emphasise that examples of 'offshored' jobs flowing back to Britain, America and
other countries are still rare. The net flow, meanwhile, remains heavily in
India's favour. Chris Gentle, head of research in the UK for Deloitte, a firm
of management consultants, predicts that hundreds of thousands of jobs
will migrate to India from higher-cost Western economies. In 2006 he predicted that by 2010 a further 150,000 jobs would have been transferred
to India from Britain alone. 'There is increasing eradication of people and
paper in service industries,' he said. 'Service industries are now exposed
to the full forces of international competition and globalisation. Anything
that goes down a wire is up for grabs.'[13] The Indian outsourcing industry
emphasises, moreover, that the bad publicity given to some aspects of
call centres, and their unpopularity with some customers, should not be
taken to reflect the fortunes of the sector as a whole. Call centres, in many
respects, represent a halfway house between direct contact with customers in branches and fully automated services. First Direct, part of the bank
HSBC, began life in Britain in 1988 as a telephone-only retail bank with no
branches. In 2000 it began encouraging its customers to shift to online
banking. By 2006, 840,000 of its 1.2 million customers were using internet
banking and 460,000 used some form of text-message banking, 75 per
cent of its customer contacts being electronic.

Even where the customer is unaware that functions have been outsourced to India, however, it is not all plain sailing. In Britain trade unions
have regularly campaigned against the offshoring of jobs, warning firms
that it is a false economy. There have been controversies on data-protection
grounds about outsourcing the administration of National Health Service
medical records to India. Unison, the public-sector union, warned in June
2006 that something as straightforward as sending patient records to
India for typing was risky because of frequent errors. While hospital sec-
retaries had supporting medical notes as a check, and could query any
doubtful words directly with doctors, overseas transcribers operated in a
potentially dangerous vacuum. It is important to recognise that some of
this kind of response is undoubtedly straightforward protectionism. It is
the job of unions to warn against changes that threaten the jobs of their
members. In Britain in general, however, the backlash against outsourcing
has been relatively mild, partly because it has been accompanied by rising

employment. There has been more tension over a much more visible trend – rising economic migration into Britain.

In America, however, outsourcing has been a hot political topic. Early in 2004 Gregory Mankiw, at the time chairman of George W. Bush's Council of Economic Advisers, caused a storm when he wrote the following in the annual Economic Report of the President:

> One facet of increased services trade is the increased use of offshore outsourcing in which a company relocates labour-intensive service industry functions to another country. Whereas imported goods might arrive by ship, outsourced services are often delivered using telephone lines or the Internet. The basic economic forces behind the transactions are the same, however. When a good or service is produced more cheaply abroad, it makes more sense to import it than to make or provide it domestically.[14]

Mankiw, for his trouble, was accused by CBS News of 'political ineptitude', and by Tom Daschle, then the Democrat Senate minority leader, of spouting 'Alice in Wonderland' economics. Even Dennis Hastert, the Republican House Speaker, said Mankiw's analysis 'fails a basic test of real economics'. John Kerry, the unsuccessful Democrat presidential candidate in the 2004 election, had attacked 'Benedict Arnold' CEOs, who had outsourced jobs overseas, pledging changes in America's tax laws if he was elected to make it less advantageous for them to do so. While insisting he was a free trader at heart, he said: 'What I am against is unfair tax laws that practically compel US companies to move operations overseas. I'm against a distorted tax code that rewards business leaders for shutting down American factories and laying off American workers.'[15]

Kerry lost the election, but anti-outsourcing sentiment in America survived his defeat. Less visible, perhaps, than the loss of manufacturing jobs to China (and before that, Japan), outsourcing has nevertheless provoked anger and action. More than 300 bills have been introduced at state level in America with the aim of restricting outsourcing by companies or government agencies. Most states have seen such bills introduced, although not generally enacted. Their role, in the main, has been to offer local politicians an opportunity for grandstanding, and to show they are concerned about job losses, both actual and potential. By the spring of 2006 only twelve such bills had made it into law, usually imposing minor restrictions on outsourcing by government and official agencies. Experts say, however, that other legal changes in some states, setting new standards for firms on data protection and data security, could have a more insidious effect on outsourcing. The issue is serious enough for Thomas Donohue, president of the US Chamber of Commerce, to have declared: 'We will lead the fight to keep our own markets flexible and open – opposing measures that would restrict outsourcing or make it more difficult for foreign investors to in-source capital and jobs to the US economy.'[16]

The economic arguments in favour of outsourcing to lower cost economies are powerful. They free workers in advanced economies to move up the value chain into higher productivity jobs. They help alleviate shortages of workers and skills. They provide benefits to shareholders in the form of higher profits, and to consumers in lower prices (Indian-provided services and Chinese-produced manufactured goods are identical in their economic impact). Studies suggest that roughly 80 per cent of the benefits of outsourcing accrue to the country doing it, and only 20 per cent to the host economy. That is not, however, the way it looks on the ground. The victims of outsourcing are easily identified, and make their discontent known. Those who benefit, on the other hand, make up a much more diffuse group, and do not tend to shout about their gains. It is one of the oldest political dilemmas, which applies to many situations, but its result is that outsourcing gets a bad press. Thus Paul Craig Roberts, a prominent supply sider and free marketeer, who was assistant secretary to the Treasury in the Reagan administration, repeatedly attack outsourcing, as, for instance, in March 2006:

> The jobs record for the past five years tells a clear story. The BLS [Bureau of Labor Statistics] payroll jobs data contradict the hype from business organizations, such as the US Chamber of Commerce, and from 'studies' financed by outsourcing corporations that offshore jobs outsourcing is good for America. Large corporations, which have individually dismissed thousands of their US employees and replaced them with foreigners, claim that jobs outsourcing allows them to save money that can be used to hire more Americans. The corporations and the business organizations are very successful in placing this disinformation in the media. The lie is repeated everywhere and has become a mantra among no-think

economists and politicians. However, no sign of these jobs can be found in the payroll jobs data. But there is abundant evidence of the lost American jobs. Information technology workers and computer software engineers have been especially heavily hit by offshore jobs outsourcing. During the past five years [January 2001–January 2006], the information sector of the US economy lost 645,000 jobs or 17.4 per cent of its work force. Computer systems design and related activities lost 116,000 jobs or 8.7 per cent of its work force. Clearly, jobs outsourcing is not creating jobs in computer engineering and information technology. Indeed, jobs outsourcing is not even creating jobs in related fields ... Oracle, for example, which has been handing out thousands of pink slips, has recently announced two thousand more jobs being moved to India. How is Oracle's move of US jobs to India creating jobs in the US for waitresses and bartenders, hospital orderlies, state and local government and credit agencies, the only areas of job growth?[17]

How big is the risk of a serious political backlash? It is probably fair to assume, as McKinsey does in its projections for Nasscom, that once the outsourcing genie has been let out of the bottle, it will stay out, although the rate of future offshoring is hugely uncertain. Certainly, the rate of outsourcing to India appeared to have slowed in the final few months that this book was being written (late 2006). Against that, there is no let-up in the pressure on companies to reduce costs. That would survive, and could be enhanced by, a global economic downturn. The biggest political challenge, perhaps, would be in controlling the backlash during a period of rising Western unemployment.

India Goes Offshoring

One intriguing possibility is that India's IT and outsourcing companies use the strong domestic base they have established to themselves move work to other countries. In 2005 Gartner, an IT research consultancy, suggested India could lose market share as a result of the loss of its labour cost advantage. Rising wages in the outsourcing sector – driven by shortages of people with the right kind of skills and fierce competition for them – together with infrastructure problems, could result in its share of the global outsourcing market halving within a few years, Gartner warned. In response, Ananda Mukerji, chief executive of ICICI OneSource (the firm that announced call centres in Northern Ireland) suggested the threat was overdone:

> While wages in India are rising, I think it is an inevitable result of the high growth the industry is facing at the moment. I don't really see this as a competitive threat for three reasons. The first is India has a significant lead over other countries and the overall maturity of the industry in terms of its scale, size, depth and width of capabilities would be hard to replicate in the short run. Secondly, India has moved beyond pure labour arbitrage, and the combination of skills and experience the industry has developed, along with its relatively low cost base (albeit eroding), is a very compelling proposition. Thirdly, I think Indian BPO companies are also going to take advantage of the newer (and lower cost) locations which are coming up and become truly global players.[18]

The third of his suggestions is the most intriguing. The idea of Indian businesses becoming global outsourcing players on the back of the expertise they have built up is logical enough. The notion of them taking that expertise and using it to outsource to countries other than India, in significant numbers, opens up new possibilities. It underlines, if nothing else, the speed with which competitive advantage can move on in a globalised world economy. Barely has the world got used to services being outsourced to India, than a new phenomenon suggests itself. Can it be that the most serious backlash in the future will be when jobs are outsourced *from* India?

The Other Ninety-nine Per Cent

India's IT industry is fast-growing, dynamic and exciting. Its impact on the rest of the world has been more obvious, in recent years at least, than the rest of the economy put together. It has made a disproportionate contribution to export earnings, punching well above its weight. But while it may be the poster boy for modern, outward-looking India, the sector is still a minnow in relation to the country as a whole. India has a working-age population of just under 700 million. In 2006 it had just over 400 million in employment (both organised and unorganised – the latter being outside the system of employment taxes, social security and most labour regulations), as well as nearly 42 million officially registered as unemployed. Less than a tenth of Indians in jobs, it should be said, are in organised-sector employment, underlining the economy's still undeveloped status. Set against this large working-age population, the IT industry has 1.3 million direct employees, according to Nasscom, with a generously estimated 3 million others indirectly employed, or owing their jobs to the industry. That equates, taking the widest measure of employment (direct and indirect combined), to under 1 per cent of India's work force working in and around the 'new' India. Even less flatteringly, just 0.1 per cent of the country's total population is employed directly in IT and outsourcing. Indian Railways, a quiz question favourite because it is one of the world's largest employers, has more than 1.6 million regular employees, 300,000 more than the Indian IT industry. The sector is, of course, growing and will continue to do so, assuming it can avoid most of the pitfalls outlined above, but even with 2.3 million directly employed by 2010 – which Nasscom expects – it will still represent a tiny job market élite. What does the rest of the country do, and is it any good at it?

Part of what it does, and always has done, is make things. One of the criticisms of the post-independence period was the neglect of the country's traditional industrial strength in favour of large-scale national champions, often state-owned. Even so, manufacturing contributed significantly to economic growth in the 1970s and 1980s. It still does, accounting for about 17 per cent of GDP and more than half of exports, though it has been something of a poor relation since the early 1990s, when the emphasis has been on services, with China clearly leading the way in manufacturing. Even so, some three-quarters of foreign direct investment into India is related to manufacturing and there are some success stories. The Hero Group, started by the Munjal brothers in the 1950s, is currently the world's largest manufacturer of motorcycles and, in the 1980s, became the biggest manufacturer of bicycles, the transport of choice for many Indians, though it subsequently lost that crown to Taiwan-based Giant Manufacturing. For Hero, as for other Indian manufacturers, low labour costs are not enough. The drive for efficiency and higher productivity has had to be pursued with as much vigour as in any of the advanced industrial countries. Indeed, the suggestion that cheap labour provides them with a free ride rankles with Indian businesses. They have always had cheap labour, they point out, but only now are they putting it to work. Bajaj Auto, which manufactures scooters and motorcycles, as well as the three-wheeled auto rickshaws that are a characteristic sight on the country's roads, made 2.4 million vehicles with its work force of 10,500 in 2005. In the immediate post-liberalisation period in the early 1990s, it was producing less than half that number of vehicles with more than double the work force.

The real problem with Indian manufacturing is that there is not enough of it, something the government is desperate to change. Stories of successful manufacturing firms improving their efficiency by shedding labour are gratifying for owners and shareholders, but they are the last thing the politicians want to hear. While China is pursuing the classic development model of shifting workers from the land to work in factories, India has been pursuing a different strategy, and not by choice. The 'Indian model' is effectively bypassing manufacturing as a source of jobs, implying that migrants from rural areas will make their way directly into service-sector jobs. It is a tall order, and probably will not work – leaving India without an engine of jobs' growth – which is why the government is determined to double manufacturing's share of the economy to between 30 and 35 per cent. Manufacturing growth has indeed accelerated in recent years, though not by enough to suggest this ambitious target will be easily achieved. Generating new manufacturing jobs is often easier said than done. During 2006 Buddhadeb Bhattarcharjee, the communist chief minister of West Bengal, was locked in a battle with local farmers over a plan to build an assembly plant for Tata Motors' new small car. Thousands of farmers and their labourers refused to accept compensation for the loss of their livelihood because they feared there would be no jobs for them at the new factory.

Back to the Land

Away from the gleaming new offices and well-manicured campuses of India's IT sector is another part of the economy. Often separated by just a few miles from the 'new' India, the old India still dwarfs it in terms of economic impact. Hundreds of millions of farmers and their families are, as the Indian government's official website puts it, 'the mainstay of the Indian economy'. 'Agriculture and allied sectors contribute nearly 25 per cent of gross domestic product (GDP), while about 65–70 per cent of the population is dependent on agriculture for their livelihood,' it notes.[19] Indian agriculture is, on the face of it, a considerable success story. Long before the country was showing itself off to the world as a high technology centre, Indian agriculture was benefiting from the 'Green Revolution' of the 1950s – the introduction of high-yielding crops, better fertilisers and improved irrigation – and raising output. Between 1950 and 2000 combined production of rice, wheat and coarse cereals rose from 121 kg per head of population to 191 kg, an increase of more than 60 per cent. Projections suggest that, partly by extending the harvested areas, notably for cereals, in Uttar Pradesh, Punjab, West Bengal, Haryana, Madhya Pradesh and Bihar, but most importantly by further increasing crop yields, further significant production increases will occur. By 2026, for example, the Indian government expects cereal output to reach 266 million tonnes a year, up 45 per cent on its late 1990s' level, fruit production to rise by 150 per cent and vegetables by 70 per cent.

These are impressive figures, though from a relatively low base, and are regarded as attainable by most independent experts. Indian agriculture typically raises its output by 1 to 2 per cent a year, though that varies hugely from year to year depending on whether the monsoon is favourable. This is a long way behind the 8 per cent growth rate of the economy as a whole, but it is vital to India's future. As Amresh Hanchate and Tim Dyson of the LSE put it:

> It is clear that the country will be able to feed its rising population, though population will remain a major influence on Indian agriculture in the period to 2026. Nevertheless, we expect that average levels of food consumption will improve somewhat; the average diet will be a little richer, especially in vegetables, fruits, and milk. But increasing agricultural mechanization and urbanization mean that patterns of human activity are changing fast: obesity is already a significant and growing problem in the major towns ... India will certainly contain many undernourished people in 2026, but probably fewer than existed at the start of the century.[20]

That is the good news about Indian farming. Unfortunately, it is more than balanced by the bad news.

Still Hungry

India's farmers may be doing their job in meeting most of the food needs of the country's growing population, but serious problems of malnutrition and undernourishment persist. Even after years of strong economic progress, India has the largest absolute number of undernourished people in the world, and the incidence of child malnutrition is also among the world's highest, higher in fact than in most sub-Saharan African countries. A third of babies are born underweight. More than a fifth of the world's poor (living on less than a dollar a day) are in India, on the government's own admission, and 75 per cent live in rural areas. The United Nations' Special Rapporteur on the Right to Food, Jean Ziegler, reported after a mission to India in August and September 2005, that 'although famine has been overcome, millions of Indians still suffer from chronic undernourishment and severe micronutrient malnutrition, especially women and children and people of lower-caste scheduled castes and tribes. Starvation deaths have not been fully eradicated, nor has discrimination against women and against lower castes. Corruption, impunity and a wide range of violations including forced labour, debt bondage and forced displacement (destroying people's access to productive resources) remain serious obstacles to the realization of the right to food.'[21] Part of the problem, as with many things in India, is bureaucratic inefficiency and poor infrastructure. Even when food is produced, it is often wasted while being transported. In 2000, many died of starvation in Rajasthan, which was hit by a severe drought, at the same time as food was rotting in government storage facilities.

The rural population, which bears the brunt of undernourishment and malnutrition, made its disquiet known in the 2004 general election, being mainly responsible for voting out the reformist coalition government under Atal Behari Vajpayee, the BJP leader. Vajpayee's non-Congress government was seen as favouring the rapidly growing middle class and ignoring the plight of the rural poor. That may have been unfair, but it reflected a growing sense that economic development has been unsustainably uneven in its benefits. 'With its surging economy and a new middle class of about 300 million, the growing divide between urban and rural people is rousing political tensions, too, as the downside of India's economic boom becomes ever more acute,' wrote Taimur Ahmad, introducing an interview with Manmohan Singh, Vajpayee's successor. 'Growth has been restricted to a relatively narrow band of industries, and in the countryside, home to three-quarters of the population, living conditions have not, by and large, improved meaningfully.'[22] For Singh, whose background in planning and development meant he was acutely aware of the problem, the key was to maintain a rapid rate of economic growth of 8–10 per cent and spend more on education, health and infrastructure. 'Our basic problem is to get rid of chronic mass poverty, ignorance and disease,' he said. 'This still afflicts millions of our people, and this change can be achieved only by a sustained increase in the overall growth rate of the economy.' For many of India's rural poor, however, what they see as Singh's 'trickle-down' prosperity will come too late.

The End of the Road

In the summer of 2006, the Indian government announced an aid package worth several hundred million dollars for cotton farmers in the western state of Maharashtra. The aid followed a two-day trip by the prime minister to the cotton-growing Vidarbha region of the state, where a failed crop, falling prices and the crushing burden of debts had led nearly 500 despairing farmers to commit suicide since the start of the year. The aid package, with similar assistance intended for farmers in Andhra Pradesh, Kerala and Karnataka, offered a combination of debt write-offs and assistance with irrigation and seed purchases. Up to 18,000 farmers in the four states had taken their own lives in the five years from 2001. In a gruesome twist, many chose to do so by taking highly toxic organophosphate pesticides. The story of one of them, Subhash Mamidwar, was retold by the *International Herald Tribune*, just ahead of Singh's tour of Vidarbha. Mamidwar was among the 95 per cent of the 3.4 million farmers in the region struggling with heavy debts. He owed 40,000 rupees – about $900 – to the bank and 100,000 rupees to moneylenders and, like many others in the region, had been caught out after investing in what was supposed to be a new wonder crop, as British journalist Amelia Gentleman explained:

> Two years ago a new genetically modified seed, Bt, was introduced
> into India, and enthusiastically endorsed by the local government. Its
> manufacturer, Monsanto, said it was resistant to boll weevil – the main
> cotton pest – and required just two sprays of insecticide for every crop,
> instead of the usual eight. The modified seed sold for about four and
> a half times the cost of normal seed, but many farmers opted to buy it
> because they believed it was indestructible and would give a higher yield.
> They were devastated when many of the Bt cotton plants were afflicted in
> November with a reddening that destroyed much of the crop. Rain at the

wrong time was considered part of the problem, and that left the farmers with unusually high debts. Since most of these farmers have debts to the banks on which they have long since defaulted, they are forced to borrow from local moneylenders at exorbitant rates of interest. Some of the rates may go as high as 100 per cent a year.[23]

India's urban–rural divide is regarded by many commentators, and by the government, as one of the most serious problems the country faces, and one of the most significant obstacles to sustained development. Hopes that world-trade liberalisation would provide a breakthrough for Indian farmers, pushed tirelessly during the World Trade Organisation's problematical Doha round by Kamal Nath, India's commerce and industry minister, struggled with the reluctance of Europe and America to make enough concessions (in the case of Vidarbha, by cutting subsidies to US cotton farmers). One significant problem for farmers, however, is the lack of a properly functioning internal market for their products. Many sell straight to the state purchasing monopoly, at controlled prices that leave little or no profit margin, even in years when the crops are good. Chronic underinvestment in the country's agricultural infrastructure – in contrast to China's heavy investment in irrigation – and appalling roads leave farmers fighting a losing battle before they have started.

The problem of rural development goes to the heart of India's economic future. 'India lives in her villages,' said Mahatma Gandhi in 1924. He was right then, and he is mainly right now. While urbanisation has increased enormously in the half century and more since Gandhi's death, most of its population does still 'live in her villages'. Imaginative ideas have been put forward for lifting rural India out of poverty. Atanu Dey and Rajesh Jain, two Indians who returned to the country after pursuing successful careers in the United States – Jain became a self-made IT millionaire – have been powerful advocates for the so-called RISC model, developed by Dey at the University of Berkeley. The Rural Infrastructural and Service Commons (RISC) approach aims to solve the 'villages' problem of rural India, which Dey characterises as an inability to exploit economies of scale. India's 700 million countryside dwellers can never migrate to the cities, Dey argues, so some of the advantages of the cities have to be taken to them. He proposes a network of 6,000 rural hubs, each serving around 100,000 people (who would only be a 'bicycle commute' away). Whereas providing services such as good roads, broadband and reliable power supplies, even sanitation and proper policing, is not economically viable for tiny villages, it could be for these rural hubs. 'Economic development is a cause and consequence of urbanisation,' says Dey. 'The urbanisation of 700 million people of rural India through migration to the cities is impossible, and so is the urbanisation of 600,000 villages where they live. RISC attempts to urbanise the rural population and do so without the insanity of keeping them confined to tiny villages.'[24]

More conventionally, the government's position paper for its 11th Plan, five-year plans being one of the enduring legacies of the Nehru era, set out proposals for addressing the problems of rural credit (farmers often being forced to borrow expensively from moneylenders) and poor irrigation. In the end, though, the Planning Commission sees growth as the solution to rural distress. 'One of the major challenges of the 11th Plan must be to reverse the deceleration in agricultural growth ... to a trend average of only 1.5 per cent,' it said. 'This deceleration is undoubtedly at the root of the problem of rural distress that has surfaced in many parts of the country. A second green revolution is urgently needed to raise the growth rate of agricultural GDP to around 4 per cent.'[25]

Dynasties

If Gandhi's villages are integral to the Indian economy, what about those bulwarks of the country's commercial and industrial life, the great business dynasties? Out of the shadows of British rule, the family-owned business conglomerates, typified by the Birlas and the Tatas, came to epitomise – and monopolise – India's economy. The history of the family conglomerates, the business dynasties, are in large part the modern economic history of India, intertwined with its emergence from colonial rule. Jamsetji Tata established his private trading firm in 1868, expanded into textiles in the 1870s and in 1903 opened the Taj Mahal hotel and tower in Mumbai, claimed to be India's first luxury hotel, and built by Tata after he was refused entry to the nearby British-run Watson's hotel. It is a wonderful story and appears to be true; the Indian being snubbed by the snooty British and then outdoing them. Today, the hotel, which has hosted 'Maharajahs and Kings', remains one of India's most prestigious, while, according to its own description, 'offering panoramic views of the Arabian Sea and the Gateway of India, the hotel is a gracious landmark of the city of

Mumbai, showcasing contemporary Indian influences along with beautiful vaulted alabaster ceilings, onyx columns, graceful archways, hand-woven silk carpets, crystal chandeliers, a magnificent art collection, an eclectic collection of furniture, and a dramatic cantilever stairway'. But then Tata was a remarkable man. By the time of independence, the Tata Group's corporate reach extended into iron and steel, electricity, chemicals, soaps, detergents, cooking oils, the airline industry and a wide range of light- and heavy-engineering products.

The Birlas were arguably even more closely integrated into the India story. G. D. (Ghanshyam Das) Birla inherited a business that started life when his grandfather left the small town of Pilani in Rajasthan to build a successful trading firm, specialising in cotton and other products, in Bombay (Mumbai). G. D. Birla, born in 1894, decided at the age of sixteen to try to break into the Scottish monopoly of jute production and trading. Having struggled against some underhand tactics employed by the British, he successfully established a jute production factory after the First World War. The Birlas were on their way to becoming a dominant force within Indian commerce and industry. Along the way, 'GD' became an adviser to Mahatma Gandhi on economic policy, though he easily outlived his friend, surviving as one of the great patriarchs of Indian business until 1983. The conglomerates prospered even as the 'Hindu rate of growth' and the bureaucratic controls of the 'licence Raj' held India back. Tata and Birla are the oldest of the business dynasties, but they have been joined by others, before and around the time of independence, including Reliance (the Ambanis), Mahindra & Mahindra, Bajaj, Thapar, the Amalgamations Group, Arvind and Ramco.

The business dynasties had fingers in every commercial pie and were instrumental in ensuring that others did not grab too big a share of it. It is fair to say the big business families were responsible for bolstering successive Indian governments in their reluctance to liberalise, particularly where foreign investment in India was concerned. India's relatively poor showing in attracting foreign investment – certainly in comparison with China – owes much to the traditional hostility of the country's business establishment. Why allow others to claim a share of the pie? This helped fashion policy under Nehru, and under later prime ministers. The cold breath of international competition, particularly from the early 1990s, exposed some of the family-owned conglomerates to pressures many of them were ill-equipped to withstand. When this triggered family disputes, the shockwaves were felt throughout Indian business.

Ambani Wars

The death in July 2002 of Dhirubhai Ambani, founder and chairman of the Reliance conglomerate, India's largest private-sector company, triggered the most important of these family disputes. It is hard to overstate Ambani's contribution to the Indian economy. The conglomerate he built came to be responsible for 3.5 per cent of the country's GDP and 6 per cent of its exports. One in four Indians who owned shares had shares in Reliance, and Ambani was credited with establishing a shareholder democracy. His death resulted in a bitter battle between his sons, Mukesh and Anil. Mukesh was the steady one, the safe pair of hands. Anil, flashy and flamboyant, was a member of parliament and appeared to have sacrificed business in favour of politics. He was also married to a Bollywood star, which made for great copy; nothing less that a real-life soap opera at the highest levels of Indian business. Anil accused his brother of corporate governance violations, including stock manipulation. A three-year battle resulted in a deal, said to have been brokered by their mother, Kokilaben, which left Mukesh in charge of Reliance Industries, the main business, dominant in the petroleum and petrochemicals sector. Anil, meanwhile, took charge of new businesses, which included holdings in energy, finance and mobile telephony. Anil also received $1 billion in cash.

For some, the dispute that almost tore the Ambanis apart was evidence that the old business dynasties were on their way out. 'The battle of the Ambani brothers is not an isolated case,' said one account. 'They follow the five Modi brothers, who controlled a fast-growing conglomerate with holdings from sponge iron to chemicals before splitting up in 1989; today the Modi name hardly figures in Indian business. Earlier, conglomerates controlled by the Mafatlal and Birla families broke up in succession struggles, and have since fallen from the top ranks of Indian business. There are still sterling family names: like Hero and Tata. But as a class, there seems to be more dysfunction than future in family empires.'[26] That may be taking it a little too far. John Ward, an expert in family businesses at the Kellogg School of Management, Northwestern University, notes that the family dynasties remain, as far as India is concerned, 'the backbone of the economy',[27] and have a significant presence in most industrial sectors, including petrochemicals through Ambani (Reliance); steel (Tata, which reinforced its global ambitions by acquiring the larger Anglo-Dutch firm of Corus in 2007); auto manufacturing (also Tata, plus Mahindra and Birla); telecommunications (Tata, Ambani); and consumer products (Godrej). Times are changing. The new India on show to the outside world has been exemplified by new, high-technology businesses, many of which came well after the dynasties. The conditions that favoured the rise of the family dynasties, particularly in the post-independence period, are changing. Apart from deregulation of the economy, which has a lot further to run, new firms are no longer necessarily held back by a lack of capital – an important source of the dynasties' power. The National Stock Exchange of India, based in Mumbai, was incorporated as recently as 1992, and has grown to become the world's third largest in terms of the number of transactions. Its rise, and its role in supplying capital to both new and established businesses, parallels the economic emergence of modern India.

Tata Adapts

Among the names making the headlines in India's highly successful IT and outsourcing story, however, one stands out as having a business pedigree that is very much 'old' India. Tata Consultancy Services (TCS) is India's biggest outsourcing firm, and is Asia's largest software firm, and provides clear evidence that a business dynasty dating back nearly a century and a half has moved with the times. Even by the standards of India's conglomerates, the Tata Group's reach into different sectors (it accounts for nearly 3 per cent of GDP) and countries is unusual. Its empire consists of 93 companies, including traditional Indian businesses such as Tata Tea, the world's second largest tea producer; Tata Consultancy Services; Tata Steel; a chain of international hotels operating under the Indian Hotels brand; a motor-manufacturing arm which is bringing low-cost cars to Indian buyers; and energy businesses, including solar power. The group employs 220,000 people and has more than 2 million shareholders and a market capitalisation of more than $40 billion. Tata has built on its traditional roots to expand in India and outside. Between 2000 and 2005 it acquired Tetley Tea in Britain, Daewoo Commercial Vehicles of South Korea, NatSteel of Singapore and The Pierre Hotel in New York. It has also responded to changing economic circumstances, drastically cutting the number of workers involved in steel production since the early 1990s to remain competitive, for example, but it has done so without provoking serious industrial disputes. While Indian industry has regularly suffered industrial unrest, Tata Steel has gone for more than three-quarters of a century without a strike.

Perhaps the most interesting thing about Tata, and India's other outward-looking companies, is that they are not prepared to rest on the laurels of a booming home market but are expanding rapidly overseas. In November 2005 the Washington-based International Finance Corporation (IFC), the World Bank's private-finance arm, presented research at a conference on 'Southern Multinationals' held, appropriately enough, at Jamsetji Tata's Taj Mahal hotel. The conference, which used the Tata Group as one of its case studies, was presented with IFC evidence showing that South–South foreign direct investment was growing at five times the rate of traditional North–South investment from industrialised countries to the developed world. 'India – and Indian companies – in just a few short years have come to the forefront of outward investment by emerging market nations,' said Assaad Jabre of the IFC at the conference. 'The emergence of Southern multinationals as global champions, and influential players in dominating ever more sectors, should not come as a surprise. This is a natural outcome of a process that started nearly sixty years ago – the slow but progressive freeing up of global trade and investment across borders and regions.'[28]

Tata is in some respects an unlikely global champion for India, and few would have been surprised had it declined as a business force. When, in 1991, Ratan Tata was appointed chairman of Tata Sons, the group holding company, a common view was that he was too gentle and reticent to be successful. But he pursued a strategy of bringing in expertise from outside to help run the company's businesses; in 2006 there was no other Tata on the company's two key decision-making boards. Tata's approach also appears to have developed into what may be a gentler, more humane, way of doing business. 'A new kind of multinational is emerging out of India,' claimed one account. 'It is the Tata Group, a family conglomerate that has gone professional without losing its old-school values. Forged from both India's struggle for independence from Britain and the influence of early-20th-century Fabian socialists, Tata is a ferocious competitor with a very liberal touch. Consider: one of the largest of its 32 businesses, Tata Steel, has cut almost half its work force since 1990 to become the lowest-cost competitor in this industry – yet has kept its promise to pay all laid-off workers full salary until retirement.'[29]

Ratan Tata himself, who will reach the firm's compulsory retirement age of seventy-five in 2012, after which the group is likely to be run from somebody outside the family – for the first time in its history – insists this approach is good business. The company's overseas forays, including a $3 billion power, steel and coal investment in Bangladesh, that country's biggest ever inward investment, and a series of projects in Africa, should assist in the economic emergence of these economies. 'We look at countries where we can play a role in development,' Tata says. 'Our hope in each is to create an enterprise that looks like a local company, but happens to be owned by a company in India.'[30]

Consuming Passions

India, with its 1.1 billion people, predicted by the United Nations to rise to more than 1.6 billion by 2050, represents a consumer market of mouth-watering potential for business. As with China, it is seen as the new frontier for multinational retailers and consumer-goods firms around the world. In one respect, however, India has already achieved pre-eminence – as the world's biggest consumer of gold. According to the World Gold Council, consumer demand for gold in India in 2005 was 590 tonnes, bigger than in any other market. Gold, typically 22 carat – high-grade – is given as a gift at Diwali and other festivals and at weddings, where it is traditional to shower the bride with gold which then remains her property. About half of India's gold demand comes from poorer, rural areas. A casual glance at India's trade figures might suggest this is a society obsessed with personal decoration. Both Britain and Belgium are significant exporters to India but, in both cases, the export figures are boosted by trade in diamonds. In recent years there has been an on–off campaign in India to get one particular diamond exported to India. The Kohinoor, the spectacular 105-carat gem that forms part of Britain's Crown Jewels, is kept safely under lock and key in the Tower of London. It was seized by the great Sikh warrior Ranjit Singh on an Afghanistan campaign in 1813 and given by his successor to Queen Victoria. Some historians say that this was an illegal expropriation typical of the colonial period. Singh is said to have willed it to a Hindu temple in Orissa, but the British ignored his wishes.

To be fair to India, most of the diamonds it imports are re-exported as cut or polished stones. Indian exports of gems and jewellery (including gold jewellery) totalled $17 billion in 2005, America being a particularly important market. But the willingness of Indians to splash out on gold may be an indication, along with others, that this is a different kind of consumer market to China. India is a younger country, more flamboyant; perhaps less worried about putting money aside for later.

Never mind precious metal, consumer businesses sense a different kind of gold rush as rising prosperity brings rapidly increasing demand. Perhaps because of this, even a reforming Indian government has been keen to ensure that foreigners do not gain all the spoils. The liberalisation of Indian retailing has proceeded much more slowly than other sectors, because of political pressure to protect small family stores, though the effect will also be to help larger Indian firms. Mukesh Ambani, officially India's richest man in 2006, is planning a $25-billion expansion in mass-market retailing, selling food, clothing and other products, as well as travel and other services, in local stores, supermarkets and speciality shops, through a subsidiary, Reliance Retail. 'Organised retail will have a profound impact and it will be a path-breaking initiative to touch the lives of rural people, who are yet to be touched by the economic development that the country is witnessing,' Ambani said. 'As organised retailing gains momentum, Reliance is committed to make investments as necessary.'[31] That means, according to the company, building 1,000 hypermarkets and 2,000 supermarkets in the space of four years together with – and this may be the really ambitious part – an efficient distribution system throughout urban and rural India.

The Indian consumer market is certainly hot. Driven by a rapidly expanding middle class, India has been experiencing a consumer boom to match the broader economic boom. In the summer of 2006, there were 5 million new mobile-phone subscribers each month and an estimated 450 shopping malls were under construction. India is movie mad, hence the success of Bollywood, and is also the world's biggest television market. The key thing about the Indian market, however, is its potential.

Big Spenders?

The rise of the Indian consumer has already made the country one of the top ten retail markets in the world. By 2010, according to projections by

McKinsey, the Indian market for consumer goods could be worth $400 billion a year, propelling it into the top five. According to McKinsey's analysis, there are three distinct segments among Indian consumers. At the very top is a relatively small élite – 1.2 million households – of wealthy city dwellers, sophisticated purchasers of branded, global products, and indistinguishable from their counterparts in other countries. At the bottom are what it described as 'struggling households, the 110 million on family incomes of $1,500 to $4,000 a year'. Close to and below these are other groups, including 'destitute' households that are poorer still. For the majority of families at the bottom of the pile, consumption means little more than the basic necessities of life. 'The real drivers of the growing consumer goods market occupy the centre section of the pyramid, among India's 40 million middle-income households, which purchase more than just the basics,' said McKinsey. 'In this "aspiring India", a typical family comprises five people, lives in a city, and has an educated head of household who is an employee or a small business owner earning an average of about $30,000 (adjusted for purchasing power parity). Such a family often lives in a small apartment, has a bank account, and owns a television, a refrigerator, and a motorcycle or small car. These aspiring middle classes are growing by about 10 per cent a year, and are expected to comprise 65 million households by 2010.'[32]

Catching Them Young

It is easy to get excited about the Indian market and the spectacular growth rates being recorded for sales of white goods and electronic products, admittedly from a low base, and for the potential for a passenger-vehicle market which has now passed 1 million a year in cars and utility vehicles. The excitement is not just because of fast-rising prosperity but the fact that much of it, particularly that which comes from earnings in IT and outsourcing sectors, is in the hands of young people, 18–35-year-olds, who spend rather than save. India is a young country, with 70 per cent of the population under the age of thirty-six. There will be more on what some see as the country's decisive demographic advantage below.

The Indian market is never straightforward, however. Some international brands have achieved considerable success, while others have struggled. Lee, the US jeans maker, has built a market from almost nothing, even as Levi Strauss has struggled. Hyundai has prospered with a car tailormade for India, the Santro, outperforming General Motors, Ford and Toyota. LG, another South Korean firm, leads the market against Sony and the other Japanese manufacturers. Reebok signed up Indian cricketers to publicise its products, stealing a significant march on Nike. 'Most multinational companies are run by a global manual but those that have succeeded in India have shredded this manual and taken the "when in India, go local" approach,' says Harid Bijoor, a marketing consultant.[33] Successful brands in India are those that have adapted to the market. Nokia's bestselling Indian version of its 1100 mobile phone has been adapted with a dust-resistant keypad, an anti-slip grip and a built-in flashlight. Samsung, which like LG has prospered, makes a washing machine with a special memory chip that allows it to resume the cycle after a power cut – all too frequent in India – and has a special rinse cycle to prevent saris becoming knotted and creased. Perhaps the most surprising story, reflecting a multinational successfully adapting to local conditions, has been that of McDonald's, which opened its first restaurant in the country in 1996 and ten years later had seventy-six, of which twenty-six were in Delhi. How could McDonald's succeed without selling beef or pork products, the staples of its menu? A glance at its Indian menu reveals how: it includes no beef or pork, but instead 'Veg Pizza McPuff', 'McAloo Tikki Burger', 'McVeggie Burger' and, famously, the 'Chicken Maharaja Mac'.

Products in the Indian market have to be cheap; this is still a low-income country. The rapid rise in mobile-phone use owes much to the fact that call charges are among the lowest in the world. Nearly half of Indians now use shampoo, up from fewer than a fifth in the space of ten years, thanks to the fact that the manufacturers started marketing them in low-cost, single-wash sachets; less of an outlay than a bottle for a shopper on a tight budget. In many ways the market is still extraordinarily under-developed. Just over 1 per cent of the population uses credit cards, and only 5 per cent of women use beauty products. The distribution network, despite the ambitious plans of Reliance and others, will still be dominated by about 12 million 'kirana' stores, the equivalent of America's 'mom and pop' stores – small, family-owned shops which the government is keen to protect. Infrastructure shortcomings will not easily be overcome. The biggest unknown is the extent to which a relatively free-spending Indian middle class will come to typify the country as a whole. Many Indians will remain very poor for the foreseeable future, particularly in rural areas.

On the Slow Road

Vineet Agarwal of the Transport Corporation of India, a freight firm, knows all about the shortcomings of India's road network. Describing the travails of a lorry travelling the 2,150 kilometres from Kolkata to Mumbai, he provides an account of a journey of epic proportions. The lorry is loaded in central Kolkata at two in the afternoon but cannot leave the city until ten at night because of restrictions on freight traffic. Traffic jams mean a 180-kilometre journey to the border of West Bengal takes until the following evening, by which time the crossing is closed for the night. A two-hour wait at the border crossing the next morning is followed by another to cross from Jharkand into Orissa. So it goes on, a journey peppered with border delays and hold-ups at toll booths. By the time the lorry rumbles within sight of its destination in Mumbai, more than a week has passed; it is the morning of day eight, the average speed was just 11 kilometres per hour, and thirty-two hours have been spent waiting at borders and toll booths.[34] What this story illustrates, apart from India's characteristically jammed roads and slow-moving traffic, is that the country is anything but a single market. The border delays are in part a reflection of the snail's pace at which the bureaucracy operates but they also show, quite literally, that each state is a law unto itself.

Failing States

India is made up of twenty-eight states, six union territories and Delhi, the capital, but economically it could be a set of separate countries, divided by difficult border crossings. Economic disparities between states are striking, if unsurprising when examined in any detail. *Per capita* incomes in Delhi are five times those in Bihar, not only the poorest, but also one of the most populous states. Predominantly agricultural states, dependent on the land, are economically constrained by the low rate of growth of agriculture. For states which are home to industry, services and, more particularly, the IT and outsourcing growth industries, the sky appears to be the limit. Some critics say the widening of disparities between states is the result of the freebooting capitalism of the post-1991 reform era. Nehru's Fabian socialism may not have created the most efficient economy in the world (far from it), but it was fair. Guided from the centre, the Planning Commission could direct investment where it was needed. But in a modern era of private-sector investment that is no longer possible. There is, it should be said, an element of truth in this. Bihar, which borders Nepal in north-eastern India and has a population of 83 million – equivalent to a large country – has always struggled. But its struggle, relatively speaking, has got worse since 1991. *Per capita* economic growth in the 1980s of 3 per cent a year dropped to below 2 per cent annually in the 1990s, when much of the country was experiencing a growth revival.

States like Bihar represent very much the old India, heavily dependent on agriculture, weighed down by class and caste conflict, high unemployment and grinding poverty. Income is more equally distributed in Bihar, but there is less of it to go round. *Financial Times* journalist Jo Johnson, visiting Muzaffarpur in Bihar, noted that 55 per cent of the under-fives in the state are chronically underweight. At a time when India is attempting to lift itself into the first rank of nations, large parts have not changed at all. 'India's dismal progress in reducing malnutrition is an indictment of its ability to deliver basic public services,' he wrote. 'A lack of official accountability in a relatively small number of states is seen as the overarching problem. As with many of India's social problems, a small number of districts account for a large share of the burden. The four states of Bihar, Uttar Pradesh, Madhya Pradesh and Rajasthan account for 43 per cent of cases and have prevalence rates [of malnutrition] that are falling more slowly than in the rest of the country.'[35]

The two Indias – one modern, urban and increasingly wealthy; the other poor, backward and scratching around for a living – often exist side by side within states. The poorest states, however, lack even oases of prosperity. How much has corruption and bad governance to do with the continued economic failings of some states, or are some problems too big to be solved? In India, at state as well as national level, the task for politicians often involves steering a fine line between what looks to be a bold reform agenda and what is politically acceptable. In the mid-1990s Chandrababu Naidu seized power from his father-in-law in Andhra Pradesh, southern India's most populous state, and pursued an aggressive agenda of modernisation and reform. Under Naidu, Hyderabad developed as the 'Cyberabad' revival to Bangalore and came to symbolise successful state-level reform. Bill Clinton and Tony Blair feted 'the CEO of Andhra Pradesh', which he turned, some said, into a laboratory for accelerated economic reform, with policies of privatisation, deregulation and a shrinking state sector. *Time* named him South Asian of the Year. But what was good for the IT sector, and for Hyderabad, was not good for Andhra Pradesh's farmers, whose suicide rates soared, or for its poor. When, in May 2004, Naidu went down to a landslide defeat, critics saw it as just reward for the highly uneven effects of his policies. 'In throwing him out of their lives, the voters of the Indian state of Andhra Pradesh may have destroyed the world's most dangerous economic experiment,' wrote George Monbiot, the Third World campaigner and environmentalist.

> During the hungry season, hundreds of thousands of people in Andhra Pradesh are now kept alive on gruel supplied by charities. Last year, hundreds of children died in an encephalitis outbreak because of the shortage of state-run hospitals. The state government's own figures suggest that 77 per cent of the population have fallen below the poverty line. The measurement criteria are not consistent, but this appears to be a massive rise. In 1993 there was one bus a week taking migrant workers from a depot in Andhra Pradesh to Mumbai. Today there are thirty-four.[36]

Even in a reform-minded country there are limits. Some state politicians prefer to run things as they have always done. Others, perhaps, try to drive the reform process too fast, and crash.

Permanently Left Behind?

The differences in economic performance between Indian states are not just a matter of intellectual curiosity. The poorest states are also those where population is projected to grow fastest, with 60 per cent of India's projected 600 million increase in population by 2050 likely to occur in just three states: Bihar, Uttar Pradesh and Madhya Pradesh. At the level of the major states, there are three Indias: the chronically poor states; middle-income states such as Andhra Pradesh, West Bengal, Kerala and Karnataka; and the richest: Punjab, Maharashtra, Haryana, Gujarat and Tamil Nadu. India's richest states have *per capita* income levels between three and four times those of the poorest, Bihar. Catriona Purfield, in an International Monetary Fund working paper, calculated that over the three and a half decades from 1970, all the poorest states, plus Kerala, grew more slowly than the national average. The fastest-growing rich and middle-income states achieved growth rates twice the rate of the poorest.

The wealthier states, on top of this, were 50 per cent more effective in reducing poverty.[37]

The poorer states appear to lose out on virtually every measure. They are much less effective at creating private-sector jobs – the poorest, most populous states account for a 40 per cent (and rising) share of the population but less than a quarter of jobs in the organised sector. Their position, moreover, appears to be getting worse. Bihar, Uttar Pradesh and Madhya Pradesh had more private-sector jobs in the early 1970s than in the early twenty-first century. For the organised jobs that exist in the poorest states, four-fifths are in the public sector. Nor are capital and labour movements narrowing the gap. The poorest states are in the wrong place, being mainly located in the less accessible central and northern regions, and investors do not like them. The five richest states have around 55 per cent of India's private-sector capital stock, compared with 15 per cent for the five poorest. About half of foreign direct investment goes to a few rich states. Nor does the flow of people help much; only 6 per cent of rural migration and 20 per cent in urban areas is across state borders. People become literally trapped in poverty, unable to afford to travel to work. Differences of language, caste and culture also stop the poor from advancing.

Can India's impoverished states do anything to lift themselves up, or are these barriers to growth and prosperity insurmountable? The economic buttons Indian states need to press to achieve better growth are familiar ones. The IMF would like them to reduce the size of the state; diversify away from over-reliance on agriculture and basic industries; invest in education, particularly female literacy; reduce excessive worker protection to make labour markets more flexible; and improve their infrastructure, particularly transport. Few would disagree with these aims. As always, though, they are easier said than done.

A Mixed Bag

This chapter has described some of the enormous strides made by India in recent years. In IT and outsourcing India has established a comparative advantage and exploited it successfully. Much more so than in the case of China, Indian businessmen have become powerful advocates for their country and its possibilities. This is true not just of Indian-based businessmen but also of expatriates like the London-based steel magnate Lakshmi Mittal, ranked by *Forbes* magazine as the world's fifth richest man in 2006.

He grew his own Mittal Steel into the world's biggest steel company, acquiring Luxembourg-based Arcelor after a hard-fought battle. Mittal, like the great Indian diaspora that helped shape Silicon Valley, provides a living testament to the skills and entrepreneurial abilities waiting to be tapped in India. But what does the fact that Mittal and others have chosen to make their fortunes outside India tell us? Are non-resident Indians, like the Scots who did so much to build the British Empire, able to prosper precisely because they are not operating on home turf?

Pankaj Mishra, writing in *The New York Times* in July 2006, soon after America's most influential foreign policy journal *Foreign Affairs* had declared India to be 'a roaring capitalist success story', offered a more sober view. Mittal, having built his empire outside India, was 'as much an Indian success story as Sergey Brin, the Russian-born co-founder of Google, is proof of Russia's imminent economic superstardom', Mishra wrote.

> The increasingly common, business-centric view of India suppresses more facts than it reveals. Recent accounts of the alleged rise of India barely mention the fact that its *per capita* gross domestic product of $728 is just slightly higher than that of sub-Saharan Africa and that, as the 2005 United Nations Human Development Report puts it, even if it sustains its current high growth rates, India will not catch up with high-income countries until 2106. Nor is India rising very fast on the report's Human Development index, where it ranks 127, just two rungs above Myanmar and more than 70 below Cuba and Mexico. Despite a recent reduction in poverty levels, nearly 380 million Indians still live on less than a dollar a day … Many serious problems confront India. They are unlikely to be solved as long as the wealthy, both inside and outside the country, choose to believe their own complacent myths.[38]

The picture Mishra painted was gloomy in the extreme, citing some of the evidence quoted in this chapter on rural poverty, income inequalities and farmers' suicides. But he also drew in the communist insurgencies in parts of central and northern India, and growing caste and class conflicts as signs that the price the country may be paying for a largely 'jobless' recovery could be widespread political instability. Could India's economic success be undermined by its lack of inclusiveness, the fact that too many are being left behind? Is the glass half full, or half empty? It is the big question about India. Optimists see the successes achieved so far as the shape of things to come. The IT sector's emergence on the global scene and the rapid expansion of the country's middle class are symbols of an economy that has cast off its shackles and has no way to go but up. India will, on this view, experience a reduction in poverty levels as dramatic as anything that has happened in China, not so much trickle-down as a great wave of prosperity washing down on the rural masses. Or could it be that India is destined to be an economy of 'pockets' – great prosperity and business success co-existing with extreme poverty and economic failure? That, certainly, is a fair description of India now. Anybody who has seen the drive and enthusiasm of the business leaders forcing the 'new' India along has to be optimistic. Anybody who has experienced some of India's more traditional failings will always be inclined to temper that enthusiasm with realism. The truth about India's prospects lies somewhere between the two extremes. The economy has broken free and will probably never sink back into its old languor, but many problems remain, and will do so for a very long time. Economic growth is solving many ills. Others, however, will stay.

6

China versus India

'We may not be able to reach where the Chinese are today, but there is no reason why we should not think big about the role of foreign direct investment.'

Manmohan Singh

'An economic litmus test is not whether a country can attract a lot of foreign direct investment but whether it has a business environment that nurtures entrepreneurship, supports healthy competition and is relatively free of heavy-handed political intervention. In this regard, India has done a better job than China.'

Yasheng Huang

'China has shackled its independent business people. India has empowered them.'

Tarun Khanna

Competing Giants

So far, apart from charting China and India's journey through economic history at the beginning, this book has described their development and prospects separately. In many ways that is a sensible approach. The histories of the two countries have at times been intertwined but their differences outweigh any similarities. Although Indian government ministers try to have it both ways, insisting it is not a race between the two giants, while at the same time pointing up every instance where India appears to be doing better. Don't compare us with China, they say, then proceed to do so themselves. That is perhaps inevitable for a country that is playing catch-up. The Indians still cannot quite understand why, when the two countries were at a similar stage of development not that long ago, China caught the growth bug first. In the 1980s, when South Korea was breaking on to the world economic stage, the first question to visitors from ministers and officials was: 'How do you compare South Korea with Japan?' Now something similar is happening between India and China. The Chinese government, it should be said, pays rather less attention to India than vice versa.

So why do we compare them? It is because they are big, and because they are hard to ignore. Size of population is the common factor linking China and India; they are the only two countries in the world with populations of more than 1 billion. There are plenty of other smaller, rapidly emerging economies which could be compared with either China or India. Pakistan, for example, can boast Indian-style growth rates. It does not, however, pass the size test. Another common factor is that both emerged on the global economic stage at more or less the same time. That was by no means pre-ordained. Indeed, even allowing for the fact that India quietly enjoyed a good rate of growth in 1980s, the impression was that China was on her own. In foreign direct investment, where China receives ten times as much as India, that remained the case even after India's watershed reform year of 1991.

The emergence of two very large countries experiencing sustained periods of economic growth simultaneously is unusual, perhaps unique. China alone would give the rest of the world plenty to digest and adapt to. Combine China's rise with that of India and the globe has seen nothing like it since America's emergence in the nineteenth century. Some like to see it as a single phenomenon; the rise of 'Chindia'. Others prefer to focus on the implications. 'Accelerated growth and structural transformation in China and India have created two giant, industrial powerhouses in the 21st century global economy,' said Haruhiko Kuroda, president of the Asian Development Bank, in June 2006. 'The rise of such large economies within a short time span is unprecedented. And like all truly monumental accomplishments, the contributions of, and consequences for, other members of the regional and global communities are profound.'[1] A stylised view of patterns of economic development would characterise the nineteenth century as European, the twentieth as American and, though we are only a few years into it, the twenty-first century as belonging to China and India. Whether it will be in reality is a question for the final chapter. In the meantime, what can be said about the respective strengths and weaknesses of the two countries? If this is the great race of our age, who is likely to win?

Divided by Ideas

For decades, development economists anguished over the ideal model for lifting countries out of poverty. If nothing else, China and India prove that the search for a single model is a vain one. Both, as we have seen, have reduced poverty; China rather more successfully than India. But, as noted above, were it not for population and their joint emergence it is doubtful anybody would seek to draw comparisons between the two. One is a centrally planned economy, controlled by a Communist Party which reaches into every nook and cranny of its people's personal and business lives. China's growth miracle has been achieved by the relaxation of some of the Party's controls, somewhat in the manner of a maiden aunt unbuttoning her stays, but many restrictions remain in place. India, by contrast, is a bustling, messy, sometimes near-anarchic democracy. J. K. Galbraith, the noted economist and wit, who died in 2006 at the age of 97, was appointed US ambassador to India by John F. Kennedy, serving in the early 1960s. He memorably described India as a 'functioning anarchy'. When the leadership of the Chinese Communist Party wants something done it gets it done, from grandiose infrastructure projects – the pride of China's economy – downwards. When India's political leaders want something done they hope and pray it will happen but are well aware that the gulf between political decisions and practical reality is often very wide. India's democratic system has a habit of punishing politicians who display too much reformist zeal. One internet discussion of India's growth potential drew the response from a contributor that the only way to rid Indian politics of incompetence and corruption was to take away the vote from the lower castes.

Rights and Responsibilities

To China's critics, the Communist Party is sitting on a powder keg of unrest that will one day explode, with disastrous consequences. In 2005 there were 87,000 officially admitted 'mass incidents', in protest at everything from corruption and taxes to dreadful working conditions and environmental damage. Protestors also rose up in response to a phenomenon directly related to the country's economic expansion: the seizure without compensation of farmland for factory and office developments. Property rights are not respected much in China and neither are human rights – it executes as many convicted prisoners as the rest of the world put together. In 2005 China put 1,770 people to death out of a world total of 2,148. Many such sentences arise directly out of social unrest, together with state persecution of the Falun Gong spiritual movement, the Uighur community in the Xinjiang Uighur Autonomous Region and the Tibetan people. Torture is widespread. There is a thriving trade in the export of the organs of executed prisoners for transplant. China has moved on from the Mao era, but not as much as it would like the rest of the world to think. Bodies such as Amnesty International say that far from improving as the economy has opened up to the world, repression in China is getting worse. The prospect of large numbers of visitors to the country for the 2008 Beijing Olympics has intensified official efforts to clamp down on unrest and ensure 'troublemakers' are kept well out of the way, human rights' monitors say.[2]

India has a better story to tell on human rights. The death penalty remains in force but in 2005, for example, seventy-seven people were given the death sentence but no executions were actually carried out. India, like China, has examples of social unrest related to economic progress. In September 2006 the police shot three people protesting over the closure of illegal shops in New Delhi. In Mumbai slum dwellers have risen up against efforts to bulldoze their homes, enforced by police brutality. Soon after the start of the reform process in 1991, Mumbai was rocked by the riots of 1992 and 1993, in which 900 people died. There is simmering unrest in some rural areas. Labour disputes and strikes are common. There is nothing like the extent of repression that there is in China, however. Where the Indian authorities can be most strongly criticised is in turning a blind eye. In the Gujarat riots of 2002, triggered by the burning to death of fifty-nine Hindus on a train at Godhra, police stood by

as Hindus inflicted horrific violence, rape and murder on Muslims, including women and small children. Nearly 800 Muslims died (along with 250
Hindus), some as a result of barely imaginable brutality, and tens of thousands of people were displaced. The train fire was later officially found
to have been an accident. As well as failing to intervene, the police were
accused of actively assisting the Hindu rioters. Religious and caste tensions continue to rumble away in India and occasionally flare up. The
July 2006 Mumbai train bombings in which more than 200 people died
were credibly blamed on Islamic militants, with the possible assistance of
Pakistan's intelligence services, said to be taking revenge for the oppression of India's Muslim minority.

Monumental Changes

The differences between the two countries are tangible in other ways.
Communist China used to put up monuments to the people's struggle,
typified by the monolithic structures in and around Beijing's Tiananmen
Square. Now it constructs monuments to its version of capitalist development in the form of ever-higher skyscrapers. India is not there yet, and
may never be, as one writer described it. 'On a late evening along Marine
Drive, Mumbai's answer to the Shanghai Bund, dancer-beggars prowl with
monkeys, extorting coins from passers-by,' he wrote. 'Deep potholes pit
the sidewalk and the sea gently laps a crumbling wall. It is quaint but it
does not feel like a city of the future. Shanghai was a bit like Mumbai until
the Chinese government did what the Indian government cannot do: in
the 1990s its planners, brushing aside any pre-existing claims, cleared the
way for developers to construct in barely 10 years the gleaming, futurist
metropolis of Pudong, across the river from the Bund.'[3] The contrast is
apt. China is able to use a steamroller to force through economic development while India has to rely on some sort of democratic consensus.

   Which one works best? Is Indian *laissez-faire*, admittedly tempered by
the operations of a fearsomely intrusive bureaucracy, a better long-term
bet than Chinese one-party rule? Could it be that China's model is more
efficient at achieving economic lift-off but that India's has more staying
power? Could it be that both will need to change dramatically if they
are to achieve the status of advanced economic nations? The hard statistical evidence so far favours China, and not just on inward investment.
India's growth rate over the period 1999–2005, just over 6 per cent a year

(though with an acceleration to 7–8 per cent in later years), compares with a Chinese annual growth rate of over 9 per cent – something that has been sustained, on average, since 1978. During 2006 China's growth rate was an impressive 10.7 per cent. China's economy is roughly twice the size of India's, however they are measured.

India's Claims

Does focusing on China's current superiority give the wrong impression? Yes, according to two authors who, in 2003, advanced what was then the deeply unfashionable view that India's long-term prospects could be better, largely because of differences in their economic and political systems. Yasheng Huang of MIT and Tarun Khanna of the Harvard Business School argued that China's success in attracting inward investment – one of the country's apparent strengths – could instead be a sign of weakness, an inability to foster genuine entrepreneurial activity. They asked: 'What's the fastest route to economic development? Welcome foreign direct investment (FDI), says China, and most policy experts agree. But a comparison with long-time laggard India suggests that FDI is not the only path to prosperity. Indeed, India's home-grown entrepreneurs may give it a long-term advantage over a China hamstrung by inefficient banks and capital markets.'[4] Part of their argument was that China's economy, and her export strength, rides largely on the back of foreign-owned, foreign-run operations. 'Made in China' production, in other words, far from representing the efforts of indigenous entrepreneurs, managers and designers, is mainly the product of decisions by multinationals to gain access to the country's supply of cheap labour. Foreign investment has been a substitute for domestic entrepreneurial activity, not a spur for it. The difference in approach is no accident. China, its domestic entrepreneurs driven underground or out of existence by years of political repression and an absence of opportunity, had little choice but to tap into foreign capital. For India, in contrast, the suspicion of multinational business ingrained in the national psyche by the East India Company extended to its own diaspora, the Indians who had achieved entrepreneurial success abroad after independence. Why should they come back and claim the spoils? Reformist India thus provided a 'more nurturing environment' for domestic entrepreneurs and bred world-beating firms such as Infosys and Wipro, according to Huang and Khanna. China has a formidable infrastructure to support manufacturing activity: a rapidly growing network of motorways and trunk roads, large and generally efficient ports and modern airports. But India, which lags well behind in these areas, has what they describe as 'much stronger infrastructure to support private enterprise'. 'Its capital markets operate with greater efficiency and transparency than do China's. Its legal system, while not without substantial flaws, is considerably more advanced.'[5]

For critics of China like Huang and Khanna, the performance of China's centrally driven economy not only flatters to deceive but contains the seeds of significant problems to come, in particular related to the banking and financial system. 'In the early 1990s, when China was registering double-digit growth rates, Beijing invested massively in the state sector,' they wrote.

> Most of the investments were not commercially viable, leaving the banking sector with a huge number of nonperforming loans – possibly totalling as much as 50 per cent of bank assets. At some point, the capitalization costs of these loans will have to be absorbed, either through write-downs (which means depositors bear the cost) or recapitalization of the banks by the government, which diverts money from other, more productive uses. This could well limit China's future growth trajectory. India's banks may not be models of financial probity, but they have not made mistakes on nearly the same scale … India's economy is thus anchored on more solid footing.[6]

Hard and Soft

The idea that India's 'soft' skills and less-directed economy are creating a tortoise that will ultimately outrun the 'hard' Chinese hare is an alluring one for many people. India as a free-market democracy is more like today's successful advanced economies, while China has more in common economically with the failed communist states of Russia and eastern Europe, combined with levels of over-investment that were a characteristic of many Asian economies when they were struck by financial crisis in 1997–8. Hugo Restall, editor of the *Far Eastern Economic Review*, in a 2006 article entitled 'India's Coming Eclipse of China', suggested that China had done well in achieving 'easy' economic growth but, partly because of the nature of its political system, would struggle to maintain that over the medium and long term. 'Here is where the contrast between Indian democracy and Chinese authoritarianism really comes into play,' he argued.

China has done well by picking the low-hanging fruit, the easy reforms in which there were many winners and few losers. For instance, by freeing farmers to produce their own crops 25 years ago, rural incomes rose and the supply of food in the city improved. Allowing prices to fluctuate with supply and demand corrected gross misallocations of resources. But more recently reforms have required difficult choices, such as laying off state workers. So far, Beijing has continued to press ahead. But it is facing a rising tide of discontent, with about 75,000 public demonstrations a year. The benefit of authoritarianism was supposedly that China could make decisions for the greater good without being stymied by the objections of a minority. Yet it is becoming increasingly unclear whether the Chinese government can retain the consent of its people. China's embrace of globalization was never built on a solid foundation, and thus a public backlash against the government could bring the whole edifice down.[7]

India's plus points, according to Restall, include not only the nurturing of domestic entrepreneurs highlighted by Huang and Khanna, but also far greater efficiency in the use of capital by Indian businesses, avoidance of the over-investment trap (India's saving ratio, averaging 25 per cent in recent years, is half China's and the country has not been flooded by foreign direct investment), and a greater commitment to the rule of law and respect for intellectual property rights. Most of all, India's advantage lies with its people. 'Demographically, India is a young country, with more than 40 per cent of the population under the age of 20 – that's 450 million people, as compared to 400 million in China,' he wrote. 'More important than their ability to work is their ability to think: The generational divide in India is pronounced, with the young by and large uninterested in the zero-sum socialist ideas of their elders. It's also revealing that they are pursuing advanced education with a zeal that was formerly thought of as a Confucian trait – American universities enrol 80,000 Indian students, compared to 62,000 Chinese.'[8] The demographic factor is an important one, and will be considered in further detail below. To what extent, however, are commentators and analysts engaging in wishful thinking? Are India's prospects being boosted because it has a political system more conducive to Western tastes?

Red Tape

India, as Restall concedes, is a less open economy than China, with average tariff levels more than twice as high. The faltering progress of the World Trade Organisation's Doha round (the Doha Development Agenda) means India will not be in a rush to reduce trade barriers. China's authoritarian approach has resulted in discontent, but it has also permitted the imposition of labour-market flexibility (which critics would see as an absence of workers' rights). Such flexibility, however achieved, is usually regarded as an essential 'supply-side' condition for sustained economic growth. It is, however, sadly lacking in India. A hangover from the days of Nehru's Fabian socialism is that hiring and firing rules are highly restrictive, with an array of central and state labour laws. Medium and larger companies, employing over 100 people, require prior government approval before reducing staff or closing down part of an enterprise. Even getting rid of unsuitable workers at the end of a probation period can require approval. In the nature of the Indian system, such approval is often slow in coming, unless the relevant official's palm is greased with cash. Restrictive laws have not greatly hampered the fast-expanding IT services and outsourcing sectors of the Indian economy and they have not prevented industrial restructurings in the past. But they help explain why India has been unable to fulfil her potential as a manufacturing nation.

Those who favour India over China are in tune with the views of some in the international business community. While still the poor relation in terms of foreign direct investment, India scores best among the BRICs (Brazil, Russia, India and China) for the quality of her business environment, despite those restrictive labour laws. The World Economic Forum's 2006 Global Competitiveness Report placed India 43rd, against China's 54th place, and India was the highest placed among the BRICs economies. This was in contrast to the rival Institute for Management Development's 2006 rankings. Its World Competitiveness Scoreboard put China in 19th place and India in 29th. If this shows some indecisiveness among multinational firms and analysts about the potential of the two countries, that fairly reflects the true position.

Population Expansion

Half a century ago China and India were both very populous countries, with populations of 555 million and 358 million respectively in 1950. Though there were worries about over-population in both countries at the time, occasioning policies to control the growth in numbers, few could have guessed at the extent of the rise that occurred. One authoritative 1954 projection projected a 2001 Indian population of 667 million. The actual figure was over 1 billion. Both countries will continue to see significant population growth, at least for a time, though their paths will diverge. According to the United Nations, China's population was 1.32 billion in 2005 and will rise to 1.39 billion in 2015 and 1.44 billion in 2025. Then, however, it will reach a plateau before declining gently to 1.39 billion by the middle of the century. That is when India will come into her own. The UN projects a rise in India's population from 1.1 billion in 2005 to 1.26 billion in 2015 and 1.4 billion in 2025; closing the gap on China but remaining slightly smaller (if small can ever be used to describe a population numbering well over a billion). Between 2025 and 2050, however, India is expected to gain nearly 200 million people, its population rising to 1.59 billion, out of a global total of 9.1 billion. By then India will be comfortably ahead of China in population. Will that be a good thing? Many see this as a key advantage for India, its supply of labour continuing to increase rapidly at a time when China's working-age population will be starting to decline. It may not be that simple. Both countries have demographic advantages and disadvantages.

Will China Grow Old before It Gets Rich?

An undeniable fact is that India has a much younger population than China and that, as a result of past population policies, China faces potentially serious demographic problems. Two things stand out about China's situation in the early years of the twenty-first century. One is that it is now in a 'demographic sweet spot', with a rapidly rising working-age population as a result of sharp falls in infant mortality two to three decades ago. Just over a tenth of China's population (11 per cent in 2004) is 'elderly', aged sixty and over. The second thing is that this will not last. By 2015 China will have a declining working-age population. By 2040 nearly a third of Chinese will be aged sixty and over. The country will face an unusual economic race, summed up in the question: Will China grow old before it gets rich? Add in a third demographic dimension, the imbalance between young men and women (a significant surplus of men) – the result of the country's one-child policy – and it starts to look rather a mess.

China is a poorish country with a demographic profile similar to many advanced economies. Its projected age distribution in 2050, for example, is roughly similar to Britain's. What is typical for the older industrial countries is, however, unusual for a developing economy. A 2004 report, 'The Greying of the Middle Kingdom' by Richard Jackson and Neil Howe, put China's ageing problem into stark perspective. 'A young nation is about to grow old,' they wrote.

> Thirty-five years ago, there were eight working age adults aged 15 to 59 in China for every elder aged 60 and over. Today there are six. Thirty-five years from now, assuming current demographic trends continue, the number will fall to just two. By then, there will be twice as many elders over the age of sixty as children under the age of fifteen. The rapid ageing of its population will test China's ability to provide a decent standard of living for the old without imposing a heavy burden on the young.[9]

One Child

China's ageing population, Jackson and Howe pointed out, is the result of two factors: declining fertility and rising longevity. The figures are dramatic. In 1970, when Mao still ruled, China's fertility rate was nearly six, implying that many births per woman during her child-bearing years. By the early twenty-first century it had dropped to less than two, below the replacement rate – that needed to maintain a stable population in the long term – of 2.1. Official policy played a part in the decline; in the 1970s families were encouraged to limit themselves to no more than two children, a strategy that evolved into the one-child policy of the early 1980s. In Beijing and Shanghai, the one-child policy appears to operate to the letter, with a fertility rate of just over one. Rural birth rates are higher, because in many cases mothers who give birth to girls are urged to 'try for a son' and are allowed to do so, but they remain sharply lower than in the past. The earlier high birth rate, as in many poor countries, was partly a product of high infant mortality rates. The low birth rate, enforced with financial penalties, reveals a highly effective population control policy. Now, at both ends of the age range things have changed. Fewer children are dying in birth, infancy and childhood, while more old people are living longer. Since the People's Republic was formed, just over half a century ago, average life expectancy has risen from 41 to 70; again a very dramatic change. These are big and beneficial shifts. Chinese life expectancy is the envy of most poor countries, but such shifts have consequences.

How serious a problem is this for China? Jackson and Howe pointed out that on the central demographic projections of the United Nations there will be an 18 per cent reduction in the working-age population by 2050. It could be worse. On the UN's 'low fertility' scenario, assuming a decline in the birth rate to 1.35 (similar to or slightly above several south-east Asian countries now), the working-age population would shrink by more than a third by the middle of the century. More certain is the prospect that, almost whatever happens, there will be more than 400 million Chinese people over sixty by 2050, with 100 million of them aged eighty and over. For them, it is essential that China does indeed get rich before it gets old. Most people in China have neither pension provision nor health-care coverage, which helps explain the very high rate of individual saving. The 'barefoot doctors' of the Mao era did much to reduce child mortality, providing most people in rural areas with health care. The doctors, however, were victims of economic reform. Only a tiny minority of the rural population now has access to government-funded health care.

The combination of China's ageing population, a weak pensions and health-care system and the one-child policy has also given rise to the so-called '4-2-1' problem'. China's youngsters, so full of optimism now, can apparently look forward to a life in which they will take on the burden of caring and providing for two parents and four grandparents. There will, of course, be no siblings to help share it out. There is also what could be a damaging, even destabilising, imbalance between the sexes. China's 2000 census reported a ratio of 116.9 boys being born to every 100 girls, compared with a norm across most countries of 105. The ratio of infant boys to infant girls was even higher at 117.8 (more boys survive childbirth). These figures may be exaggerated, reflecting under-reporting of female births by families desperate to have more children. But they also reflect one of the dreadful consequences of the one-child policy: the abortion of female foetuses. They may also reflect female infanticide, at least to some degree. The shortage of girls will help reinforce China's demographic problem, eventually reducing the number of marriageable women. And, while Chinese men desperate for wives can turn to foreign brides imported from countries such as North Korea and Vietnam, this is hardly a permanent solution to the girl shortage. As Jackson and Howe put it:

Gender imbalance has sometimes played a role in igniting social unrest in the past – most notably during the Nien Rebellion in the mid-1800s, when bands of surplus bachelors turned to brigandage and insurrection. Even more ominous than the shortage of brides, however, is the looming shortage of daughters-in-law. The missing brides of today, after all, will become the missing caregivers of tomorrow, for while it is the son who bears responsibility for caring for his aged parents in Chinese culture, it is the daughter-in-law who actually does the caring.[10]

China's demographic problem is, on the face of it, easily solved. A relaxation of the one-child policy would quickly start to make inroads into both China's ageing population and the serious gender imbalance. In 2006, however, Zhang Weiqing, minister of the State Commission of Population and Family Planning, said it was the state's long-term policy to stabilise the birth rate at its present low level and that it would be strictly implemented in the nation's 11th Five-Year Plan (2006–10) and beyond. Rejecting rumours of a relaxation of the policy, he said it had succeeded in limiting China's population, perhaps by 300 million, preventing an even greater population burden on the country's economic development, environment and resources.

Young India

Unlike China, India appears to have an ambivalent attitude to population growth. It was one of the first countries in the world to introduce policies aimed at controlling population growth – the original National Family Planning Programme dates back to 1951 – but ministers also emphasise the country's demographic advantage. A young and rapidly growing population may signal a failure of the family-planning regime (which continues, despite its lack of success), but it provides a contrast with China, and suggests not only long-term growth in Indian markets but also, perhaps more importantly, in the labour force. But which country has got it right – China, which is concerned about the pressure on resources and dividing economic gains among an ever-larger population, or India?

It was in Beijing, of all places, that an Indian businessman summed up what he regarded as his country's most significant advantage. 'Yes, they've had most of the inward investment and their infrastructure is fabulous,' he said, referring to China. 'But they have huge problems because of their ageing population. Our young people are our big advantage.' That is certainly the way many would like to see it. The India Brand Equity Foundation, the Confederation of Indian Industry body which has successfully promoted the country overseas, puts it succinctly in its advertisements: 'Youngest and fastest growing population of consumers and professionals,' it said. 'Consumer demand growing five times faster than the economy. Rising aspirations of a rapidly growing middle class. Assured long-term demographic dividend – 70 per cent of Indians are less than 36 years old. Spiralling growth in services and retail adding young income earners. India: Fastest Growing Free Market Democracy.'[11] It is easy to get excited about India's demographic dividend. Its demographic sweet spot has still to arrive. In 2000, 36 per cent of India's population was under 14 years old, 60 per cent was aged 15–64, conventionally defined as working age, and fewer than 5 per cent of people were 65 or over. By 2025, according to projections from the Population Research Centre at Delhi's Institute of Economic Growth, the share in the population of children (0–14) will have dropped to just over 26 per cent and the 'pensioner' share will be slightly higher, at more than 6 per cent. The biggest gain will be in the working-age population, up to more than two-thirds of the population. The 'dependency ratio' – the ratio of dependants (children and pensioners) to people of working age – will thus have fallen significantly. This is what champions of the Indian economy are talking about when they cite the country's demographic advantage – a huge bulge of working-age people making their way through the population over the coming decades.

Faith

In May 2000, a baby girl, Astha (Hindi for faith), was born to a poor New Delhi couple. She was, officially, the one billionth Indian, taking the country's population above that symbolic figure for the first time. Behind the celebrations, however, there were also concerns. 'The one billionth baby, symbolically selected and born at Safdarjang hospital, represents the human being that brings India's population up to 1 billion. Thus this baby is very special and very unique,' said Michael Vlassoff, the representative in India of the United Nations Population Fund.[12] 'But 42,000 other babies are also being born in India today on May 11, as they are on every day. What world will they inherit? Will their hopes and aspirations be fulfilled?' For the UN the concern was that India would not have the food and water to provide for its huge population. This is the traditional worry about India and it begs the question: When will India's huge and growing population turn from being a national burden, and a source of mass poverty, to becoming an economic advantage? Any visitor to India is struck by its sheer weight of population; street people and slum dwellers number an estimated 7 million in Mumbai alone. India has one of the highest population densities in the world: 324 people per square kilometre, according to the 2001 census. In states like West Bengal, which includes the teeming city of Kolkata, population density is 904 people per square kilometre, with Bihar close behind on 880. If this weight of numbers is one worry about India's supposed demographic advantage, there are others.

Young Unemployed India?

A demographic dividend is only worth having if it is successfully exploited. The big fear is that India's economic growth will be insufficient to mop up the rapid expansion of the working-age population that is in prospect. As already touched on, India's job market is unusual in two respects. One is that the lion's share of employment is outside the organised sector, which accounts for fewer than 40 million workers in a population of 1.1 billion. Most people who are in jobs – more than 90 per cent – are in the unorganised sector, which is like a giant black economy, outside the reach of labour laws and the income-tax system. Nor is this merely a stage of development. During the 1990s, in other words in the post-reform period, organised-sector employment grew by just 4 per cent, while unorganised-sector employment rose by more than 30 per cent. The other unusual feature is that the economy appears to be skipping a normal stage of economic development. India's manufacturing sector is not big enough or successful enough to absorb rural workers. The usual flow, from 'primary' agriculture into 'secondary' industry and 'tertiary' services barely exists. Many of India's rapidly growing service-sector companies, meanwhile, require well-educated recruits. Poorly qualified rural workers will be of little use. Without the engine of manufacturing employment, India could be facing trouble. Some certainly think so. The India Labour Report 2006, produced by TeamLease, the country's leading employment agency, projected an unemployment level of 211 million by 2020 – 30 per cent of the workforce – with 9 in every 10 of the unemployed being young people. This, it said, was on the basis of extrapolating current variables forward.

'There will be a large number of people in 2020 in the labour force who will require a range of employment opportunities,' it said. 'If current trends continue, it will lead to widespread unemployment. This is a problem facing mostly the youth (and currently the children) of India, which will have substantial negative socio-economic ramifications in many unpredictable ways.'[13] The report had an agenda, which was to make the case for a substantial relaxation of labour laws at national and state level. Even if only partly true, however, it makes for a worrying prospect: probably the world's biggest-ever youth unemployment problem.

The closer India's supposed demographic advantage is examined, indeed, the less impressive it looks. India's children suffer deprivation – up to 50 per cent are malnourished – and poor or inadequate education. Some 60 million children do not have access to education and millions more receive only cursory schooling. Under two-thirds of Indians are literate, and many of them to only the most basic standards. In addition, as Nicholas Eberstadt of the American Enterprise Institute has pointed out, population growth is highly uneven. The parts of India that are driving the country's economic development have low levels of population growth, while in the poorer areas of the north population continues to rise rapidly. This is exactly as would be expected. Poor people, particularly in rural areas, have large families, partly as insurance against high levels of infant mortality, Prosperity brings with it smaller family size. 'Sub-replacement fertility already prevails in most of India's huge urban centres – New Delhi, Mumbai (Bombay), Kolkata (Calcutta), Chennai (Madras) among them,' wrote Eberstadt, adding: 'By 2025, South India's population structure will be aging unmistakably. In places like Kerala, Tamil Nadu and Karnataka, median age will be approaching a level comparable to Europe's in the late 1980s.'[14] This, as he put it, will have significant implications for India's boom cities. Indeed, it casts a shadow over the country's whole economic prospects. 'Bangalore – like the rest of the Indian South – is part of what may soon be known as Old India: While its labour force is relatively skilled, it is also older, and absolute supplies of available manpower will peak and begin to shrink,' Eberstadt argued. 'Other parts of India, by contrast, will have abundant and growing supplies of labour, but a disproportionate share of that manpower will be entirely unschooled or barely literate. Educated and aging, or untutored and fertile: This looks to be the contradiction – and the constraint – for India's development in the decades immediately ahead.'[15]

So who comes out best when it comes to population? Like two heavy-weights trying to slug it out to the finish but ending up supporting one another's weight, it has to be said that neither China nor India can deliver a knockout blow. Neither country has a demographic profile anybody would envy. China's ageing population will be a burden and will inhibit its economic development but, perhaps sensibly, the authorities have taken the decision to confront that problem in the coming decades, rather than allow the population to grow and have to deal with the consequences of over-population later. As for India, its population growth could turn out to be a boon if it solves the problems of low literacy levels, a long-running skills mismatch and how to generate the tens of millions of jobs its growing population will need. In the absence of such solutions, India's demographic advantage is a mirage. The beneficial effects of a young and growing population on the country's prosperity will be outweighed by the negative consequences of over-population. There are those who argue, indeed, that India will come to envy China's one-child policy.

Politicised Capitalism

What about India's second supposed advantage, that it has been able to foster a genuine entrepreneurial spirit, in contrast to China? Has China's appetite for foreign direct investment stifled rather than stim-ulated domestic enterprise? Add to that the all-embracing influence of the Chinese Communist Party, widespread corruption at local level and sapping uncertainty about the enforceability of property rights and China appears to have none of the ingredients in place for a genuinely entrepre-neurial economy. Such shortcomings have been recognised. A few years ago Accenture, the management consultancy firm, surveyed executives in China on the theme of 'liberating' the entrepreneurial spirit.[16] Most saw America and, interestingly, Japan as role models of entrepreneurial econo-mies. Only 3 per cent thought China was the world's most entrepreneurial economy, while most saw significant barriers to enterprise, with 83 per cent citing an aversion to risk and failure, 79 per cent the tax system and 69 per cent government legislation.

The Chinese economy is nothing, however, if not fast-moving. The idea that China lacks entrepreneurial spirit sits uneasily alongside the fact that the global Chinese diaspora includes more than its fair share of entrepre-neurs, large and small. It is also the case, as we saw earlier in the book, that its shift to a path of strong, sustained economic growth owes much to the liberation of the entrepreneurial spirit, particularly in rural areas. Indeed, a more accurate picture is one in which that spirit has survived even when the authorities have tried to bear down on it. The 'informal' sector of the economy, which thrives to this day, has provided an outlet for enterprise which the government has either ignored or been unaware of. The informal economy extends to informal banking services, bypassing state banks that were traditionally both financially creaky and bureaucratic. Michael Gonzalez, writing in the Heritage Foundation's annual Index of Economic Freedom in 2006, lauded the system of underground or informal finance that oils the wheels of the Chinese economy. He described what to outside observers looked like a library or magazine-reading club, known as the 3D Club, but which was an illegal bank. 'The 3D was just a particularly ingenious example of a phenomenon that makes up the very sinews of capitalism in China,' he wrote.

> Without 3D and the many permutations of what is generically known as 'informal finance', China's capitalist revolution would have been stillborn. This is no hyperbole. Economists estimate that the money taken in as deposits by 3D and other 'shadow banks' goes on to finance fully three-fourths of private-sector needs. 3D is also a particularly poignant example of human creativity and of how freedom seeps into every crevice that government abandons, either because it lacks enforcement capacity or the will to use it. In China, back-alley banks do most of the intermediation between savers and private businesses.[17]

According to Gonzalez, 'the informal finance phenomenon is proof of how the entrepreneurial spirit of the Chinese people shines through any crack in the great wall of repressive government'.

The other factor, stressed by many China watchers, is the deterministic nature of the Chinese Communist Party's approach to economic development. Encouraging entrepreneurialism may not have been the first choice of the authorities but what counts is what works. William Overholt, Asia Policy Chair at the Rand Center for Asia Pacific Policy, argues that Hu Jintao becoming Chinese president in 2003 completed a process in which entrepreneurialism, having been on the political fringes or kept underground, became central. The aim of the Chinese leadership was to create 'a dominant middle class entrepreneurial society. They have one of the five most entrepreneurial societies on earth today. They have put in place nine people who have bought the whole nine yards of globalization, to an extent you won't see even in Washington, DC.'[18] The proof of the pudding, for some, is the increasing impact of Chinese firms on the global economy. As if to underline China's global ambitions, some of its biggest companies have been reaching out to become significant global players. There is a caveat here. Most of China's big companies are state-owned enterprises, which to some is a contradiction in terms. Even so, *Fortune's* Global 500 list for 2005 included sixteen Chinese names, up from eleven in 2002, and well above India's five. Some of the more significant names included Lenovo, which acquired IBM's personal computer division, Haier, TCL Corp., Huawei, China National Offshore Oil Corporation (CNOOC) – unsuccessful in its attempt to take over America's Unocal – Nanjing Automotive and China National Petroleum Corporation (CNPC).

Significant though these names may be, it is important not to overstate their importance, nor to get carried away with the idea that China has forged a new style of company organisation that will work in the long term. The fundamental contradictions between political controls and economic freedoms remain. Yasheng Huang of MIT describes the system China has evolved as 'commanding-heights capitalism' and dismisses claims that it has been transformed into a fully functioning market economy. Excessive state interference is a barrier to true enterprise all over the world, and China is no different. Victor Nee and Sonja Opper, in a 2006 paper for the World Bank, define China's system as 'politicized capitalism', in which the state not only sets the regulatory framework in which firms operate but also interferes directly in their decisions. They argue that this should be viewed as a transitional stage or 'hybrid economic order', implying that it should be viewed as a phase in China's economic development, not its final resting place. It is often forgotten that there was a high degree of direct state interference during the early years of the take-off stages for Japan, Taiwan and South Korea. China could go the same way, though there is no firm evidence yet that the state will relax its grip. As long as this is the case, Nee and Opper argue, China's form of capitalism will deliver inferior performance. 'In contrast to the common view that close state–firm relations have actually contributed to China's remarkable growth trajectory, our results suggest that politicized capitalism is not associated with beneficial effects on the firm's performance when state bureaucrats are directly involved in influencing decision-making in the firm,' they wrote.[19]

Banking Woes

For critics of China, the banking system is an economic catastrophe waiting to happen. China's state-owned banks, they argue, operate in a way that would have driven any properly run financial institution to bankruptcy many years ago. The network of dodgy loans that link state-owned banks and their counterparts in commerce and industry represent an economic 'house of cards' that could collapse when the merest pressure is exerted. Non-performing loans – those which are not being serviced by customers and may never be repaid – could be as high as 40–50 per cent of the total, according to independent estimates (mainly those published outside China). One day, they will be exposed as such, critics argue, and a large part of the economic miracle will be shown to have been built on the shakiest of foundations. The banking system is indeed a source of vulnerability for China's economy, though there is evidence that the problem is being tackled. At least twenty-five foreign banks have taken stakes in Chinese banks, bringing with them both capital and the greater rigour of Western banking methods. The authorities, while conceding that banking reform is needed and that much lending is on thin or non-existent margins, queries outside estimates of the proportion of non-performing loans, which it puts at 13 per cent. The banks are also being knocked into financial shape in preparation for stock-market listings, mainly in Hong Kong. Because international investors insist on higher financial standards, this, it is argued, provides the spur for a thorough financial spring clean. Several Chinese banks have listed in Hong Kong. The Industrial and Commercial Bank of China's October 2006 initial public offering led to a record one million share applications from investors. Retail investors made applications for nearly eighty times the shares on offer.

Entrepreneurial Spirit

In many ways the obstacles to entrepreneurship in India are as formidable as those in China. For China's repressive regime and 'politicized capitalism', read India's corruption and bureaucracy (characteristics it shares with China); a creaking infrastructure; ambiguous attitudes to business; a tax system that heavily penalises individual success; and caste and religious differences. On the plus side, though, are a legal system which protects property rights, the English language, a much stronger private-sector tradition, freedom of speech and of the press, and stable democracy. India also has deeper and more efficient capital markets. The Bombay Stock Exchange (BSE), as it still calls itself, in Mumbai, India's financial capital, dates back to 1875, and is Asia's oldest, pre-dating Tokyo by three years. There are twenty-two stock exchanges in India in all. The BSE has more than 6,000 stocks listed, with a combined market capitalisation of over $450 billion, and its Sensex index of leading shares is closely followed around the world. The rise of Indian stock markets has paralleled the economy's climb.

China, in contrast, has failed to develop sophisticated and liquid stock markets. Shanghai, with its state-of-the-art international airport, modern transport system, space-age World Financial Center and stunning skyline, provides living proof that there is more to establishing successful financial centres than concrete and glass. A few years ago, it was common to talk of the eclipse of Hong Kong in favour of Shanghai. Such talk is now rare. The official aim is still to make Shanghai a leading global financial centre, but it is now accepted that this is a long-term goal. Shanghai's experience from 2001 to 2005, when share prices halved and stockbrokers who had offered guaranteed returns to investors were badly exposed, set back the cause of investor-led capitalism in China for years. In September 2006 Chen Liangyu, the city's Communist Party secretary, was removed from office by Party leaders for alleged corruption involving allegations of illicit investment of hundreds of millions of dollars of pension-fund money in property and infrastructure. This, and Shanghai's experience more generally, is a reflection in microcosm of China's problems; overbearing bureaucracy combined, paradoxically, with weak regulation. Fewer than 1,000 firms are listed on the Shanghai market. China's best companies go further afield, with official approval, to Hong Kong, Singapore, London or America's NASDAQ, where listing requirements are tougher and provide much more of a spur to managers.

This may, in time, improve Chinese corporate performance. But as far as stock-market investors are concerned, Indian firms have so far been a better bet. An analysis by *Business Week* of financial data from Standard & Poor's, the rating agency, showed that over the period 1999–2003 Indian companies, in general, outperformed their Chinese counterparts on the two key measures of return on equity and return on capital employed.[20] Faced with greater competitive pressures than their equivalents in China, Indian firms are under much more pressure to perform. They also have to keep their investors happy. Chinese companies quoted in Hong Kong, so-called Red Chips, performed better than those confined to the mainland exchanges of Shanghai and Shenzhen. The directors and managers of Indian quoted companies, reliant on raising capital on the Bombay Stock Exchange or one of the country's other exchanges, are obliged to be efficient in their use of it.

When it comes to the numbers game, India has its own case to make in other ways. A wider international listing of companies by turnover, the *Forbes* 2000, had twenty-seven firms from India in its 2005 rankings, compared with twenty-one from China. Prominent Indian names included Reliance Industries, Tata Consultancy Services (and Tata Iron and Steel and Tata Motors), Infosys, Wipro, Bharat Heavy Industries and ICICI Bank. An earlier *Forbes* listing, of the world's 200 best small companies, had thirteen from India and only four from China. There is undoubtedly something powerful stirring in India. INSEAD, the international business school, calls it an 'entrepreneurial explosion' which will see great businesses founded over the next ten to twenty years. Martin Feldstein, head of the Council of Economic Advisers under Ronald Reagan and now a distinguished professor of economics at Harvard, takes the view that there has been a national mood change in India. Politicians, officials and opinion-formers in India used to look askance at China's dictatorship and dismiss comparisons between the two countries. Now, he argues, they have taken a leaf out of China's book, particularly its single-mindedness, and are directing their efforts towards fostering enterprise. 'The optimistic mood in India's business community, the desire for reforms by the top leadership of the government, and the growing number of relatively middle-class households provide a force for change and a source of support for new entrepreneurial activities,' he wrote. 'If the political leaders can now persuade the traditional opponents of reform that growth can benefit their constituents and that better new jobs will replace the old, India will see decades of remarkable achievement.'[21]

Small is Not Beautiful

A key feature of successful entrepreneurial economies is not just having strong large companies but having thriving smaller firms; small and medium-sized enterprises (SMEs). Smaller firms drive innovation and employment, embodying a nation's entrepreneurial drive. During the Nehru–Gandhi era, however, India took this too far, giving SMEs a degree of protectionism, including the exclusive right to produce certain products, which restricted larger firms, preserved inefficiencies and hampered the country's economic development. Before the liberalisation of 1991 small businesses that appeared to fit better with India's 'village' philosophy avoided the suspicion with which larger firms, and even more so foreign businesses, were regarded by the Indian people and their political leaders. Even in the post-liberalisation era, such attitudes have not entirely disappeared. The reluctance of successive governments to open up Indian retailing too quickly to foreign competition reflects a determination to protect small-scale family stores.

Does India have a thriving SME sector? Most of the focus for the 'new' India has been on successful larger firms, some of which started small relatively recently, such as Infosys and Wipro. The nature of the software and IT services sectors is such that there are many thousands of innovative small firms with considerable potential. There is also, however, a long tail of less successful Indian SMEs, many caught between two stools. They have lost the protection they received under the 'licence Raj', but are beset by inefficiency and a lack of innovation. They employ nearly 30 million people in nearly 3 million businesses and contribute around 40 per cent of industrial output. At least a third of India's direct exports emanate from them. But competition, where it has been introduced, has not been kind to them. Many still rely on expensive finance from the unorganised sector, the informal moneylenders. This is changing, though perhaps not rapidly enough. According to one assessment, from the government's own ministry for small-scale industries: 'SMEs in India, which constitute more than 80 per cent of the total number of industrial enterprises and form the backbone of industrial development, suffer from the problems of sub-optimal scale of operation and technological obsolescence. Indian SMEs are facing a tough competition from their global counterparts due to liberalisation, change in manufacturing strategies and turbulent and an uncertain market scenario.'[22] Smaller firms in India spend little on research and development, product development and innovation. They also suffer from the fact that managerial talent is spread thinly.

India certainly has the potential for a highly entrepreneurial economy. As with the country's youthful population, this should be an advantage over China. Neither, however, gives India a killer blow, and for similar reasons. In neither case is India leveraging these potential advantages because of familiar shortcomings, particularly in the education system. It is also a question of attitude. Rather than embark on the precarious journey to become a successful entrepreneur, many educated Indians prefer the security of a government job, for security, salary and, as the *Financial Times* journalist Edward Luce argues, the opportunity for benefiting from backhanders. 'For all but the Anglophone élite, who have exploited new opportunities for themselves since 1991, a job with the government is the most coveted there is,' he writes. ' "Government job," said Virender, when I asked what career he most wanted. "Government job," had said his nephews and nieces, who seemed surprised I needed to ask. "Government job," said every villager introduced to me by Nikhil and Aruna in Sowangar a few months earlier. For the overwhelming majority of Indians, having a government job is not merely a question of security, although the fact that you cannot be sacked is a large incentive. Nor is it just a question of gaining a higher social status, though that is also a big attraction to most people. To the majority of Indian villagers, a government job is in the first place an instant leapfrog into a higher standard of living.'[23]

Saving Grace

The China growth story has been characterised by record levels of foreign direct investment (FDI) – ten times the amount attracted by India – and a high domestic saving rate – equivalent to 45 to 50 per cent of gross domestic product – with the stock of savings having built up to more than $1,000 billion. This is, in many respects, the classic east Asian model of economic development, the first stage of which is investment for export, the second the development of domestic markets. The question about China's investment and savings is not whether they are enough but whether they are too much. There is also an issue about whether China has 'bought' inward investment too expensively, offering tax and other incentives that may not just be unfair to competitor economies but will be difficult to sustain in the long term.

India is a different story. The country's failure to attract sufficient FDI, arising partly from traditional Indian hostility to international capital, is well known and is something recent reform-minded governments have tried to rectify, so far with only limited success. India, with a shaky budgetary position, is in no place to offer large-scale fiscal incentives to attract footloose global companies. Not only that but, in what looks like a double disadvantage, India's domestic savings are also significantly lower than China's. Manmohan Singh, the prime minister, has expressed his hope that both will rise strongly: FDI because of the opening-up of the economy to capital inflows; savings as a result of India's demographic profile. A young country with a high proportion of working-age people should, in theory, save more, because of the declining proportion of dependants.

In 2006, Singh celebrated the fact that India's saving rate increased to 29 per cent of GDP, and suggested this could be the shape of things to come. But India's rate of saving and investment, broadly 25–30 per cent of GDP, seems unlikely to converge on the 35–40 per cent rate typical of east Asian economies such as South Korea and Malaysia during their most rapid development periods, let alone China's higher rate. How big a constraint is this? Deepak Mishra of the World Bank put the question straightforwardly: 'Can India attain East Asian growth with a South Asian saving rate?'[24] Why does China save more than India? It is not, as is commonly thought, just because Chinese households are safeguarding themselves against the march of time – the country's rapid ageing – while Indian families do not need to bother. Household savings, which average about 22 per cent of GDP in India, are higher relative to the size of the economy than China's, which are around 15 per cent. The differences come from saving by corporations and enterprises – nearly 25 per cent of GDP in China and only 5 per cent in India – together with saving by government. Public-sector saving is 10 per cent of GDP in China but fluctuates around zero in India.

Can India grow strongly, say at 8 per cent a year, without raising saving and investment rates? India does not, it seems, need to replicate China's level of savings. Because its bias has been towards service industries, which are less capital-intensive than manufacturing, its requirements have been lower. At the skilled end of the work force, India has invested in human capital – people – more than in machines. But India, Mishra argues, does need a somewhat higher level of savings and would be unwise to rely much on demographics to deliver them. Household saving, which would be most likely to respond to such factors, is already high by international standards and appears to have reached a plateau. In two respects, however, India needs to be more like China. It must attract a higher level of inward investment and it must put its public finances in better shape. As he concludes: 'India could grow at eight per cent, if it can ensure prudent fiscal outcomes and undertake domestic reforms to attract external capital to fill its emerging saving–investment gap.'[25]

Building Blocks

The scale of China's ambition, and its ability to convert it into large-scale spending on infrastructure projects, is extraordinary. Between 2006 and 2010 it will spend more on new and upgraded airports than even during the infrastructure boom of the previous fifteen years. The programme includes forty-two new airports, bringing the national total up to 190 by 2010, with Beijing, Shanghai and Guangzhou being significantly upgraded as international airports and Chengdu, Wenming, Xi'an, Wuhan and Shenyang becoming important regional hubs. China's commercial aircraft fleet – nearly 900 in 2006 – will rise to 4,000 by 2020, according to Civil Aviation Administration. China's road network is being transformed by perhaps the biggest building programme in history, recalling the Romans and the construction of the interstate highways in post-war America. Already China is second only to the United States in the size of its road network. That is just the shape of things to come. By the mid-2030s more than 90,000 additional kilometres of expressways/freeways (roads with a speed limit of 120 kph) are planned, implying that in three decades China will add the equivalent of the current US freeway network. Its new highways will stretch from the Himalayas to the Gobi desert.

What about the vehicles that will run along these roads? Official projections suggest that by 2020 the country will be the world's biggest manufacturer of cars, of which a significant proportion will be for the home market. China may not compare itself very often with India, though it does model itself in many respects on America. British journalist James Kynge, in his 2006 book *China Shakes the World*, drew the novel comparison between the fast-growing industrial city of Chongqing and the bustle, noise and pollution of Chicago at the dawn of the American age.[26]

Even more than airports and roads, the scale of China's ambition, and the ability of the state to ride roughshod over the kind of objections that a democratic government faces, were demonstrated clearly by the $25-billion Three Gorges Dam project in Hubeil province in central China on the Yangtze, the world's third longest river. Three Gorges, the largest hydroelectric dam in the world, is one of the modern wonders of the world, if you like that sort of thing. The span of the dam, construction of which was completed in May 2006, is two kilometres, while its reservoir will extend for 600 kilometres upstream once the project is finished in 2009. In the West we are used to planning inquiries and compulsory purchase orders around large-scale public works projects. Three Gorges, however, took things to a new level, with 1.3 million people displaced, many forcibly and with no compensation or offer of resettlement. Those who complained were threatened with arrest or were subject to violence. The project itself, which ran up huge cost overruns, some of them due to the technical problems encountered, was branded a disaster by environmental campaigners, When the area was flooded, it submerged factories, mines and waste dumps, spreading their toxic contents down the river. In the summer the reservoir will turn into a festering bog of effluent, silt, industrial pollutants and rubbish, and a breeding ground for mosquitoes, bacteria and parasites, with possibly disastrous consequences for health. The dam is also inflicting damage further downstream and could severely harm fishing in the East China Sea, which is among the world's largest fisheries.

So China marches on, even at a significant cost to human rights and the environment. Economic progress requires electricity, and the Three Gorges Dam will provide plenty of it. In India, by contrast, the effort to improve the country's infrastructure is a much statelier one. Local disputes stand in the way of what businesses regard as essential improvements, as we saw in the case of Bangalore. Meanwhile, the government in New Delhi cajoles and persuades in its efforts to inject a new urgency into the task of getting an infrastructure suitable for the twentieth century, let alone the twenty-first. 'The most important area where the government can help India's entrepreneurs is by addressing infrastructure deficiencies,' wrote Manmohan Singh in 2006.

There is no doubt that India has large gaps in physical infrastructure compared with our competitors in East Asia and even Southeast Asia.

We need to bridge the gap in electricity generation, roads, railways, telecommunications, ports, airports, and urban mass transport if our potential is to be realized. The investment required to close the infrastructure gap is huge – current estimates suggest that we will have to spend $250 billion on infrastructure over the next five years, far more than the public purse can afford. We propose to supplement public resources by using public–private partnerships (PPPs) as much as possible, and we are evolving strategies that will enable us to do so.[27]

A third to a half of India's roads are unpaved. Journeys on paved roads are long, frustrating and unpredictable, severely hampering business. There is some progress. The 'Golden Quadrilateral', a new 5,000-kilometre highway network linking Delhi, Kolkata, Chennai and Mumbai, is said to be India's biggest infrastructure project since independence, with the first leg completed in 2006. It too has drawn comparisons with the construction of America's interstate highways. More is needed to get India moving, however, than providing roads. The standard tourist advice to visitors to the country is: 'Don't hire a car.' Even with an Indian driver, the journeys are hair-raising, and frequently interrupted by incidents, arguments and accidents. India's gleaming new roads, where they exist, have to battle with some of the peculiarities of Indian tradition, which include the obligatory wandering sacred cows, herds of goats or other animals, bicycles, slow-moving motorcycles creaking under the weight of their baggage, and camel-drawn carts. Highly erratic driving habits, with sudden, inexplicable manoeuvres, complete the picture.

How big a drawback are India's acknowledged infrastructure shortcomings? From the prime minister down, everybody recognises the problem. How many potential inward investment projects have been lost on the limousine ride from the airport at Delhi or Mumbai into the city centre? China presents an efficient face to the world, India one of barely organised chaos. China spends ten times as much on roads as India and freight journeys by rail are a third of the cost per kilometre. China has a huge infrastructure advantage. It is easy, however, to overstate the effect of modern buildings and smart new roads. It has not, as noted above, turned Shanghai into a global financial centre. A study led by K. C. Fung of the University of California has suggested that in the case of China, 'soft' infrastructure, which it defines as economic reform and liberalisation, has been more important in attracting inward investment than 'hard' infra-structure.[28] That offers reassurance for India, though it also throws out a challenge. India has to get its soft infrastructure right to compensate for its other failings. So far the record on that has been mixed, particularly when it comes to opening up protected sectors to inward investment.

Resource Hunger

China's hunger for energy and commodities is well documented, hence its particular interest in Africa, as well as Latin America. China has been buying up much of Africa and accounts for much of the world's growth in com-modity demand. From 1999 to 2005, China was responsible for two-thirds of the rise in demand for metals, and by 2006 was consuming a quarter of global metals' output. It uses just over an eighth of annual world oil sup-plies, and was responsible for 25 per cent of growth in demand between 1999 and 2005. India is not a bit player when it comes to commodities and energy – it is the world's fifth largest energy consumer (China is the second, after America) – but its impact has been much less significant.

Which is best placed when it comes to resources? China was, until relatively recently, self-sufficient in energy, and a net exporter of coal. That is changing, and gradually China's domestic oil production – about 180 million tonnes a year – has become insufficient, so that in 2005 about 40 per cent of the country's oil needs were met by imports. Coal self-sufficiency continues. Periodically there is optimism in the Chinese official press about new oil and gas discoveries, usually in the South China Sea. Mainly, though, even if these discoveries are taken through to production, they will merely compensate for declining output at Daqing and the other big oil fields in eastern and north-eastern China. India is more dependent on energy imports, relative to demand, than China – importing about a third of its needs. India produces nearly all the coal it uses but only a third of the oil. In 2005 the Indian government signed a $40-billion deal to import 7.5 million tonnes of liquefied natural gas annually from Iran over twenty-five years. An Iran–Pakistan–India gas pipeline has been on the drawing board since the early 1990s. There have been significant recent oil discoveries in India, notably in Rajasthan. For the foreseeable future, however, India will need to import energy.

Ask any question about India's economy and the answer is likely to be 'infrastructure'. Power cuts punctuate everyday life. Power theft is endemic, with at least a third of the country's electricity unpaid for. One official estimate suggested that over 40 per cent of Delhi's electricity is stolen. Households tap illegally into electricity supply lines, and not always just poor and slum households; so too do factories. The situation is typically chaotic, perhaps typically Indian.

Apart from energy, India is rich in iron ore – hence the national disappointment at the relatively poor performance of manufacturing – as well as zinc and aluminium (bauxite). But India is poor in copper, tin, nickel and zinc. China can boast self-sufficiency in tin and zinc but needs to import all the other major metal ores. India is better placed than China when it comes to food self-sufficiency, and is a big net exporter of some food commodities, notably tea and coffee. The main concern, in both cases, though, is whether changes in domestic eating patterns to Western-style diets, with more consumption of wheat and meat, will lead to bigger demands on world markets. So far, the China factor – and to a lesser extent, the India factor – has been mainly felt in markets for hard commodities and oil, rather than soft commodities.

Heat and Dust

Plan a visit to India and there are certain months you are advised to time your trip. November to March is usually favoured. The monsoon season and the stifling heat rule out May to September for all but the hardiest tourists. This is when the élite of the British Raj used to retreat to the relative cool of the hill stations, and it is when today's Indian élite tries to time its travel elsewhere, to Europe or America. Traditionally, economists have regarded climate as an important factor in economic development. David Landes, in his *The Wealth and Poverty of Nations* (1998), came down in favour of cultural explanations for development but he also cited climatic factors, quoting a diplomat's observations that in countries like India the effects of the hot weather were enervating, and the consequences in terms of people's ability to work significant. How much, in these days of air-conditioned offices and limousines, is India's climate still a negative? Not least because air conditioning is always under threat from power cuts, and sitting in traffic for a 'short' four-hour journey is not pleasant even in an air-conditioned car, the Indian climate has not suddenly disappeared as a factor.

Neither have the pressures on India's health-care system. During the late summer and autumn of 2006 the country was hit by a dangerous outbreak of Dengue fever, which even made it into the prime minister's official residence, infecting both his grandson and his son-in-law. The mosquito-borne fever, which struck down more than 10,000 people and led to hundreds of deaths, added to the strain on the Indian health service, which suffers from rates of absenteeism as high as 40 per cent among health workers, the world's biggest HIV case load and the return of polio, which was thought to have been more or less eradicated.

Partners in Grime

The rest of the world frets about the rise of India and China for economic reasons. But it also worries, perhaps even more, about the environmental consequences. Can the planet cope with China and India as big energy consumers? And which of them is more vulnerable on this score? In the spring of 2006, a thick grey-black cloud drifted over northern China, before reaching Seoul, the South Korean capital. From there the noxious cloud of soot and poisonous chemicals made its way across the Pacific to America's west coast. Higher levels of sulphur compounds and carbon were detected by researchers in California, Oregon and Washington, in some cases in the form of visible deposits on their monitoring equipment. Scientists monitoring air quality at Lake Tahoe in California said the cloud was the dirtiest they had seen outside urban areas. Things are even worse at home – coal-related pollution is blamed for 400,000 premature deaths a year in China. This is one Chinese export nobody wants, and it is growing. China, rich in coal but poor in oil, burns more of it than the United States, the European Union and Japan put together. Projects like Three Gorges are not enough. Every week or so, a new coal-fired power station opens in China and, despite Beijing's declared commitment to clean coal technology, most use old, polluting designs. 'This is the great challenge they have to face,' says David Moskovitz, an energy consultant and adviser to the Chinese government. 'How can they continue their rapid growth without plunging the environment into the abyss?'[29]

In 1990, when the former East Germany was opened up to the West as a result of German unification, visitors were staggered by the amount of environmental degradation that had occurred during the communist era. Multiply East Germany many times over and you begin to get an idea of the scale of the problem in China. One of the more notorious incidents was in

November 2005, when an explosion at a PetroChina plant in the Jilin province in north-east China deposited at least 100 tonnes of highly toxic and carcinogenic benzene into the Shonghua river, forming an 80-kilometre-long slick. As it meandered more than 300 kilometres downstream to the city of Harbin, the capital of Heilongjiang province, the reaction was one of near panic, with many of the city's 4 million residents trying to leave as drinking water supplies were cut off for days. That was the reaction, too, across the border in Russia, where, as in America, serious pollution has also been an unwanted import from China. In March 2006, Zhou Shengxian, director of China's State Environmental Protection Administration, warned of the risk of 'disastrous consequences', particularly from the thousands of chemical plants along the Yangtze and Yellow rivers, unless anti-pollution efforts are stepped up.[30] Even without accidents, the picture is grim. The Yangtze provides drinking water for a twelfth of the world's population, yet water from a quarter of its tributaries is not even suitable for spraying on crops in fields, such are the levels of pollution. In the booming industrial city of Chongqing, as in other cities, many people lack running water. Officially, 70 per cent of China's rivers and lakes are polluted, more than 100 cities suffer from serious water shortages and 360 million people lack access to safe drinking water.

Poison

When it comes to environmental problems, it is usually the case that anything China can do, India can do worse, or at least as badly. One of the world's worst environmental disasters, at Bhopal in Madhya Pradesh in 1984, resulted in the deaths of more than 15,000 people and injuries to 550,000 (these are the numbers of victims, and in the case of the deaths, those victims' families to whom compensation has been paid), when deadly methyl isocyanate gas escaped from a Union Carbide pesticides plant in the heart of the city. It was a modern-day horror story. The gas, heavier than air, brought painful death to some victims through a rapid build-up of fluid in the lungs (pulmonary oedema), and left others blind or suffering from poisoning that will result in fatal diseases later. It is hard to imagine the scale of the panic when it started spreading on that fateful night of 3 December 1984. Victims recall waking in the dark, in the middle of the night, coughing and retching, and then of trying to escape through the frenzied crowds on the streets, the transport system having given up. Many of those who died were trampled in the rush to get away. Bhopal is, on one level, a simple story of that callous disregard of an American-owned multinational for the people of a poor country in which it was operating. Safety standards were well below those at Union Carbide's US plants and probably not properly observed. Local people had no knowledge of the deadly chemicals in their midst. Union Carbide paid $470 million into a fund for victims at the end of the 1980s and was considered to have got off very lightly; most of those affected received just a few hundred dollars.

There is another aspect to Bhopal, however. Two decades after the disaster, the site and its surroundings are still contaminated with toxic waste, local politics and disputes over who should pay delaying the clean-up work. As the monsoon rains have continued to pour on to the factory, cancer-causing chemicals have washed down into the drinking wells. The poor people of the city, forced to live near the plant, are still falling ill and dying as a result of doing so. Like a chemical Chernobyl, Bhopal is still killing people and the victims are still campaigning for justice. It is a reminder of the limits of India's new prosperity.

In 2006, Coca-Cola and Pepsi were banned from sale by the Indian state of Kerala, after their drinks were found to contain dangerously high levels of pesticides. It looked like a blow against corporate wrongdoing by US multinationals, albeit on a relatively minor scale, though the ban was soon overturned by the courts. In reality, India is capable of generating her own environmental problems, and on a huge scale. Greenpeace has claimed that there are 'a thousand Bhopals' all over India and has identified a number of 'toxic hotspots', including Eloor in Kerala, Kodaikanal in Tamil Nadu and Patancheru in Andhra Pradesh.[31] They follow a similar pattern: large-scale, heavily polluting chemical plants, many of which use obsolete technology, which appear to be able to damage the environment with impunity. India has environmental laws; the Environment Protection Act, rushed through in 1986 in direct response to Bhopal, established the Ministry of Environment and Forests. As with so many things in India, however, laws are one thing but enforcement is another. Faster economic growth has meant that, in most cases, environmental problems have got worse. It is an area, perhaps among many, where India's famous bureaucracy is ineffectual. Evidence assembled by America's Energy Information Administration (EIA) suggests that India's big cities (it has more than twenty with populations of over a million) are among the world's most polluted, particularly Delhi, Mumbai, Kolkata and Chennai, with urban air quality in general among the worst in the world. Of the 3 million premature deaths worldwide annually as a result of air pollution, India accounts for more than any other country. Rising car use and unchecked industrial pollution mean the problems are getting worse, not better. This is despite the adoption of tough standards on car and commercial vehicle emissions. Despite this, particulate levels in Delhi from diesel have been measured at ten times the legal limit. The job of replacing old, polluting vehicles with cleaner, newer ones has been a tough one. India, like China, has a problem with emissions from coal-fired power stations, and from burning coal directly. India's problems are not as acute as those of China, but they are real enough. Between 50 and 60 per cent of the country's energy needs are met from coal and lignite.

It is possible to take an optimistic view of India and China's environmental impact, as I shall argue in the final chapter. For the moment, however, the issue is whether and by what means both countries can grapple with the immediate environmental consequences of economic growth. It is hard to choose which of the two has the more serious problems. Chinese officials have suggested that pollution costs the equivalent of 10 per cent of GDP, though the first experimental 'green GDP' measure, released in September 2006 by the State Environmental Protection Administration and the National Bureau of Statistics, suggested that in 2004 it was just under 97 per cent of conventionally measured GDP, implying an annual environmental pollution cost of about $64 billion. Both bodies admitted, however, that the measure was not yet comprehensive.

The 10 Per Cent Club

Though China and India are big, but also so different, it is a curiosity of their simultaneous emergence that they appear to fit reasonably snugly together. China's comparative advantage is in manufacturing, though it is keen to expand more into services. India's is in services, though it is desperate to be more successful in manufacturing. The story of the past decade or so could have been very different if they had been competing head-to-head in either manufacturing or services. Who knows, the 'China effect' on worldwide prices of manufactured goods could have been even bigger, as could the 'India effect' on competition in services.

Both countries have advantages and disadvantages. The message of this chapter has been that those advantages and disadvantages often cancel each other out, both within and between the two countries. Thus, China's impressive achievements in building a modern infrastructure are offset by its failing to establish a 'soft' infrastructure, and by the role of the state. Even after a quarter of a century of growth, and the years of large-scale inward investment, international business remains wary of the Chinese government. Wal-Mart, perhaps the biggest single beneficiary of trade with China (on its own it would be the country's fourth largest trading partner), announced reluctantly in 2006 that it would allow trade-union representation in all its Chinese operations. The move came after pressure from the officially backed All-China Federation of Trade Unions, and would not have happened without the approval of the Chinese Communist Party. India, meanwhile, has a potential demographic advantage, in its young and growing population, but risks squandering that advantage through educational and other failings. The big risk is of a generation, not of skilled and enthusiastic young workers, but of the poor and unemployed.

When it comes to hard numbers, India's ambitions are clear. From the prime minister down, a single figure stands out. India wants to achieve a sustained growth rate of 10 per cent a year. A 10 per cent growth rate is not only 'eminently feasible' said Manmohan Singh, but also necessary, not least to mop up the rising working force. 'We need growth, we need jobs, we need income and we need security,' he declared, warning that 'history will judge us harshly' if the bold decisions needed to achieve it were not taken.[32] As it happens, India did not achieve 10 per cent growth during 2006, but China did easily. This was strong, even by Chinese standards, but not necessarily atypical. An economy that has grown by between 9 and 10 per cent annually since 1978 has often slipped into double figures. To be fair to India, it also did pretty well, growing by close to 9 per cent. In 2006, both India and China benefited from the strongest run for the global economy since the early 1970s, and their symbiotic relationship with the rest of the world – both contributing to and benefiting from global economic growth. The world is tilting to the east, and China and India are part of that shift.

Can India achieve the 10 per cent growth its political leaders and businessmen so desperately want? Robert Prior-Wandesforde, in a detailed assessment for HSBC in 2006, suggested more modest ambitions are in order. Even at 8–9 per cent growth, India's economy is exceeding its 'speed limit', he suggested, and could result in significant inflationary pressures. India runs 'twin' deficits, both the current account of the balance of payments and the budget deficit being in the red. Nobody is suggesting there will be a re-run of the 1991 crisis that forced the country's change of economic direction, but some vulnerability remains. Prior-Wandesforde acknowledged that India has come a long way, and could comfortably sustain a growth rate of about 7 cent.

> If everything were to develop perfectly, we estimate that trend growth could rise to 8.5 per cent in 10 years' time. This, however, is the dream scenario and, importantly, doesn't take full account of the many impediments to growth. India's seemingly irresistible growth force is set to meet the proverbial immovable object in the form of the country's infrastructure problems. An apparent improvement in the quantity and quality of primary education masks underlying difficulties, power will remain a big problem in the context of a world with finite natural resources, while roads, railways and ports require vast expenditure.[33]

The dream of sustained 10 per cent growth, he suggested, would remain just that.

Poor Relation?

India is playing catch-up, and seems destined to continue to do so for some time. Even 8.5 per cent growth, which depends on India doing a lot of things right, would be lower than China has averaged over the past three decades, to the frustration of the politicians in New Delhi and the businessmen of Mumbai, Chennai and Bangalore. That is also the view of other economists who have studied India's potential. Their conclusion is that while 8 per cent is achievable, 10 per cent is probably not. That looks hard on India, after three decades of having to play second fiddle to China. The bank Goldman Sachs, which has done more than any other organisation to draw the world's attention to the changes being ushered in by the BRICs economies, says: 'Both are moving towards their long-term potential faster than we anticipated. However, if we were forced to choose between the two, our most objective assessment would be that China is, at this point in time, slightly better positioned to deliver on its potential than India.'[34] That does not mean China will always grow faster than India. There is an element of the tortoise and the hare about the two. The Goldman Sachs projections have China's growth slowing to 5 per cent by 2020, and 3 per cent by 2050 – roughly in line with what the successful advanced industrial economies achieve now. India, in contrast, is seen as averaging 8 per cent growth over the period to 2020. India, in other words, should soon be growing faster than China. By the middle of the century, India could have overhauled America in GDP terms, and be second only to China in the world. She will still, however, be the poor relation, GDP *per capita* being well below Chinese levels.

Political Tensions

Numbers matter and they matter a lot to politicians and businesses interested in growing markets. What also matters, however, is the quality of growth and whether it maintains social cohesion. Is China addicted to growth, in the sense that any slowdown would expose even more serious social tensions than the tens of thousands of protests that already occur each year? Or will those social tensions themselves force the government to rein back, go easier on liberalisation and turn inward? China gets pulled both ways; the people's expectations versus the people's fear of change – the hunger for even greater prosperity among those doing well in the new 'capitalist' era against the anguish of those being left behind, or forced to endure grim lives to maintain the economy's competitiveness. At the World Economic Forum's 2006 China Business Summit in Beijing, a series of scenarios were presented for China in the years to 2025. One, 'Unfulfilled Promise', sees the authorities struggling to contain internal dissent and being forced to backtrack on liberalisation and reform. Instead of striding to the top of the global economic heap, China becomes something of an economic backwater; still growing but no longer capable of conquering the world. Joe Studwell's thesis in his 2002 book *The China Dream* – that Westerners hoping to profit from the opening-up of a huge Chinese market of middle-class consumers will always end up disappointed – would once again have been proved correct. India faces similar tensions. The gap between the urban middle classes and the rural poor is growing. Finding jobs for a rapidly growing population will be an enormous challenge for a country which, despite pockets of considerable wealth, remains poor. It might not take too much for India to sink back into mediocrity and isolationism. The Indian equivalent of the World Economic Forum's take on China's 'Unfulfilled Promise' is a 2025 scenario called 'Bolly World', a dream sequence in which the hero – India – dazzles the world for a while, attracts the money men from overseas but then settles back into complacency. There is no trickle-down, the rural and urban poor remain untouched by prosperity, and India looks back a quarter of the way through the twenty-first century only on missed opportunities.

It could happen, to either or both of the two countries. One could thrive while the other struggles. Because India's 'miracle' is of more recent vintage than China's, there is more nervousness in India about whether it can be sustained than in China. Perhaps the best way to look at China and India, after all, is as partners rather than outright competitors. It may be that they will stand or fall together. As we will see in the final chapter, the potential for that partnership is formidable. The risks of disappointment, however, remain.

7

Ten Ways China and India will (and won't) Change the World

'The emergence of China, India, and the former communist bloc countries implies that the greater part of the earth's population is now engaged, at least potentially, in the global economy. There are no historical antecedents for this development. Columbus's voyage to the New World ultimately led to enormous economic change, of course, but the full integration of the New and the Old Worlds took centuries. In contrast, the economic opening of China, which began in earnest less than three decades ago, is proceeding rapidly and, if anything, seems to be accelerating.'

Ben Bernanke, US Federal Reserve Board Chairman

'With growing competition from China and India, having the best educated, best-skilled and best-trained workforce in the world is not for Britain an option in a global economy, but a necessity.'

Gordon Brown, UK Chancellor of the Exchequer

'If Bush wants to tout his record, he should do it somewhere where the Bush economy has actually created jobs, like India ... or China.'

Jay Leno, comedian

China and India provoke fear and uncertainty in almost equal measure. No self-respecting Western politician in the early twenty-first century can avoid including at least a reference to them in speeches. By mentioning China and India they are demonstrating awareness, not only of modern-day realities, but also that they are alert to the effects of the emergence of these two giants – both good and bad – on their voters. In one respect China and India are convenient shorthand for globalisation, but they are much more than that. They are used both as a wake-up call and an excuse. Think we are spending too much on education? Look at the number of graduates produced annually by China and India; well over 2 million each. Criticising our record on jobs? We are doing our best but there are forces out there, exemplified by China and India, nobody can do much about. Businesses play similar games. China and India have destroyed pricing power, so shareholders should be grateful for the profits they have managed to generate. And yes, if you can't beat them you have to join them; shifting production or back-office work there, however much the unions protest. This is, it appears, the new reality.

We have come a long way in this book. It started with those British businessmen worried about whether they could ever make a living again, through ancient India and China to their rise in the modern era and their bursting on to the world stage, stunningly, in recent years. What does it mean, and what lessons should we draw? There are many, but I want to focus on ten, some reassuring, some less so. Nobody can say precisely how these two countries will develop, and how the rest of the world will respond and develop around them. It is possible, however, to come to some broad conclusions.

1. They are the biggest thing to hit the world economy

Economic fashions come and go. In the 1980s it was common to laud the German and Japanese economic models as being superior to what many saw as the flaky and divisive Anglo-Saxon approach. Then in the 1990s Germany and Japan embarked on a period of economic stagnation and nobody cited them very much. Their turn may come again. Around 1997, a spate of books on the miracle economies of Asia, like South Korea, Taiwan and Singapore, this time focusing on the superiority of *their* approach, languished on the bookshelves when the Asian financial crisis of 1997–8 set them back for years. So a book about China and India has to be modest in its claims. Nothing seems capable of stopping them but plenty of experts said that about Japan at the end of the 1980s. Even without making overblown claims about what might happen, however, it is possible to lodge a big claim about what has already happened.

Already China and India have had a bigger impact on the world economy than Britain did when it emerged as the first industrial nation in the eighteenth and nineteenth centuries, or even than America did in the final decades of the nineteenth century and the early twentieth century. That may seem hard to credit. Britain's industrial revolution, which showed the way for the countries of Europe and made possible the transition from predominantly agricultural economies, was profound in its impact, heralding the enormous increases in wealth of the modern era. The period 1870–1914, the so-called 'second industrial revolution', saw new and more efficient industrial methods emerging, notably production-line mass manufacture in the United States which, combined with the opening-up of America, also transformed the global economy. Big though China and India are, their re-emergence perhaps even qualifying as a third industrial revolution, it is hard to say that they are qualitatively as important as those earlier developments. Mostly, after all, we are talking about a geographical shift in patterns of economic activity, not entirely new ways of doing things.

Even allowing that – though some would argue that information technology, efficient telecommunications links and the free flow of capital does amount to a revolution as profound as the earlier ones – China and India's claims to fame are quantitative, not qualitative. A World Bank study, *Dancing With Giants*, published in 2006, drew on Angus Maddison's historical data and concluded that neither Britain nor America had administered as large a shock to the world economy as modern China. Add in India, so far still the junior partner, and the impact does seem unique, the nearest parallel being the United States in the period 1820–70, just ahead of the second industrial revolution. The key to it is the pace of growth. China started in 1978 with less than 3 per cent of the world economy but then proceeded to grow at a 9–10 per cent rate for a quarter of a century, three times faster than the global average. Britain and America during their golden ages typically only grew at twice the rate of the global economy. Modern-day export-led economies like Japan burst on to the scene in the 1950s, 1960s and 1970s almost as impressively as China. But they failed to sustain it as long as China seems likely to do, leading the World Bank authors to conclude: 'China is arguably the largest shock we have seen thus far, and her growth and that of India are projected to continue. In short, even though China is not the dominant force in the world economy, the shock she is administering to it is unprecedented.'[1] Add in India and something special is indeed happening.

Others are more cautious about concluding that nothing like this has ever happened before. Jonathan Anderson, chief Asian economist at the global investment bank UBS, thinks that in both style and impact China and India are following a well-established pattern. Japan and the Asian tiger economies increased their share of the world economy from 4 to 13 per cent in the twenty years from 1965. China is on track to treble its share of global output over a twenty-year period. India, now discovering the importance of a higher saving rate, will similarly adopt the Asian template, focusing on export-led growth. 'The bottom line is that China's growth is impressive but by no means unprecedented,' he argues. 'Quite the opposite. Whether we look at trade, GDP or industrialization, the mainland has been treading a path laid out earlier by other Asian economies and is, at best, simply matching the dynamism of Japan and the Asian tiger economies. Obviously the world faces challenges from a rising China, but it has faced these before.'[2] That is a key point, which I shall return to shortly.

Perhaps the decisive statistic on the unprecedented impact of China and India was provided by Richard Freeman of Harvard University and the National Bureau of Economic Research. What he describes as 'One Big Fact' is that: 'In 2000 as a result of the collapse of communism, India's turn from autarky, China's shift to market capitalism, the global economy encompassed 6 billion people. Had China, India, and the former Soviet empire stayed outside, the global economy would have had 3.3 billion people.'[3] Taking labour force estimates from the International Labour Office, Freeman was able to get to a doubling of the global workforce, mainly as a result of China and India. Thus the 'before' and 'after' picture was of a worldwide work force of 1.46 billion in 2000, swollen to 2.93 billion as a result of China (760 million), India (440 million) and the ex-Soviet states (260 million). Nothing like this has ever happened before. Even at the end of the nineteenth century America's population was only 76 million, about a fifth of the population of Europe. Its impact was proportionately much smaller.

What matters, of course, is what happens next. The book will end by looking in greater detail at the prospects and pitfalls for China and India, but it seems clear that even on cautious assumptions their impact will continue to grow. According to the World Bank they contributed a combined 16 per cent of global growth between 1995 and 2004, while America was responsible for 33 per cent. Even using growth numbers that could be said to flatter America (3.2 per cent annual growth, compared with 6.6 per cent in China, 5.6 per cent India), the China–India contribution rises to 20 per cent over the period 2005–20, against 29 per cent for America. Those, as the World Bank admits, are conservative estimates and do not take account of an important effect – the tendency of the currencies of successful emerging economies to rise (thereby automatically increasing their share of the global economy). They demonstrate, however, the power of compound interest. If economies grow faster than the average, their contribution to that average will rise and their share will grow.

2. But they are not as big as they seem

Having said that China and India are the biggest thing to hit the world economy, it may seem perverse to argue that we should not be over-impressed with their size. The most impressive thing about them, and the thing that unites them, is population. Two hundred years ago the earth was populated by 1 billion people. Today, of course, China and India have more than that number each. It is a useful exercise to try to visualise that number of people, or indeed that number of anything. Most of us can manage 1,000 without much trouble, or even 100,000; the spectators that can be fitted into a good-sized football stadium. A million is harder; perhaps think of a well-attended march, roughly those who turned up for the Stop the War march in London ahead of the invasion of Iraq in March 2003. But imagine a billion? That is impossible. More than a quarter of the world's hundred biggest cities are in China and India. And they are growing all time. 'Every year, 8.5 million Chinese peasants move into cities,' wrote journalist Jonathan Watts.

Nowhere is the staggering urbanisation more evident than in Chongqing. Never heard of it? This is where the pace and scale of urbanisation is probably faster and bigger than anywhere in the world today. This is the Coketown of the early twenty-first century. Set in the middle reaches of the Yangtze, this former trading centre and treaty port has long been the economic hub of western China. But after its government was given municipal control of surrounding territory the size of many countries, it has grown and grown, becoming what is now the world's biggest municipality with 31 million residents (more people than Iraq, Peru or Malaysia). The population in its metropolitan areas will double from 10 million to 20 million in the next 13 years.[4]

Impressive and rather disturbing though these figures are, it is important to put these huge populations into perspective. The reality of life for most Chinese is not urban living (which itself can be exceedingly grim) or gleaming new factories owned by American or Japanese multinationals. For the majority – an officially estimated 750 million – it is the often grinding poverty of rural life. There are few rural idylls in China, but mainly a struggle to survive and a desire to escape to the cities where the streets appear to be paved with gold. Even in 2030, according to the Chinese government's own estimates, 600 million people will still live in the country. They are not the world-beating competitive labour force the rest of the globe fears, though some will continue to provide the 'factory fodder' for China's industrial expansion. They are the country's long and inefficient tail, a population burden. This is even more the case in India, where more than 70 per cent of the population lives in the countryside, and where the rural population grew by no less than 200 million over the period 1981–2001. The odd thing about India's economic emergence, indeed, is that it has not been accompanied by more rapid urbanisation. The explanation is that, in the absence of large-scale employment opportunities in manufacturing (and nothing like the demand for construction workers for infrastructure work as in China), there have not been the jobs for them to go to.

The central point is that, easy though it is to get blown away by China and India's billions, it is more useful to think of the much smaller parts of the economy which are, in fact, competing with the rest of the world. China is growing beyond the 'enclave' economy consisting just of the operations of multinationals in the coastal areas which take advantage of low labour costs and tax breaks, but there is a long way to go. Much of Chinese business consists of barely reformed state-owned enterprises no more capable of taking on the world than were their East German equivalents when they were exposed to the harsh light of international competition when the Berlin Wall came down. That is even more the case for India. The world has become obsessed with an IT and outsourcing sector that employs barely 0.1 per cent of the population. Only just over 3 per cent of Indians are in organised employment. How big are the truly competitive parts of the Chinese and Indian economies? China's contribution to world GDP in 2005 was about a sixth of that of America. Allowing China a little extra because of the undervaluation of the renminbi and other factors, that suggests we should think of it as a 'productive' economy of no more than 100 million people, compared with America's 300 million. In the case of India, which accounts for less than 2 per cent of the world economy, compared with more than 28 per cent for the United States, a generous estimate would be a productive economy of 30–40 million people.

Of course, both countries have the scope to move more people into productive work, though this depends on maintaining or even stepping up the progress of recent years. The key point is that the focus on population is misleading. It is misleading in terms of the competitive threat, as it is when it comes to the size of their markets. When pundits talk about 'one billion consumers' for either China or India, a healthy dose of scepticism is in order. Perhaps the best corrective to population obsession, however, is hard economic numbers. The World Bank's illustrative projections for the contribution of the 'Giants' (China and India) over the period to 2020 are conservative but not necessarily unrealistic. And, while 20 per cent of global growth will come from them, that means 80 per cent will not. 'Over the time horizon we are dealing with, the Giants will not come to dominate the world economy,' the authors write. 'Developments in North America and Western Europe, for example, still will be quantitatively larger.'[5] Let us get excited about China and India but let us also keep our feet on the ground.

3. They will stretch the world's resources

Large populations do have one vital characteristic – they consume resources. Combine large (and growing) populations with rapid rates of economic growth and it is inevitable that China and India's claim on global resources will grow. China now outconsumes the United States in four of the five basic food and industrial commodities: grain, meat, steel and coal – oil being the only exception. In 2005 China consumed nearly 50 per cent more grain than America and nearly twice as much meat. Half of the world's pigs, it seems, are in China; pork, followed by poultry, being the meat of choice. Between them, China and India are responsible for 50 per cent of the world's rice consumption. China is the world's second biggest oil consumer, having overtaken Japan, and has America in its sights. When the biggest energy consumers gathered in Monterrey, Mexico, in October 2006 for a ministerial discussion about global warming, China, the world's second biggest energy user, and India, in fifth place, sat at the top table. China burns a third of the coal the world uses each year and is the biggest consumer, with India in third place.

The impact of China and India on the world commodities' markets is undeniable. Their emergence has provided succour for commodity market bulls who see a rising market stretching for decades ahead. If one side of the China–India effect is an increase in the intensity of global price competition, the other is the boost they have provided to fuel, raw material and, to a lesser extent, food prices. Pity the poor widget-maker in Coventry, Cleveland or Cologne caught between these two powerful forces. The long-run effect of the rise of China and India cannot be considered in isolation. It depends partly on what other countries do, in particular the United States, when it comes to energy consumption. Every 1 per cent reduction in US consumption would offset a rise of 2 per cent in Chinese demand. And, while the China effect has been clear on metals' prices (India to a lesser extent because of its smaller manufacturing sector), as has that of both countries on food prices, the impact on oil is easy to overstate. Between them they account for only 11 per cent of consumption, though that share is growing. And, while 25–30 per cent of the increase in oil consumption in recent years has come from them, that leaves the bulk of the increase coming from the conventional consuming nations.

What happens next? Between 1990 and 2005, China's oil consumption rose by between 7 and 8 per cent a year, while India's increased by 5.5 per cent annually. You can have some innocent fun extrapolating these rates of increase forward, or even by speculating on what might happen if current low levels of oil demand per head (1.7 barrels a year in the case of China, 0.7 for India; a barrel being 159 litres) rise towards Western levels, which in the case of America is around 30 barrels a year. Within half a century China would be using the whole of current world output with none left over for India, let alone the rest of the world. It will not, of course, happen like that. Nor will the breakneck increase in the use, particularly by China, of the world's cement and steel, continue. There will be infrastructure booms in the future but they will not be on the scale of the present one. China may well hand on the baton to India but its infrastructure spending will not come close to China's in ambition and scope. The China–India effect is, however, real enough. Other things being equal, their growth will mean greater pressure on resources, and higher prices, than would otherwise be the case. The Paris-based International Energy Agency (IEA) published medium-term oil market projections in the summer of 2006, partly to assess the impact of the world's new consumers.[6] Although the projections only ran until 2011, they showed that even by then Asia's oil use – just over 28 million barrels a day – would have crept ahead of North America's. They arrived at this figure despite assuming an annual decline in Japanese oil demand and despite factoring in continued growth in North America – 85 per cent of the growth in oil demand among the advanced (OECD) economies coming from the United States, Canada and Mexico. The IEA also predicted that by 2011, thanks significantly to the China–India effect, worldwide oil demand would be growing faster than supply. Something, it seems, will have to give, or high prices and oil shortages will hamper everybody.

4. But they won't destroy the planet

It is a fact of life that, while levels of energy consumption per head are much higher in the rich countries than in emerging economies, rapidly industrialising nations will always be more resource-hungry. For a given increase in economic activity, their energy use will be higher. This so-called energy intensity is higher in poorer, fast-growing economies because they have more heavy industry, use older technology and are less efficient in their use of energy. Richer, service-based economies are big energy users but their economic growth does not require oil, gas and coal to be burned in matching quantities. They also appear to be responsive to price changes. The era of really cheap oil came to an end in 1973, when the Organisation of Petroleum Exporting Countries (OPEC) exerted its market power. Since then the 'energy intensity' of GDP in the rich countries has fallen by about 40 per cent, more in some cases. On the face of it, then, the rise of China and India is bad for the planet. Their growth will require lots of energy, and it will produce lots of carbon emissions. Roughly speaking, every 1 per cent of economic growth in China and India requires an increase of 1 per cent or more in energy use, compared with half or a third of that in America, with Canada the most profligate user of energy relative to growth. The one crumb of comfort, it seems, is that India has not been more successful in developing her industrial sector. If so, the world would have even more of a headache on its hands. The previous chapter told some of the environmental horror stories in both countries and the potential impact of rising energy use on the countries themselves, their neighbours and the wider world.

It is a big issue. On the one hand it is possible to take a 'why bother?' attitude to the effect of China and India on the planet. If these two leviathans are about to spew out vast quantities of carbon for the next fifty years, like the dark Satanic mills of Britain's industrial revolution but on a vast scale, surely efforts to cut emissions in enlightened Western countries are futile? This, in a nutshell, has been the American objection to ratifying the Kyoto Protocol. Any agreement that does not impose emissions reductions on China and India is lopsided and unworkable, so put another log on the fire and fill up the SUV. There is, however, another side to the story. While China and India have not been solely responsible for the rise in global energy prices in recent years – which included an increase in the oil price from just over $10 a barrel in 1998 to nearly $80 in the summer of 2006 – they have clearly contributed to it. High energy prices mean a greater emphasis on efficiency, even where energy use is apparently immune from such factors. US motorists responded by reducing their driving when the price of gasoline hit more than $3 a gallon. More importantly, the rise of China and India has brought greater urgency to the task of containing global carbon emissions. As the scientific warnings have grown louder, so the prospect of meaningful action has increased, including in America, let by states such as California.

It is possible, indeed, to combine growing energy demand in China and India with a drop in global carbon emissions. Price Waterhouse Coopers (PWC) did just this in a set of projections looking forward to 2050 in which global economic growth could average more than 3 per cent a year but carbon emissions decline by a small amount (0.4 per cent) annually.[7] This required what PWC called 'green growth plus carbon capture and storage', the latter involving taking carbon dioxide from power plants and storing it in depleted oil and gas fields, deep underground in rock formations or in the oceans, thereby cutting emissions by up to 90 per cent. The key idea, however, is convergence of energy use – and carbon emissions – between different countries. Thus, America's share of global carbon emissions was seen as declining from 23 per cent in 2005 to 14 per cent by 2050, while China's share rises from 17 to 26 per cent and that of India from just over 4 per cent to just under 12 per cent – and this within an overall reduction in emissions of 17 per cent. Is this remotely feasible? Between 1990 and 2004 US emissions of carbon dioxide increased by nearly a fifth. This is despite the fact that the energy intensity of US growth is declining by about 2 per cent a year, although that is not enough to stabilise either energy consumption or greenhouse-gas emissions. For this trend to be reversed in America, two things have to happen. The political mood has to shift, along the lines of the green agenda being pursued in California by Arnold Schwarzenegger, who in 2006 signed legislation imposing a cap on the state's greenhouse-gas emissions. The second requirement is that America and the other advanced economies become early and aggressive adopters of energy-efficient technology, including carbon capture and storage. 'The richer OECD economies may need to take the lead in developing new technologies and reducing their emissions over the next couple of decades, given that it may not be feasible to expect much faster-growing emerging economies like China and India actually to cut their emission levels, as opposed to controlling their rate of increase, until later in their process of economic development,' PWC concluded its report.[8]

Maybe, however, China and India will also have greener growth than we tend to expect. Lester R. Brown, the noted environmentalist, in his 2006 book *Plan B 2.0*, suggests that China and India have no choice but to opt for environmentally sustainable growth, and could, in doing so, teach the advanced economies a lesson. Applying current US consumption patterns to China and India shows how they have to adopt a different model – he argues. If not, by 2031 China could have 1.1 billion cars, compared with 800 million worldwide now. Or its consumption of paper would be twice current global production. Or its oil demand would exceed present-day global production levels by nearly a fifth. 'The Western economic model – the fossil-fuel-based, automobile-centred, throwaway economy – will not work for China in 2031,' Brown writes.[9] 'If it does not work for China, it will not work for India, which by 2031 is projected to have even more people than China.' The Worldwatch Institute, which Brown founded and chairs, goes even further in its *State of the World Report 2006*. Citing examples where both countries were taking steps to accelerate the development of alternative-energy supplies, including wind power and bio fuels, together with water harvesting (from rainfall), and China's position as world leader in making and installing low-energy light bulbs, it offers an optimistic view. While China and India constitute a global environmental threat, they also offer an opportunity. 'We were encouraged to find that a growing number of opinion leaders in China and India now recognize that the resource-intensive model for economic growth can't work in the 21st century,' says Christopher Flavin, president of the Worldwatch Institute. 'Already, China's world-leading solar industry provides water heating for 35 million buildings, and India's pioneering use of rainwater harvesting brings clean water to tens of thousands of homes. China and India are positioned to leapfrog today's industrial powers and become world leaders in sustainable energy and agriculture within a decade.'[10]

5. They will flex their diplomatic and military muscles

In 2006, in what was seen as a highly symbolic move, the historic Silk Road between China and India was re-opened. The ancient road, or more correctly a series of interconnected routes, extended 8,000 kilometres across Asia to the Middle East and Europe. It brought enormous wealth and variety to the region, some of which was uncovered around 1900 when the so-called Library Cave at Dunhuang was opened, having been sealed nearly 1,000 years earlier. Its artefacts, available to view online thanks to a collaborative project between China and the British Library, provide an insight into the Silk Road's glorious past. That glory had already faded, however, when in 1962, after a territorial dispute led to a short war between China and India (in which China claimed victory), the border crossing through the Himalayan pass of Nathu La was closed, and relations between the two countries remained frosty. Whether the opening of the pass, which meanders through the Himalayas at a height of 4,000 metres, will mean that the Silk Road once more becomes an important trade route is open to doubt, though there is talk of using it to transport iron ore, food products and some industrial goods. Much more than that, however, the opening of the pass cemented what Manmohan Singh, the Indian prime minister, had earlier described as a new 'strategic partnership' between China and

India, who share a border stretching more than 3,000 kilometres. In April 2005 Singh had invited his Chinese counterpart, Wen Jiabao, to New Delhi for talks. At the start of Wen's 4-day visit, during which several agreements were signed, on trade, economic co-operation, civil aviation and technology sharing, Singh declared that a new era was dawning. 'India and China can together reshape the world order,' he said.[11]

A December 2004 report by America's National Intelligence Council looked at the growing economic and political power by 2020 of what it described as the 'arriviste' nations. China and India's emergence could be viewed in a similar way to the uniting of Germany in the nineteenth century and the advent of a powerful United States in the early twentieth century, it argued, and had the potential to 'transform the geopolitical landscape, with impacts potentially as dramatic as those in the previous two centuries'. How would this manifest itself? Firstly, in changes in the international balance of power, at least as it is formally embodied in the membership of the United Nations' Security Council and the Group of 7/8 leading industrial nations. The E (for 'emerging') 7, led by China and India and including Brazil, Russia, Mexico, Indonesia and Turkey, could become as important as the G7. The widening of the membership of the G7/G8 to take in China and India is only a matter of time, as is India's elevation to permanent membership of the UN Security Council. China, of course, has long been a permanent member, often frustrating other countries with its policy of 'non-interference', rarely backing sanctions or other actions against pariah states. The bigger question is whether the current groupings, which reflect economic and geopolitical power as it used to be, will have to be reshaped even more radically.

Secondly, both China and India will want to use their economic clout and try to guarantee that it is sustained. The National Intelligence Council sees China striving for 'great power' status, becoming the dominant political force in east Asia, while also developing into a first-rate military power 'on any measure', with spending second only to America. India's exertion of political power will be different, though perhaps no less important, increasing its leverage though international bodies through the World Trade Organisation, acting as a potential Asian counterweight to China while at the same time co-operating closely with Beijing. Both economies, hungry as they are for resources, will build close, almost colonial relationships with small commodity-producing countries. China has already been hard at work doing so. The great unknown, which is what keeps some people in Washington awake at night, let alone those in Taipei, Tokyo and Islamabad, is how Beijing and New Delhi will use their power. As the National Intelligence Council put it: 'How China and India exercise their growing power, and whether they relate co-operatively or competitively to other powers in the international system, are key uncertainties.'[12]

Transformed though China is in so many respects, some old habits die hard. National power and prestige is still seen through the prism of military might, as when Mao was running things. The difference is that, in the past, China indulged in large-scale defence spending when it could ill-afford to do so, inflicting misery and starvation on the population in order to keep the military wheels turning. Now economic prosperity means it can afford to spend on the latest technology, the official aim, as set out in its 2004 White Paper on defence, being to fight 'local wars' using information technology-based weaponry. The People's Liberation Army, with its permanent force of 2.25 million, is the largest standing army in the world. China never forgets old enmities, and may never forget its enmity with Japan, dating from the invasion of Manchuria in 1931 and the Sino-Japanese War of 1937–45. Japan, reliant on the US military presence for her security, has become increasingly nervous about the Chinese build-up, though this has not altered what many in China see as a lack of remorse in Japan for past war crimes. Every time former prime minister Junichiro Koizumi visited the Yasukuni Shrine, commemorating Japanese war heroes, the tensions increased a notch. One of the first acts of his successor, Shinzo Abe, who took over in September 2006, was to visit Beijing and express contrition for his country's wartime atrocities. An even bigger issue, of course, is Taiwan. What would happen if China pursued by military means the country's official goal of reunifying Taiwan and the mainland? Is the uneasy limbo sustainable in which Taiwan is not formally independent but as far away from reunification as ever? In March 2005, to underline its continuing claims on Taiwan, China passed an anti-secession law to prevent any move towards Taiwanese independence. This flexing of muscles by Beijing backfired, however. The European Union, which had appeared to be on the point of relaxing its embargo on arms sales to China, drew back, retaining the embargo.

In May 1974, barely eighteen months after prime minister Indira Gandhi had given her authorisation for the manufacture of a nuclear device by the Bhabha Atomic Research Centre, India's prototype bomb, nicknamed Smiling Buddha, was exploded in the Thar desert in Rajasthan. India had joined the nuclear club, unofficially and against the wishes of the existing nuclear powers, but fulfilling a 1946 pledge by Jawaharlal Nehru that his country would develop every means possible to defend itself. Nothing much happened after the 1974 test until the late 1980s, when the Indian government became aware of Pakistan's nuclear-weapons programme and Rajiv Gandhi ordered a stepping-up of India's own programme. In May 1998, in a series of tests codenamed Operation Shakti, India successfully tested a number of nuclear devices. 'India is now a nuclear weapons state,' said Atal Behari Vajpayee, the prime minister, on 14 May. 'We have the capacity for a big bomb now. Ours will never be weapons of aggression.'[13] Two weeks later Pakistan successfully tested its nuclear weapons. Despite the fact that she had surreptitiously gained nuclear status, and despite the potential powder keg of India and Pakistan as nuclear states, India has tended to escape serious international censure. Though Pakistan would disagree, partly because of the longstanding dispute over Kashmir, India tends to be everybody's favourite partner, her claims of non-aggression being taken at face value. In March 2006 George W. Bush visited New Delhi and signed a controversial deal to provide India with the technology to develop its nuclear-power programme, at the same time giving it the green light to expand its nuclear-weapons technology. India has never signed the Nuclear Non-proliferation Treaty (NPT). The *Economist* labelled the agreement 'Dr Strangedeal'. 'Aiding India's nuclear weapons programme, as this deal inevitably will, offends the NPT, which bans such help, direct or indirect, to any country not recognised as a nuclear power by the treaty (and India isn't),' it warned.[14] The White House's rationale was straightforward enough; India is a stable democratic partner in a potentially unstable region. But stable partners have proved fickle before. Saddam Hussein's Iraq was once one. If India ever turned aggressive this could be the kind of deal future generations will rue.

6. But they won't start a new Cold War

For many commentators, the rise of China, and to a lesser extent India, will bring back the superpower rivalry that ended with the break-up of the Soviet Union. China, on this view, will pursue not only her national economic interests but also her geopolitical interests, using military means if necessary. 'The Middle East is just a blip,' wrote Robert D. Kaplan in 2005. 'The American military contest with China in the Pacific will define the twenty-first century. And China will be a more formidable adversary than Russia ever was.' China, according to Kaplan, 'constitutes the principal conventional threat to America's liberal imperium'. Its navy will push out into the Pacific, challenging US hegemony, and setting the scene for 'a replay of the decades-long Cold War, with a centre of gravity not in the heart of Europe but, rather, among Pacific atolls that were last in the news when the Marines stormed them in World War II'.[15]

The Pentagon does not use quite such colourful language but its annual reports to Congress on China's military build-up have taken on a more strident tone, reflecting both concern and puzzlement. Washington cannot quite work out what Beijing is up to. Thus its 2006 annual report noted that the People's Liberation Army was 'in the process of long-term transformation from a mass army designed for protracted wars of attrition on its territory to a more modern force capable of fighting short duration, high intensity conflicts against high-tech adversaries'.[16] China had the greatest potential of any country to compete militarily with the United States 'and field disruptive military technologies that could over time offset traditional US military advantages'. Future battles may be, not over ideology, but over scarce resources. Above all, as Donald Rumsfeld, the former US defence secretary put it, why is China so secretive about its intentions? 'Why this growing investment?' he asked plaintively. 'Why these continuing large and expanding arms purchases? Why these continuing robust deployments?'

What would be India's role in any new Cold War? As George W. Bush's March 2006 deal with Manmohan Singh underlined, America sees India on its side if and when tension rises with China, or indeed in Asia more generally. US military strategy towards India has its roots in an October 2002 report, commissioned by the Pentagon, 'The Indo-US Military Relationship: Expectations and Perceptions'. Among the experts it quotes, a US admiral says that both the United States and India regard China as an enemy, 'though we do not discuss this publicly' and, according to another source: 'We want a friend in 2020 that will be capable of assisting the US military to deal with a Chinese threat. We cannot deny that India will create a countervailing force to China.' The role for India's armed forces would, in essence, be to support America. 'The US military seeks a competent military partner that can take on more responsibility for low-end operations in Asia ... which will allow the US military to concentrate its resources on high-end fighting missions,' it said.[17] If that sounds demeaning to India, it is because it is, reflecting a somewhat one-dimensional approach by Washington to foreign policy. One thing is, however, clear. Just as America, China and India seem bound to be the three biggest economic powers in the latter part of the twenty-first century, so their three-way political and military relationship will be a key one. But will it be a Cold War relationship?

If there is one thing that people have learnt about China over the years, it is never to underestimate its leadership's intelligence and adaptability. Nobody observed more closely the Soviet Union's experience during the Cold War and the fact that it emerged from it economically weakened, and forced to pursue a quasi-capitalist model and establish close ties with the West. Having engaged with the world in the economic sphere, which has been the basis of its recent success, China is not going to retreat into isolationism. Nor is China going to risk the stability of a global economy, given its own interdependence with the rest of the world. Soviet Russia had an interest in the collapse of capitalism; China does not. That does not mean China will be a meek partner. Already in dealings with America over issues such as the external value of the renminbi, Beijing has shown itself to be no pushover and has insisted it will do whatever is in its own interests. In this case, however, its interests coincide with those of other countries; a strategy of external engagement. The Chinese government was concerned as any in the West when, in October 2006, North Korea announced its arrival as a nuclear state by testing a weapon at Gilju in the north of the country. Beijing said it was 'resolutely opposed' to North Korea's action. For some, that was a sign that superpower status will carry with it responsibility. Rather than taking on the Soviet Union's mantle of Cold War warrior, in other words, China will adopt a more constructive approach.

'For its part, China will have to take on the global responsibilities commensurate with its size and influence,' wrote the Centre for Strategic and International Studies and the Institute for International Economics.

Beijing can no longer claim that a foreign policy premised on a desperate need for internal development is a purely domestic matter, particularly when it facilitates the violation of international norms by unsavoury regimes. Nor can Beijing fall back on a 'developing world' self-image to deny its own impact on international affairs. The policies and actions of a rapidly developing and globally integrated nation of 1.3 billion people necessarily will affect the management of a peaceful and stable global system. As China rises, Beijing will need to acknowledge this fact and start action in ways that reinforce international norms and that reflect a broader and more long-term concept of China's self-interest – becoming what US Deputy Secretary of State Robert Zoellick calls a 'responsible stakeholder'.[18]

Things change, and so do regimes. There is no guarantee that Beijing will continue to be as outward-looking as it is now. But crude comparisons between China and Soviet Russia seem misplaced, as does the idea that world domination is the not-so-secret Chinese plan. The military build-up may look sinister to the outside world, but it is not that surprising. Possessing military power, mainly for defensive reasons, may be enough. As Hugh Baker, emeritus professor at the School of Oriental and Africa Studies in London, put it, quoting an old Chinese saying: 'The gentleman does not fight. Were he to do so, he would win.'[19]

7. They will provide huge market opportunities

On a visit to Beijing, I was staying in a hotel attached to a new shopping mall whose stores were occupied by most of the world's luxury brands. Prada, Gucci, Armani and Ferragamo, among many others, offered their wares at prices that looked far too high for the hotel's international guests, let along the locals. But people were buying – not in huge quantities, but they were buying – and the shoppers were almost exclusively Chinese. Visitors tend to head for places like the city's 'Silk Alley' (actually Silk Street), where branded goods can be bought at lower than Western prices. Notices all around claim that these are most definitely not counterfeit items, though many international businesses suspect that – if not in Silk Street – they are prey to the so-called 'third shift' problem, where a factory producing branded goods for global companies has a third production shift, the products of which go out of the back door, destined for local markets. But for some of China's new consumers, at least, prestige matters.

Perhaps we should not be so surprised. China already has an estimated 300,000 dollar millionaires and the number is growing by about 50,000 a year. The *Hurun Report*,[20] a business magazine, publishes an annual China rich list of 500 people, the qualification for which in 2006 was individual wealth of $95 million or more. Top of the list, with wealth of $3.4 billion, was a woman, 49-year old Zhang Yin, propelled there thanks to the Hong Kong stock market listing of her company, Nine Dragons Paper. For somebody who had lived through China's past economic travails, this must have seemed like winning a hundred lotteries at once. She and her Taiwanese-born husband Liu Mingzhong had set up their business as recently as 1990, importing scrap paper from America, recycling it at the company's paper mills in Guangdong and Jiangsu and selling it on in China, mainly to retailers. Her 72 per cent stake in Nine Dragons Paper made her the richest self-made woman in the world, beating Oprah Winfrey and J. K. Rowling. In second place was Huang Guangyu, who had also made much of his money in Guangdong, China's first capitalist frontier, and who was worth $2.5 billion on the back of his GoMe business, in electronics goods retailing and real estate. A measure of China's rapidly rising wealth was that in 1999 the 50th richest person on *Hurun Report*'s rich list was worth $6 million, but by 2006 the 50th richest individual had wealth of $525 million.

A country's prosperity is not, of course, measured by the number of its super-rich. The number of dollar millionaires is rising sharply in China, but the chances of being one are roughly the same as being struck by lightning; 300,000 represents a mere 0.02 per cent of China's 1.3 billion population. China's promise of 'one billion consumers' has lured unwary businesses before, only to disappoint. This time, however, it is for real. China's newly prosperous middle classes account for 12 per cent of global luxury goods sales, third only to America and Japan. Analysts project that by 2015 nearly a third of the world's luxury goods will be sold in China, with only America ahead. Conspicuous consumption is on the rise. During 2005 Bentley sold two of its Mulliner 728 cars in China. That does not sound much, but they retail at the equivalent of more than $1 million a time in China and this was more than the company, part of Volkswagen, sold in any other market. In 2005 BMW sold nearly 25,000 cars in China. In time, China will be the biggest market for consumer products in the world. The Chinese Academy of Social Sciences estimated that in 2003 nearly a fifth of the population was middle class – more than 250 million – with that proportion growing each year. There will be economic setbacks, as discussed below, but they will not prevent China's consumer markets from growing.

Exports from China receive most of the attention, and most of the criticism, particularly in America. But imports into China have also grown strongly – by between 20 and 30 per cent annually in recent years – and will continue to do so. Between 1995 and 2005 America's exports nearly quadrupled. China is not just hungry for resources to turn into manufactured goods and sell back to the rest of the world. It is hungry for capital goods, medical equipment, sophisticated electronic products, aircraft – it is already a huge market for Boeing and Airbus – and just about anything else. China will be the world's fastest-growing large market for the foreseeable future, rapidly ticking off the records as it expands: biggest market for personal computers in 2006, broadband internet users in 2007; and so on. Through sheer weight of population and its openness to foreign trade, China will for decades be the place to be.

India is also a fast-growing market, with many of the same features as China: a rapidly-growing middle class; an expanding élite of the super-rich; and so on. Sometimes it seems that it does not matter which economic system you have, the result is the same. Rapid growth, and sudden increases in prosperity, will bring with it increasing consumption but also sharply higher levels of inequality. India has its own rich list, largely consisting of the country's business élite. Thus, in 2006 Mukesh Ambani, Reliance Industries' chairman and managing director, was worth an estimated 70,000 crore rupees. Since a crore is 10 million, this means he was worth 700 billion rupees, or roughly $15.5 billion – nearly five times as wealthy as Zhang Yin in China. Close behind him was Azim Premji, chairman of Wipro, worth more than $14 billion. India, because of its better-developed capital markets, can outgun China when it comes to the very wealthy but its middle class is, on reasonable measures, much smaller than China's, probably 40 million households. Scaling that up for size of family, India probably had between half and two-thirds of the number of middle-class people as China in 2006. Both countries will be fast-growing markets in the coming years, but a bit of perspective is useful. China imports five times as much as India; $660 billion versus $132 billion in 2005. Even allowing for China's greater appetite for commodities and fuel, this is a huge difference. China's exports, taking goods and services together, are more than five times those of India. The difference between the two, in openness to trade, is stark. As far as exporters are concerned, the Indian market is so far a mere echo of China's. The differences between consumer spending in the two countries are not so pronounced; the Chinese market is roughly twice the size of India. In some respects India has now reached the point China got to in the early 1990s, when future growth required the economy to be opened up, and that is now happening, including in areas like retailing. It will, however, take time.

8. But they will remain relatively poor

Abject poverty is much more obvious on the streets of India's cities than it is in China, and India remains more obviously a poor country. On the face of it, however, both are poor countries. On the measure used by the World Bank and other international bodies, China's Gross National Income (GNI) *per capita* is just $1,740, while India's is much lower, at a mere $720. Think about that for a second. India's *average* income is less than two dollars a day, which, given that it has quite a few billionaires and a growing middle class, means that it also has plenty of very poor people. China does better, but its average comes out at less than five dollars a day. To put this in perspective, GNI *per capita* in the world's richest country, Luxembourg, is nearly $66,000. In America it is nearly $44,000; in Britain $37,600. Britons and Americans are between twenty and twenty-five times better off than the average Chinese person, and in the case of India the comparisons are stark to the point of being embarrassing. Indians are, on average, less than half as well off as Chinese people. Britons and Americans are between fifty and sixty times as well off as Indians. No wonder, you might say, they can undercut with their low labour costs; they are paid a pittance. To put China and India's positions in perspective, they ranked 128th and 159th respectively in the World Bank's league table for *per capita* GNI. Tongans are better off, on average, than Chinese people, while the inhabitants of the Côte d'Ivoire, it seems, enjoy a better living standard than Indians. Can the world's two coming economic superpowers really be that poor?

The answer is probably not. It costs a lot more to live in Manhattan than Mumbai, or in Birmingham than Beijing. Adjusting for purchasing-power parity comparisons, China's GNI *per capita* was $6,600 in 2005, 107th in the world. That was just under a sixth of the United States ($42,000) and about a fifth of the UK ($32,700). It feels closer to the actual difference in living standards. While China has huge numbers of poor people the visitor never sees, the raw statistical comparison overstates its poverty levels. Adjusting in a similar way for India does not change the relative picture much in relation to China; Indian *per capita* GNI becomes $3,460 and is thus roughly half the Chinese level. India is also well down the global league table, in 144th place. But on this basis, Americans enjoy income levels twelve times those of Indians and Britons are nine times as well off. This feels, as in the case of China, closer to reality, again without diminishing the very real poverty experienced daily by hundreds of millions of Indians.

The central point is that, even after nearly three decades of rapid economic growth, growth that cannot be reasonably expected to continue at this rate (9–10 per cent), China is still relatively poor, measured by the country's average living standards. India's modern-era rise came later and it is even poorer. For all the talk of billionaires, millionaires and expanding middle classes, neither yet makes it into the world's top hundred in terms of average living standards, however measured. That will change, but it will not change as much as people may think. Even if everything goes pretty much right for China and India, and they grow to become the first and third largest economies in the world (with America second) by the middle of the century – or even the top two economies – their citizens will be a long way from being rich. Goldman Sachs, in its projections for the BRICs economies, factored in not only relatively rapid growth for China and India but also significant rises in their currencies.[21] Currency appreciation, which on its own will serve to close the GDP gap between countries, is a normal by-product of economic development. It has been a huge bone of contention between Beijing and Washington that the value of the renminbi has been held below what most economists would regard as a fair value. Over the long term, however, Goldman Sachs assumes that this particular dam will break, and that both the renminbi and the rupee will rise by nearly 300 per cent by 2050. On that basis, and on the basis of all the other assumptions about growth, investment and demographics, China will have a *per capita* national income of $31,400 by 2050 (in 2003 prices), with India around two-thirds of that level. China in 2050 will, on that basis, enjoy living standards somewhat lower than the UK in 2005, and only about two-thirds of current American levels. Other economies will not, of course, stand still while China and India are developing.

Factoring in growth in the advanced countries produces the result that China's *per capita* national income in 2050 will be under 40 per cent of US levels and about half of the UK. Indians, who by the middle of the century will not have barely closed the income gap with the Chinese, will be even further behind.[22]

The observation that Chinese and Indian living standards will be below Western levels until the middle of the century and beyond – and may never catch up – does not detract from the fact that these will still be very big and important economies. We do not think of Luxembourg or Bermuda as big beasts in the global economic jungle just because their *per capita* incomes are high; the reverse is true of China and India. Even the improvements in prosperity in prospect will offer enormous market opportunities and lead to worries about the capacity of the world's resources to cope. It does, however, point up two key messages. One is that, for all the worries about China and India taking over the world, Westerners will be better off than the people of these countries for the foreseeable future. The other message, perhaps less reassuring, is that the threat from these economies is not going to go away. They will continue to have a big advantage in terms of lower labour costs.

9. They will hit turbulence and trigger protectionism

The fact the competitive threat to the West will persist (alongside the huge market opportunities both countries will offer) is one reason for thinking it will not all be plain sailing for China and India. Their economic success is the product of an open global economy; China even more than India. How big is the risk to that success from a closing-down of the world economy? The present era of globalisation is often regarded as irreversible, but it is not. Protectionism is already chipping away at it. In the case of China, the European Union has imposed restrictions on imports of clothing and shoes, under anti-dumping rules intended to protect EU manufacturers (particularly in Italy) against unfair competition. Europe also complains that it is unable to gain unrestricted access to China's markets. In the US Congress, where protectionism is never far below the surface, there has been hostility to the takeover by Chinese state-owned enterprises of America's corporate assets. There was, as described earlier, opposition to Lenovo's acquisition of IBM's personal computer division, and even more to the proposed takeover in June 2005 by CNOOC, the

Chinese oil company, of Unocal of California – objections that had the effect of scuppering the deal. After the CNOOC deal collapsed, in addition, there was a backlash in Beijing, with the authorities using the episode to take a harder-nosed attitude to foreign investment, particularly that involving the acquisition of stakes in Chinese businesses. In the case of trade, Congress has mainly focused on trying to punish China for her 'unfair manipulation' of the currency. A bill sponsored by two senators, Charles Schumer (Democrat) and Lindsey Graham (Republican), postulated that the renminbi was undervalued by between 15 and 40 per cent and proposed a 27.5 per cent tariff (halfway between 15 and 40) on all US imports from China in return.

In India's case the protectionist threat is less direct. The high water-mark for the backlash against outsourcing to India appears to have been in 2004, when Democrat John Kerry targeted US firms who were moving jobs offshore during the presidential election campaign. By March 2006, *Newsweek* was able to report that the outsourcing backlash was overdone: 'What happened to the outsourcing backlash? It has been muted by the fact that India didn't suck Silicon Valley dry after all. Actually, US tech employment is growing. There are 17 per cent more tech workers in the United States today than back in the bubble days of 1999, says a new study by the Association for Computing Machinery. And the Bureau of Labor Statistics predicts that the US economy will add 1 million tech jobs over the next decade, a 30 per cent increase.'[23] The backlash has not disappeared entirely. Ségolène Royal, the French Socialist presidential hopeful for the 2007 election, pledged to take action against what she described as 'wildcat outsourcing'.[24] A bigger immediate worry for India, perhaps, are the straws in the wind that suggest that not only has the backlash been overdone but so perhaps has the potential growth of outsourcing. Estimates by TPI, an outsourcing consultancy, suggested that 2006 would see the first drop in outsourcing contracts since the market began to grow in the 1990s. The market, it claimed, was maturing and the big expansion may have already occurred.

China and India both benefit from open markets, given their competitive advantage. It is not, however, all one-way traffic. When he visited China in September 2006, Henry Paulson, the US treasury secretary, said he was concerned about rising protectionist sentiment there. Paulson's visit came after a series of moves by the Chinese government to restrict foreign investment in real estate, limit the acquisition of stakes in Chinese companies and control the operations of foreign news agencies such as Reuters, Dow Jones and Bloomberg in favour of Xinhua, the official news agency. Beijing said it was also examining sectors where local Chinese companies were subject to 'unfair' competition. Long-standing international complaints persist that the Chinese authorities have failed to clamp down on a particular type of unfair competition: counterfeiting of foreign products and illegal copying of software and entertainment. China insists it is committed to protecting intellectual property rights under World Trade Organisation rules, but many international firms are unconvinced.

The protection of intellectual property rights is also a big problem in India. The Bollywood film industry is a victim, but so too is Hollywood. Everything from car parts to medicines is faked in India. More serious is the lack of genuine trade liberalisation in many areas. India has come a long way from the closed economy of the early 1990s, when the average tariff was an astonishingly high 200 per cent. By 2005–6 it had dropped to 15 per cent for non-agricultural goods, though was still high, at between 30 and 40 per cent, for farm products. More serious are India's famous non-tariff barriers, including a stultifying bureaucracy that drives away many potential exports to India, together with the capricious use of standards – some of which vary on a state by state basis – to discriminate against foreign products. Cars imported into India still attracted a tariff of more than 100 per cent in 2006. Imports of second-hand cars are not permitted. The Indian government has also been slow to allow foreign firms into certain sectors, including retailing.

Trade wars offer one potential threat to the rise of China and India but there are others, most notably the inevitability of significant economic setbacks. Since the early 1990s neither economy has experienced a serious downturn, sailing virtually unscathed through the Asian financial crisis of 1997–8. Long runs of economic growth like this become addictive, to the point where a recession or even a period of subdued activity would be painful, the economic equivalent of cold turkey. The trigger could be a US-led global recession, or some other factor such as worldwide energy shortages. In both economies people's expectations of continually rising prosperity are high. In both, political discontent is never far below the surface. The tens of thousands of popular protests that take place in China each year are testimony to this, even during a remarkable period of economic success. Those protests could explode in a time of sharply rising unemployment. In India, there are plenty of people who have never really believed in the country's reform-led economic miracle, and would be quick to say 'I told you so'. Politically and economically, a huge test will be the ability of the Chinese regime and the Indian government to ride through a period of austerity. Boom does not have to be followed by bust but the Chinese and Indian booms will not be uninterrupted.

10. But they don't change the rules of globalisation …

Finally, should the rest of the world respond differently to China and India? Do those businessmen worried about whether they will ever be able to compete again have a point? Should bluecollar workers in steel towns unite with their whitecollar counterparts in call centres and rise up against the threat? The idea that what we are seeing from China and India is different from anything that has gone before in terms of scale is correct. What often goes with it, however, is the belief that the response should also be different. Not only are they big, and with huge cost advantages, but they are also breaking the normal rules of economic development. With the connivance of multinational companies they are gaining technology and methods that their predecessors could only have dreamt of. Not for China and India a future of being permanently left in the technology slow lane. Not for China and India a path of gradual progress, starting at the very bottom of the value chain and moving only gently up it. That would pose little threat to the rest of the world. The speed with which they are catching up has been rapid, however, reinforced by high levels of foreign direct investment, so far more into China than India. Every business is affected by their rise, and potentially every worker.

… for the poor …

How should the rest of the world respond? There are two distinct issues. The first is whether the rise of China and India has the effect of holding back poor countries. The second is whether they will end up impoverishing the world's richer nations. The effect of these two big economies on other poor countries has been mixed. In the case of Africa, which usually qualifies as the continent that globalisation left behind, China's gargantuan demand for resources, with India's only a few paces behind, has provided a significant boost. In 2005 sub-Saharan Africa enjoyed its strongest economic growth for three decades, largely on the back of rising commodity prices. On the other hand, competition in manufacturing from China and in the service sector from India risks leaving poorer African countries stuck as primary producers. In some cases the effect has been to reverse the development process, by rendering local manufacturing no longer viable. It is a big issue. Raphie Kaplinsky, in his 2005 book *Globalization, Poverty and Inequality*, notes that China and India (together with Brazil and Indonesia) differ from other developing economies in that they have sufficiently large domestic markets to be able to exploit the economies of scope and scale required for modern production systems.[25] Most other developing countries face an uncomfortable Catch 22. They are reliant on export markets to be able to drive production costs down, but it is in those very markets that they are likely to be undercut by the likes of China. The final insult is when China claims their local markets, too. Kaplinsky also notes, however, that the effect varies according to region. China's rise as a manufacturing nation has helped, not hindered, other east Asian economies. Production chains are spread across the region, with other countries often supplying the technological components that are put together by Chinese workers. India has been a more self-contained economy, but similar regional effects are occurring. Trade between China and India, for example, is growing rapidly (India is a beneficiary of China's resource demand, exporting large quantities of iron ore).

It is elsewhere in the world, notably sub-Saharan Africa and Latin America and the Caribbean, where it is hard to detect any beneficial effects of China and India's rise beyond demand for resources. If there is a 'resource curse', current patterns of globalisation are exacerbating it. It is important, however, to locate this problem where it properly belongs. Weak economic growth in Africa and Latin America, characterised by stagnant or falling *per capita* incomes, dates back to the early 1980s, when China was just emerging blinking into the sunlight and when the true 'China effect' was years away. India is similarly blameless for the problems dating back to that period. The relatively poor performance of these regions pre-dates the rise of China and India and should not be attributed to them. If poor countries need special protection against global economic forces, they should have had it to cope with the threat to their domestic markets – and the constraint on their export activity – from Europe, America, Japan and the Asian tigers. There is some evidence, indeed, that

China and India's growth will be more developing-country-friendly than that of the advanced countries. If there is a problem, the solutions are familiar ones – most particularly re-designing the international trading system so that it is fairer to poor countries. The struggle to conclude the Doha trade round did not, however, offer much encouragement in this area. Poor countries can also learn from the way China and India pursued their economic development, which in neither case followed the 'one size fits all' Washington consensus model.

... or for the rich

What about rich countries? Fear of China and India is widespread. They are lean, hungry and highly competitive, the argument goes, while the West is flabby and complacent. They will undercut us, condemning our workers to lower pay. But pay in the West can never go low enough to make up for the competitive disadvantage that the existing industrial countries face. The best they can hope to do is slow the pace of relative decline, perhaps by putting up trade barriers. Can this be right? There are certainly some gloomy prognoses around. Clyde V. Prestowitz, a former US trade negotiator and now president of the Economic Strategy Institute, is author of *Three Billion New Capitalists: The Great Shift of Wealth and Power to the East (2006)*. The problem with the way globalisation is developing, he argues, is that it is lopsided. On one side is America, with its debt-driven, consumption-based economic growth and a trade deficit of $800 billion, or 7 per cent of gross domestic product. On the other are the Asian economies, with their focus on export-led growth, which are 'characterized by relatively low consumption, saving rates of 30 to 50 per cent of GDP, government intervention in markets, managed exchange rates, promotion of investment in "strategic" industries, incentives for exports and accumulation of chronic trade surpluses along with large reserves of dollars'.[26] Prestowitz's criticism is partly directed at the rich countries, particularly America, for their 'cavalier' embracing of free trade, coupled with the absence of industrial policies to maintain competitiveness in the light of this onslaught from the East. The trade deficit, America's low saving rate, dwindling investment in scientific training and research and the risk of an 'economic 9/11' as America's foreign creditors cash in their dollar chips are all, to him, signs that global economic leadership is being handed over to China and India without a fight. For him, the current model of globalisation, with the United States as consumer allowing China and India to build their economies, even as the supply-side base of America and other industrial countries is transferred to them, is not sustainable. China and India's entry, together with the economic complacency of the rich countries, has turned globalisation from being a 'win–win' combination into something that threatens real damage.

If that is at one end of the spectrum – though, to be fair to Prestowitz, there are many who would be even more critical – there are plenty of people at the other. William Overholt of the Rand Center for Asian Pacific Policy, argues powerfully that the transformation of China from being an opponent of globalisation and a disrupter of its institutions to being a fully paid-up member of the club, is one of the most positive developments to have affected the world economy for generations. China could have been a reluctant globaliser, as Japan was until relatively recently. Instead Beijing has embraced the global economy enthusiastically and, in doing so, has established a template for others. Where did India look to for economic development until great changes were forced on its government in 1991? Indian politicians used to believe that a closed economy and the limited gains from import substitution were the way forward. China showed India the way, and is still doing so, and is showing other countries the way, too. But, as Overholt points out, the process has been far from painless in China, involving a thoroughgoing restructuring of the economy, large-scale job losses and plenty of misery. China and India have provided global growth, are offering significant market opportunities and, crucially, have allowed Western economies to expand at a faster rate than would otherwise have been the case. Critics of globalisation in the China–India era tend to ignore the China effect on manufacturing prices and the (smaller) India effect on prices in the service sector. They have resulted in lower inflation, lower interest rates and the most benign set of global economic conditions since the post-war golden age of the 1950s and 1960s. In short, the fact that China and India have opted into the global economy should be celebrated, not feared. As Overholt puts it:

> China's success is one of the most important developments of modern history, but projecting from current growth to Chinese global dominance or threats to our way of life, is just wrong. Unlike the old Soviet Union, reformist China does not seek to alter any other country's way of life.

Its economy faces world history's most severe combination of banking, urbanization and employment challenges and by 2020 a demographic squeeze that will have few workers supporting many dependents. The best outcome for us would be a China that is eventually like Japan, prosperous, winning in some sectors, losing in others. Signs that China is making rapid progress in that direction should be welcomed, not feared.[27]

Much the same goes for India, though with even less need for reassurance that New Delhi is not aiming for global dominance. The world economy has been through a period of excessive reliance on America, one consequence being the gaping US trade deficit. If, as is likely, America will need a period of slower growth to cure her imbalances, we will come to be grateful for the growth momentum provided by China and India.

In the end, as British economic journalist Martin Wolf argued persuasively in his 2004 book *Why Globalization Works*, we are back to a very old argument.[28] Each wave of globalisation brings a re-run of the 'pauper labour' fear. How can we ever compete with these low-paid workers? Won't all our jobs disappear overseas? These debates, it should be said, are being conducted at a time when employment is at or close to record levels in Britain and America and not far below it in other countries. The answer, of course, is that low-cost advantages do not last for ever. China has low wages because it also has low productivity. As productivity rises, so will wages. The same goes for India. While businesses who have outsourced activities to the subcontinent sometimes claim that productivity levels are as high there as at home, the numbers belie such claims. Were it true, the cost savings from outsourcing would be much bigger than they are. China and India fears are essentially fears based on a static analysis. How many jobs will be left in Britain, America, France or Germany if China and India retain their cost advantages while raising productivity? The appropriate way to look at it, however, is dynamically. Rising efficiency and productivity in China will not make her economy, as Wolf puts it, 'invincibly competitive' because wages will rise as well. The size of China and India's pools of labour makes us worried. We have, however, seen it all before, if not quite on this scale. Aneurin 'Nye' Bevan, the Welsh politician, famously said: 'Why look in the crystal ball when you can read the book?' China, and to a lesser extent India, frighten us with their size, their teeming masses of people. But they are just Japan, Taiwan and South

Korea in another guise. Bigger, yes, but similar. The book, the history, tells us that the world is remarkably good at absorbing new arrivals on the global economic scene and benefiting from their presence. China and India, in this respect at least, really are no different.

That is as good a message as any on which to end this book. The rise of China and India is fascinating, uplifting and, to some, very worrying. It is, at one and the same time, the biggest thing to hit the global economy and the most effective anti-poverty programme the world has ever seen. China and India are changing the way we live, and will continue to do so. Their rise changes the balance of global economic and political power. That is more than a little frightening. We look in wonderment at their enormous populations and we wonder what will happen when they live like us (to which part of the answer is that we have to change the way we live). What every business and every individual should be most worried about, however, is that their rise elicits the wrong response. The wrong thing to do would be to give in to populist fears and put up the shutters. And to say this is not to espouse any kind of ultra-conservative free-market view. Expectations have been raised among the people of China and India. Their prosperity has come from engaging with the rest of the world. There will be trade frictions and there will be protectionism, but to try and deny China and India their rightful place in the global economy – a place that looked secure two centuries ago – would be a huge betrayal.

Notes

Chapter One: The Return of History

1 Maddison, Angus (2001), *The World Economy: A Millennial Perspective*, OECD, Paris.

2 Kenoyer, Jonathan Mark (1996), 'Around the Indus in 90 Slides', www.harappa.com.

3 Robb, Peter (2005), *A History of India*, Palgrave, London, p. 27.

4 Lal, Deepak (1998), *Unintended Consequences*, MIT Press, Cambridge, Mass., p. 28.

5 Von Glahn, Richard (2005), in *China, Reference Classics*, edited by Edward L. Shaughnessy, Duncan Baird Publishers, London, p. 68.

6 Roberts, J. A. G. (1999), *A History of China*, Palgrave, London, p.10.

7 Lal (1998), pp. 34–5.

8 Desai, Meghnad (2003), 'India and China, An Essay in Comparative Political Economy', paper for IMF Conference on India/China, Delhi, April 2003.

9 Golas, Peter (2005), in *China, Reference Classics*, ed., Shaughnessy, p. 166.

10 Lal (1998) p. 39.

11 Boserup, Ester (1965), *The Conditions of Agricultural Growth*, George Allen & Unwin, London.

12 Lal (1998), p. 40.

13 Landes, David (1998), *The Wealth and Poverty of Nations*, Little, Brown, London, p. 55.

14 Landes (1998), p. 50.

15 Maddison (2001), p. 24.

16 Elvin, M. (1973), *The Pattern of the Chinese Past*, Stanford University Press, Stanford, pp. 223–4.

17 Balazs, Etienne (1968), *La Bureaucratic céleste: recherches sur l'économie et la société de la Chine traditionnelle*, Gallimard, Paris, pp. 22–3.

18 Rothermund, Dietmar (1993), *An Economic History of India: From Pre-Colonial Times to 1991*, Routledge, New York, p. 2.

19 Robb (2005), p. 49.

20 Rothermund (1993), p. 5.

21 Smith, Adam (1776), *An Inquiry into the Nature and Causes of the Wealth of Nations*, book 1, chapter 3, Methuen, London.

22 Smith (1776), book 1, chapter 3.

23 Sen, Amartya (2001), 'History and the Enterprise of Knowledge', address to the Millennium Session of the Indian History Congress, Kolkata.

24 Desai (2003).

25 Studwell, Joe (2005), *The China Dream*, third edition, Profile Books, London, p. 10.

26 Roberts (1999), pp.188–9.

27 Roberts (1999), p.193.

28 Studwell (2005), p. 21.

29 Litvin, Daniel (2003), *Empires of Profit*, Texere, New York, p. 12.

30 Litvin (2003), p. 11.

31 Das, Gurcharan (2002), *India Unbound: From Independence to the Global Information Age*, Profile Books, London, p. 66.

32 Marx, Karl (1853), 'The British Rule in India', *New York Herald Tribune*, 25 June 1853.

33 Das (2002), pp. 66–7.

34 Landes (1998), p. 228.

35 Lal (1998), p. 35.

36 Clinginsmith, David, and Williamson, Jeffrey G. (2004), 'India's De-industrialization under British Rule: New Ideas, New Evidence', NBER working paper no. 10586, June 2004.

37 Singh, Manmohan (2005), Oxford University acceptance address, July 2005.

38 Desai (2003).

Chapter Two: Enter the Dragon

1 McGinty, Stephen (2006), 'Charles and the Appalling Old Waxworks of China …', *Scotsman*, 23 February 2006.
2 McGeary, Johanna (1998), 'The China Summit: How Bad is China?', *Time*, New York, 29 June 1998.
3 McGeary (1998).
4 Alexander, Garth (1993) 'Milton vs. Barton: China; The New Experts Fall Out,' *Sunday Times*, London, 7 November 1993.
5 Alexander (1993).
6 Krueger, Anne (2005), 'China and the Global Economic Recovery', speech to the American Enterprise Institute, 10 January 2005, International Monetary Fund, Washington, DC.
7 Woodall, Pam (2005), 'From T-shirts to T-bonds', *Economist*, London, 28 July 2005.
8 *Business Week* (2004), 'Special Report – The China Price', 6 December 2004.
9 Freeman, Richard (2005), 'China, India and the Doubling of the Global Labour Force', *Globalist*, 3 June 2005.
10 Chang, Jung and Halliday, Jon (2005), *Mao, The Unknown Story*, Jonathan Cape, London, p. 337.
11 www.ebeijing.gov.cn (2006), 'Introduction to Chinese Agriculture'.
12 Wu, Jinglian (2005), 'Understanding and Interpreting Chinese Economic Reform', Thomson Higher Education, Mason, Ohio, p. 38.
13 Chang (2005), p. 451.
14 Roberts, J. A. G. (1999), *A History of China*, Palgrave Macmillan, London, p. 273.
15 Wu (2005), p. 53.
16 Chang (2005), p. 541.
17 Wu (2005), p. 58.
18 *CNN.com* (1997), 19 February 1997.
19 *Washington Post* (1997), 'China's Deng Xiaoping is Dead at 92', 20 February 1997.
20 International Committee of the Fourth International (1997), 'Deng Xiaoping and the Fate of the Chinese Revolution', 12 March 1997, www.wsws.org.
21 *CNN.com* (1997).

22 Crowell, Todd, and Polin, Thomas Hon Wing (1999), 'Deng Xiaoping, Asian of the Century', www.asiaweek.com.

23 Xinhua News Agency (2006), 'China to Spend 14 Per Cent More in Building "New Countryside",' http://english.gov.cn.

24 *People's Daily* (1992), 'Records of Comrade Deng Xiaoping's Shenzhen Tour', http://english.people.com.cn.

25 Quoted in Wu (2005).

26 Crowell and Polin (1999).

27 OECD (2005), 'China Overtakes US as World's Leading Exporter of Information Technology Goods', 12 December 2005, www.oecd.org.

28 Hornblower, Sam (2004), 'Wal-Mart and China: A Joint Venture', 23 November 2004, www.pbs.org.

29 Hornblower (2004).

Chapter Three: India Rising

1 Zakaria, Fareed (2006), 'India Rising – Special Report', *Newsweek*, 6 March 2006.

2 Wharton Knowledge Network (2006), 'Delhi in Davos: How India Built Its Brand at the World Economic Forum', http://knowledge. wharton.upenn.edu/article/1394.cfm.

3 Bajpai, Nirupam (1996), 'Economic Crisis, Structural Reforms and the Prospects of Growth in India', development discussion paper no. 530, Harvard Institute for International Development, Harvard University, May 1996.

4 Cerra, Valerie, and Saxena, Sweta Chaman (2002), 'What Caused the 1991 Currency Crisis in India?', IMF staff papers, vol. 49, no. 3, Washington, DC.

5 Bajpai (1996).

6 *Time* (1955), 'Five-Year Plan', 17 October 1955.

7 Varadarajan, Tunku (2001), 'Why the Subcontinent is Subpar', *Wall Street Journal*, 19 March 2001.

8 Das, Gurcharan (2002), *India Unbound*, Profile Books, London, pp. 98–9.

9 Thakurta, Paranjoy Guha (2004), 'Bombay Plan and Mixed-up Economy', *Hindu Business Line*, 7 September 2004.

10 Roy, Subroto (ed.) (1998), 'Milton Friedman on the Nehru/ Mahalanobis Plan, (February 15, 1956)', India Policy Institute.

11 Bauer, Peter (1998), 'B. R. Shenoy: Stature and Impact', *Cato Journal*, vol. 18, no. 1 (spring/summer 1998), New York.

12 Virmani, Arvind (2004), 'India's Economic Growth: From Socialist Rate of Growth to Bharatiya Rate of Growth', working paper no. 122, Indian Council for Research on International Economic Relations, February 2004.

13 Bhagwati, Jagdish (2005), 'India, Japan and Asia', www.ide.go.jp.

14 Tully, Mark (2002), *India in Slow Motion*, Viking, London, p. xvi.

15 Tully (2002), p. 296.

16 Tully (2002), p. 297.

17 WEF (2005), 'Global Competitiveness Report 2005', www.weforum. org.

18 Mukherji, Joydeep (2006), 'Economic Growth and India's Future', occasional paper no. 26, March 2006, Center for the Advanced Study of India, University of Pennsylvania.

19 DeLong, J. Bradford (2001), 'India since Independence: An Analytical Growth Narrative', www.j-bradford-delong.net.

20 Virmani (2004).

21 Rodrik, Dani, and Subramanian, Arvind (2005), 'From "Hindu Growth" to Productivity Surge: The Mystery of the Indian Growth Transition', IMF staff papers, vol. 52, no. 2, International Monetary Fund, Washington, DC.

22 Virmani (2004).

23 DeLong (2001).

24 Das (2002), p.199.

25 DeLong (2001).

26 Srinivasan, T. N. (2004), 'Comments on Dani Rodrik and Arvind Subramanian, "From 'Hindu Growth' to Productivity Surge: The Mystery of the Indian Growth Transition"', www.imf.org.

27 Panagariya, Arvind (2005), 'The Triumph of India's Market Reforms: The Record of the 1980s and 1990s', policy analysis, 7 November 2005, www.cato.org.

28 Commanding Heights (2001), interview with Manmohan Singh, conducted 2 June 2001, www.pbs.org.

29 Quoted in David P. Arulanantham (2004), 'The Paradox of the BJP's Stance towards External Economic Liberalisation: Why a Hindu

Nationalist Party Furthered Globalisation in India', Asia Programme working paper, December 2004, Chatham House, London.

30 Arulanantham (2004).

31 *Guardian* (2004), 'India's Rulers Concede Defeat', Associated Press, 13 May 2004, carried in the *Guardian*, London.

32 Das (2002), p. 224.

33 Ahluwalia, Montek S. (2002), 'Economic Reforms in India since 1991: Has Gradualism Worked?' *Journal of Economic Perspectives*, summer 2002.

Chapter Four: China Roars, the World Listens

1 Tyson, Laura D'Andrea (2001), 'China: Under the Glare of the Olympic Torch', *Business Week*, 13 August 2001.

2 Jan, Reena (2005), 'China's New Architectural Wonders', *Business Week*, 23 December 2005.

3 Sudjic, Deyan (2005), 'The City that Ate the World', *Observer*, 16 October 2005.

4 Sudjic (2005).

5 O'Neill, Jim (2001), 'Building Better Global Economic BRICs', republished in *The World and the BRICs Dream*, Goldman Sachs, New York and London, 2006, p.14.

6 Goldman Sachs (2005), 'China's Ascent: Can the Middle Kingdom Meet Its Dreams?', 21 November 2005, Goldman Sachs, New York and London.

7 Wilson, Dominic, and Purushothaman, Roopa (2003), 'Dreaming with BRICS: The Path to 2050', republished in *The World and the BRICs Dream* (2006), p. 26.

8 New Economist (2006), 'Can Chinese Workers Afford Chinese Goods?' 29 March 2006, www.neweconomist.blogs.com.

9 *China Economic Review* (2006), 'Battle of the Brands', May 2006, Shanghai.

10 Ernst & Young (2005), 'China: The New Lap of Luxury', September 2005, www.ey.com.

11 Lutz, Bob (2005), 'Building the World's Biggest Car Market', GM Fastlane Blog, 29 April 2005, http://fastlane.gmblogs.com.

12 *Economist* (2005), 'Dream Machines', *Economist*, 2 June 2005.

13 Goldman Sachs (2004), 'The BRICS and Global Markets: Crude, Cars and Capital', Goldman Sachs, New York and London, October 2004.

14 *China Daily* (2004), 'Private Car Ownership Sparks Problems', *China Daily*, 16 April 2004.

15 Preeg, Ernest (2005), *The Emerging Chinese Advanced Technology Superstate*, Manufacturers Alliance/Hudson Institute, Arlington, Virginia.

16 CSIS/IIE (2006), *China: The Balance Sheet*, Public Affairs, Cambridge, Massachusetts, p. 103.

17 CSIS/IIE (2006) p. 105.

18 Gilboy, George J. (2004), 'The Myth Behind China's Miracle', *Foreign Affairs*, July–August 2004.

19 Sigurdson, Jon (2006), 'China – Next Science Superpower?' www. demos.co.uk.

20 Wolfowitz, Paul (2005), statement issued on visit to China, 12 October 2005, World Bank, Washington, DC.

21 United Nations Development Programme (2005), *China Human Development Report 2005*, www.undp.org.

22 Muldavin, Joshua (2006), 'In Rural China, a Time Bomb is Ticking', *International Herald Tribune*, 1 January 2006.

23 AFL–CIO (2004), 'Key Elements of the AFL–CIO's 301 Petition Regarding the Violation of Workers' Rights in China', www.aflcio.org.

24 Rosoff, Robert J. (2004), 'Beyond Codes of Conduct: Addressing Labor Rights Problems in China', *China Business Review*, March 2004, www. chinabusinessreview.com.

25 Windle, Charlotte (2006), 'Made in China No Longer Cheap', BBC, 23 January 2006, www.bbc.co.uk/news.

26 Quoted by Windle (2006).

27 FBI (2006), 'Sister Ping Sentenced to 35 Years in Prison', 16 March 2006, www.newyork.fbi.gov.

28 Pieke, Frank (2004), 'Chinese Globalisation and Migration to Europe', working paper 94, March 2004, Center for Comparative Immigration Studies, University of California, San Diego.

29 House of Commons Home Affairs Committee (2001), *First Report, 2000–1*, 23 January 2001, House of Commons, London.

30 Quoted by Hilsum, Lindsey (2005), 'The Chinese in Africa', 4 July 2005, www.channel4.com/news.

31 Walt, Vivienne (2006), 'China's Africa Safari', *Fortune*, 7 February 2006.

32 Kaplinsky, Raphael, McCormick, Dorothy, and Morris, Mike (2006), 'The Impact of China on Sub-Saharan Africa', Asian Drivers paper, Institute of Development Studies, University of Sussex.

33 Sachs, Jeffrey D., and Warner, Andrew (1995), 'Economic Reform and the Process of Global Integration', Brookings Papers on Economic Activity, 1995.

34 Rodriguez, Francisco, and Rodrik, Dani (2000), 'Trade Policy and Economic Growth: A Sceptic's Guide to the Cross-National Evidence', Kennedy School of Government, May 2000.

35 Meacher, Michael (2006), 'Crushed by Well-heeled Global Boots', *The Times*, 8 June 2006.

36 Kaplinsky, Raphael (2005), *Globalization, Poverty and Inequality*, Polity Press, Cambridge, p. 247.

Chapter Five: India's Networked Economy

1 Friedman, Thomas L. (2005), *The World is Flat: A Brief History of the twenty-first Century*, Farrar, Straus & Giroux, New York, p. 8.

2 Interview with the author, January 2006.

3 Nasscom–McKinsey Report 2005, www.nasscom.in.

4 Quoted by David Smith (2004), 'Offshoring: Political Myths and Economic Reality'. Leverhulme Globalisation Lecture, Nottingham, 12 October 2004, www.economicsuk.com.

5 House Resolution 227 (2005), US House of Representatives, 26 April 2005.

6 Kaminsky, Jonathan (2006), 'Struggling to Keep Up: Bangalore's Infrastructure Tries to Meet Needs of Its Technology Industry', *San Francisco Chronicle*, 7 May 2006.

7 Moreau, Ron, and Mazumdar, Sudip (2005), 'Urban Renewal? Bangalore's Poor Infrastructure has Sparked a Bitter Feud over City versus Rural Needs', *Newsweek International*, 5 December 2005.

8 Thornton, Philip (2006), 'India Put on Hold as Africa Challenges to be the Latest Outsourcing Hotspot', *Independent*, 6 June 2006.

9 BBC (2006), 'Powergen Shuts Indian Call Centres', 15 June 2006, www.bbc.co.uk.

10 Alliance & Leicester (2006), 'Banking Customers Want Financial Call Centres Kept in Britain', 23 January 2006, www.alliance-leicester-group.co.uk.

11 Gibson, Yasmine (2004), 'Indian Call Centres ... the Inside Story', *Evening Standard*, 27 September 2004.

12 ICICI OneSource (2006), 'ICICI OneSource Announces Outsourcing Centres in Northern Ireland', 13 June 2006, www.icicionesource.com.

13 Pym, Hugh (2006), 'More Service Sector Jobs Set to Go to India', 7 June 2006, www.bbc.co.uk.

14 Quoted by David Smith (2004).

15 Haniffa, Aziz (2004), 'The John Kerry Interview,' *India Abroad*, 14 October 2004, www.rediff.com.

16 Donohue, Thomas J. (2006), 'State of American Business 2006', 4 January 2006, US Chamber of Commerce.

17 Roberts, Paul Craig (2006), 'A Nation Polarized Between Rich and Poor: America's Bleak Jobs Future', 6 March 2006, www.counterpunch.org.

18 Nasscom (2006), 'Face to Face with ICICI OneSource', 22 June 2006, www.nasscom.in.

19 Government of India (2006), 'Agriculture', www.india.gov.in/sectors/agriculture.php.

20 Hanchate, Amresh, and Dyson, Tim (2005), 'Prospects for Food Demand and Supply', in *Twenty-First Century India*, edited by Tim Dyson, Robert Cassen and Leela Visaria, Oxford University Press, Oxford, pp. 252–3.

21 United Nations Economic and Social Council (2006), *Report of the Special Rapporteur on the Right to Food, Jean Ziegler, Mission to India*, 20 March 2006, www.ohchr.org.

22 Ahmad, Taimur (2006), 'Solving India's Growth Problem', www.adb.org.

23 Gentleman, Amelia (2006), 'Despair Takes Toll on Indian Farmers', *International Herald Tribune*, 31 May 2006.

24 *Hindustan Times* (2006), 'The Policies We Chose Have Kept Us Poor', 26 June 2006, www.hindustantimes.com.

25 Planning Commission, Government of India (2006), 'Towards Faster and More Inclusive Growth: An Approach to the 11th Plan', http://planningcommission.nic.in/plans/planrel/apppap_11.pdf 14 June 2006.

26 Chatterjee, Sumeet, and Moreau, Ron (2005), 'Family Feuds: Colliding Sons', *Newsweek*, 4 July 2005.

27 Chandler, Clay (2005), 'Dealing with Dynasties', *Fortune International*, 31 October 2005.

28 Jabre, Assaad (2005), 'The Rise of Southern Multinationals', speech at IFC conference, Mumbai, 9 November 2005, www.ifc.org.

29 Wehrfritz, George, and Moreau, Ron (2005), 'A Kinder, Gentler Conglomerate', *Newsweek*, 31 October 2005.

30 Perry, Alex (2006), 'Shaking the Foundations: How Ratan Tata turned the Country's Oldest Conglomerate into a Global Force', *Time*, 12 June 2006.

31 Indianews.com (2006), 'Reliance Plans Massive Retail Push', 27 June 2006.

32 Bharadwaj, V.T., Swaroop, Gautum M., and Vittal, Ireena (2005), 'Winning the Indian Consumer'. McKinsey Quarterly Special Edition 2005, www.mckinseyquarterly.com

33 *Economic Times* (2006), 'When Second-best Global Brands Eye India', 7 July 2006.

34 *Economist* (2006), 'The Long Journey', 3 June 2006.

35 Johnson, Jo (2006), 'Malnutrition Stunts India's Economic Growth Ambitions', *Financial Times*, 17 May 2006.

36 Monbiot, George (2004), 'Exit Chandrababu Naidu', *Guardian*, 19 May 2004.

37 Purfield, Catriona (2006), 'Mind the Gap – Is Economic Growth in India Leaving Some States Behind?', IMF working paper WP/06/103, International Monetary Fund, Washington, DC, April 2006.

38 Mishra, Pankaj (2006), 'The Myth of the New India', *The New York Times*, 6 July 2006.

Chapter Six: China versus India

1 Kuroda, Haruhiko (2006), 'Regional and Global Implications of the Rapid Economic Growth in the People's Republic of China and India', Stanford University, 1 June 2006, www.adb.org.

2 Human Rights Watch (2006), 'Olympics and Human Rights: Beijing in 2008', www.hrw.org.

3 Giridharadas, Anand (2006), 'China vs. India: A Battle of Ideas', *International Herald Tribune*, 27 January 2006.

4 Huang, Yasheng, and Khanna, Tarun (2003), 'Can India Overtake China?', *Foreign Policy*, July–August 2003, Washington, DC.

5 Huang (2003).

6 Huang (2003).

7 Restall, Hugo (2006), 'India's Coming Eclipse of China', *Far Eastern Economic Review*, March 2006.

8 Restall (2006).

9 Jackson, Richard, and Howe, Neil (2004), 'The Greying of the Middle Kingdom', Centre for Strategic and International Studies/Prudential Foundation, p. 6.

10 Jackson (2004), p.18.

11 IBEF (2006), *India: Taking India to the World*, Global Agenda, January 2006, WorldLink Publications, London, p. 35.

12 *Guardian* (2000), 'Over-population Warning as India's Billionth Baby is Born', 11 May 2000.

13 TeamLease (2006), India Labour Report 2006, www.teamlease.com.

14 Eberstadt, Nicholas (2005), 'Old Age Tsunami', *Wall Street Journal*, 15 November 2005.

15 Eberstadt (2005).

16 Accenture (2002), 'Liberating the Entrepreneurial Spirit in China', www.accenture.com.

17 Gonzalez, Michael (2006), 'Informal Finance: Encouraging the Entrepreneurial Spirit in Post-Mao China', 2006 Index of Economic Freedom, chapter 4, www.heritage.org.

18 UCLA Asian Institute (2003), 'The New Leadership in China: What Can We Expect from Hu Jintao?' http://international.ucla.edu.

19 Nee, Victor, and Opper, Sonja (2006), 'China's Politicized Capitalism', World Bank, 29 March 2006, http://siteresources.worldbank.org.

20 Mehring, James (2005), 'Who's Got Performance?' *Business Week*, 22 August 2005.

21 Feldstein, Martin (2006), 'There's More to Growth than China', *Wall Street Journal*, 16 February 2006.

22 Kacker, Stuti (2005), 'Overcoming Barriers to Innovation for Indian SMEs', International Network for SMEs, annual conference, Barcelona, 14 April 2005.

23 Luce, Edward (2006), *In Spite of the Gods: The Strange Rise of Modern India*, Little, Brown, London, pp. 62–3.

24 Mishra, Deepak (2006), 'Can India Attain the East Asian Growth with South Asian Saving Rate?' World Bank, September 2006, Washington, DC.

25 Mishra (2006).

26 Kynge, James (2006), *China Shakes the World*, Weidenfeld & Nicolson, London, pp. 26–8.

27 Singh, Manmohan (2006), 'Enterprise to Reduce Poverty', Global Agenda 2006, World Economic Forum.

28 Fung, K. C., Garcia-Herrero, Alicia, Lizaka, Hitomi and Siu, Alan (2005), 'Hard or Soft? Institutional Reforms and Infrastructure Spending as Determinants of Foreign Direct Investment in China', University of California, Santa Cruz.

29 Bradsher, Keith, and Barboza, David (2006), 'Pollution from Chinese Coal Casts a Global Shadow', *The New York Times*, 11 June 2006.

30 *China Daily* (2006), 'Minister: China Risks Environmental Disaster', 13 March 2006.

31 Greenpeace (2006), 'Toxic Hotspots', www.greenpeace.org/India.

32 *Hindu* (2005), 'Manmohan Singh Targets 10 Per cent Growth', 30 November 2005, www.hindu.com.

33 Prior-Wandesforde, Robert (2006), 'India: Pitfalls and Possibilities', HSBC Global Research, London, July 2006.

34 Goldman Sachs (2006), 'China versus India?' *Global Economics Weekly*, 1 February 2006.

Chapter Seven: Ten ways China and India will (and won't) Change the World

1 Winters, L. Alan, and Yusif, Shahid (2006), *Dancing With Giants*, World Bank, Washington, DC, p. 7.

2 Anderson, Jonathan (2006), 'China's True Growth: No Myth or Miracle', *Far Eastern Economic Review*, September 2006, Hong Kong, p.14.

3 Freeman, Richard B. (2004), 'Doubling the Global Work Force: The Challenge of Integrating China, India, and the Former Soviet Bloc into the World Economy', presentation, Institute for International Economics, 8 November 2004, www.iie.com.

4 Watts, Jonathan (2006), 'Invisible City', *Guardian*, 15 March 2006.

5 Winters (2006), p. 5.

6 IEA (2006), 'Medium-term Oil Market Report', Paris, July 2006.

7 Hawksworth, John (2006), 'The World in 2050: Implications of Global Growth for Carbon Emissions and Climate Change Policy', Price Waterhouse Coopers, September 2006.

8 Hawksworth (2006).

9 Brown, Lester R. (2006), *Plan B: Rescuing a Planet Under Stress and a Civilization in Trouble*, Earth Policy Institute/W. W. Norton, New York, p.11.

10 Worldwatch Institute (2006), 'State of the World 2006: China and India Hold World in Balance', 11 January 2006, www.worldwatch.org.

11 Lancaster, John (2005), 'India, China Hoping to "Reshape the World Order" Together', *Washington Post*, 11 April 2005.

12 National Intelligence Council (2004), 'Mapping the Global Future', December 2004, www.foia.cia.gov.

13 Joshi, Maroj (1998), 'Nuclear Shock Wave', *India Today*, 25 May 1998.

14 *Economist* (2006), 'From Bad to Worse', 20 July 2006.

15 Kaplan, Robert D. (2005), 'How We would Fight China', *Atlantic Monthly*, June 2005.

16 United States Department of Defense (2006), 'Annual Report to Congress: Military Power of the People's Republic of China', Washington, DC, 2006.

17 Quoted in Bidwai, Praful (2005), 'India Moves towards a New Compact with the United States', Foreign Policy in Focus, 14 July 2005, www.fpif.org.

18 Centre for Strategic and International Studies/Institute for International Economics (2006), *China: The Balance Sheet*, Public Affairs, Washington, DC, pp. 159–60.

19 Luard, Tim (2004), 'China Takes Place on World Stage', 21 October 2004, www.bbc.co.uk.

20 *Hurun Report* (2006), '2006 China Rich List', www.hurun.net.

21 Wilson, Dominic, and Purushothaman, Roopa (2003), 'Dreaming with BRICs: The Path to 2050', Goldman Sachs, New York, London, 1 October 2003.

22 Hawksworth, John (2006), 'The World in 2050', Price Waterhouse Coopers, www.pwcglobal.com, March 2006.

23 Naughton, Keith (2006), 'Outsourcing: Silicon Valley East', *Newsweek*, 6 March 2006.

24 Seager, Ashley (2006), 'Outsourcing of Labour to Poorer Countries Eases as Market Shrinks', *Guardian*, 14 October 2006.

25 Kaplinsky, Raphael (2005), *Globalization, Poverty and Inequality*, Polity Press, Cambridge.

26 Prestowitz, Clyde (2006), 'The World is Tilted', Issues 2006, www.newsweek.com.

27 Overholt, William, H. (2005), 'China and Globalization', testimony presented to the US–China Economic and Security Review Commission, 19 May 2005, www.rand.org.

28 Wolf, Martin (2004), *Why Globalization Works*, Yale University Press, Yale.

Acknowledgements

This book is the result of very many conversations and interviews, with experts too numerous to mention. I have also drawn liberally, and I hope fairly, on the research of others. Thanks to all who helped. At Profile Books, my thanks to Andrew Franklin, Penny Daniel and their colleagues for their help and support, and to Sally Holloway for diligent copy-editing. This is my third book with Profile and, as always, they have been a joy to work with. At home, my thanks always to Jane, and to Richard, Thomas, Emily and Elizabeth. I hope, in return, the book tells them something about how the world is changing.

Index